Investigating Pragmatics in Foreign Language
Learning, Teaching and Testing

SECOND LANGUAGE ACQUISITION
Series Editor: Professor David Singleton, *Trinity College, Dublin, Ireland*

This series brings together titles dealing with a variety of aspects of language acquisition and processing in situations where a language or languages other than the native language is involved. Second language is thus interpreted in its broadest possible sense. The volumes included in the series all offer in their different ways, on the one hand, exposition and discussion of empirical findings and, on the other, some degree of theoretical reflection. In this latter connection, no particular theoretical stance is privileged in the series; nor is any relevant perspective – sociolinguistic, psycholinguistic, neurolinguistic, etc. – deemed out of place. The intended readership of the series includes final-year undergraduates working on second language acquisition projects, postgraduate students involved in second language acquisition research, and researchers and teachers in general whose interests include a second language acquisition component.

Other Books in the Series
Language Learners in Study Abroad Contexts
  Margaret A. DuFon and Eton Churchill (eds)
Early Trilingualism: A Focus on Questions
  Julia D. Barnes
Cross-linguistic Influences in the Second Language Lexicon
  Janusz Arabski (ed.)
Motivation, Language Attitudes and Globalisation: A Hungarian Perspective
  Zoltán Dörnyei, Kata Csizér and Nóra Németh
Age and the Rate of Foreign Language Learning
  Carmen Muñoz (ed.)
Investigating Tasks in Formal Language Learning
  María del Pilar García Mayo (ed.)
Input for Instructed L2 Learners: The Relevance of Relevance
  Anna Nizegorodcew
Cross-linguistic Similarity in Foreign Language Learning
  Håkan Ringbom
Second Language Lexical Processes
  Zsolt Lengyel and Judit Navracsics (eds)
Third or Additional Language Acquisition
  Gessica De Angelis
Understanding Second Language Process
  ZhaoHong Han (ed.)
Japan's Built-in Lexicon of English-based Loanwords
  Frank E. Daulton
Vocabulary Learning Strategies and Foreign Language Acquisition
  Višnja Pavičić Takač
Foreign Language Input: Initial Processing
  Rebekah Rast
Morphosyntactic Issues in Second Language Acquisition
  Danuta Gabryś-Barker(ed)
Language Learners with Special Needs: An International Perspective
  Judit Kormos and Edit H. Kontra (eds)

For more details of these or any other of our publications, please contact:
**Multilingual Matters, St Nicholas House, 31-34 High Street
Bristol, BS1 2AW, England**
http://www.multilingual-matters.com

SECOND LANGUAGE ACQUISITION 30
Series Editor: David Singleton, *Trinity College, Dublin, Ireland*

Investigating Pragmatics in Foreign Language Learning, Teaching and Testing

Edited by
Eva Alcón Soler and Alicia Martínez-Flor

MULTILINGUAL MATTERS
Bristol • Buffalo • Toronto

Library of Congress Cataloging in Publication Data
Investigating Pragmatics in Foreign Language Learning, Teaching and Testing
Edited by Eva Alcón Soler and Alicia Martínez-Flor. 1st ed.
Second Language Acquisition: 30
Includes bibliographical references and index.
1. Language and languages–Study and teaching. 2. Pragmatics–Study and teaching.
3. Second language acquisition. I. Alcón Soler, Eva. II. Martínez Flor, Alicia.
P53.62.I58 2008
418.0071–dc22   2008012755

British Library Cataloguing in Publication Data
A catalogue entry for this book is available from the British Library.

ISBN-13: 978-1-84769-085-2 (hbk)
ISBN-13: 978-1-84769-084-5 (pbk)

Multilingual Matters
UK: St Nicholas House, 31-34 High Street, Bristol, BS1 2AW.
USA: UTP, 2250 Military Road, Tonawanda, NY 14150, USA.
Canada: UTP, 5201 Dufferin Street, North York, Ontario M3H 5T8, Canada.

Copyright © 2008 Eva Alcón Soler, Alicia Martínez-Flor and the authors of individual chapters.

All rights reserved. No part of this work may be reproduced in any form or by any means without permission in writing from the publisher.

The policy of Multilingual Matters/Channel View Publications is to use papers that are natural, renewable and recyclable products, made from wood grown in sustainable forests. In the manufacturing process of our books, and to further support our policy, preference is given to printers that have FSC and PEFC Chain of Custody certification. The FSC and/or PEFC logos will appear on those books where full certification has been granted to the printer concerned.

Typeset by Datapage International Ltd.
Printed and bound in Great Britain by the Cromwell Press Ltd.

Contents

The Contributors vii

Preface
Amy Snyder Ohta xi

Introduction
1 Pragmatics in Foreign Language Contexts
   Eva Alcón Soler and Alicia Martínez-Flor 3

Part 1: Investigating How Pragmatics Can Be Learned in Foreign Language Contexts
2 Language Socialization Theory and the Acquisition of Pragmatics in the Foreign Language Classroom
   Margaret A. DuFon 25
3 Talking with a Classroom Guest: Opportunities for Learning Japanese Pragmatics
   Yumiko Tateyama and Gabriele Kasper 45
4 Pragmatic Performance: What are Learners Thinking?
   Tim Hassall 72
5 Learning Pragmatics in Content-based Classrooms
   Tarja Nikula 94
6 Computer-mediated Learning of L2 Pragmatics
   Marta González-Lloret 114

Part 2: Investigating How Pragmatics Can Be Taught in Foreign Language Contexts
7 Using Translation to Improve Pragmatic Competence
   Juliane House 135
8 Effects on Pragmatic Development Through Awareness-raising Instruction: Refusals by Japanese EFL Learners
   Sachiko Kondo 153
9 Enhancing the Pragmatic Competence of Non-native English-speaking Teacher Candidates (NNESTCs) in an EFL Context
   Zohreh R. Eslami and Abbass Eslami-Rasekh 178

v

Part 3: Investigating How Pragmatics Can Be Tested in Foreign Language Contexts

10 Investigating Interlanguage Pragmatic Ability:
    What Are We Testing?
    Sayoko Yamashita 201

11 Raters, Functions, Item Types and the
    Dependability of L2 Pragmatics Tests
    James Dean Brown 224

12 Rater, Item and Candidate Effects in Discourse
    Completion Tests: A FACETS Approach
    Carsten Roever 249

The Contributors

Eva Alcón Soler, senior lecturer at University Jaume I, has been working on discourse and language learning since 1993. Her research has covered, among others, interlanguage pragmatics, lingua franca communication, interaction and second language acquisition. Her publications include *Intercultural Language Use and Language Learning* and several special journal issues: Communication, Cognition and Second Language Acquisition (*Communication & Cognition* 30, 1997), Discourse Analysis and Language Learning (*Australian Review of Applied Linguistics* 16, 2000), The Role of Interaction in Instructed Language Learning Contexts (*International Journal of Educational Research* 37, 2002) and Pragmatics in Instructed Language Learning (*System* 33, 2005).

James Dean ("JD") Brown is Professor of Second Language Studies at the University of Hawai'i at Manoa. He has spoken and taught courses in more than 30 countries ranging from Brazil to Yugoslavia. He has also published numerous journal articles and book chapters (on language testing, curriculum design, research methods and program evaluation) and authored or co-authored numerous books (on reading statistical language studies, language curriculum, language testing, language testing in Japan, testing L2 pragmatics, performance testing, criterion-referenced language testing, using surveys in language programs, doing research, language test development, ideas for classroom assessment, connected speech and heritage language curriculum).

Margaret A. DuFon is an Associate Professor of Linguistics at California State University-Chico. She received her PhD in Second Language Acquisition from the University of Hawai'i-Manoa. Her current research interests include interlanguage pragmatics, second language socialisation, language and identity, and classical Malay folktales. Her research has focused on the acquisition of Indonesian language during study abroad. Her co-edited (with Eton Churchill) volume *Language Learners in Study Abroad Contexts* includes her work on 'The Socialization of Taste during Study Abroad in Indonesia'.

Zohreh R. Eslami is an Assistant Professor of ESL Education in the Department of Teaching, Learning and Culture in the College of Education at Texas A&M University in College Station. Her research interests include cross-cultural pragmatics, pragmatics of Persian language, interlanguage pragmatics and sociocultural issues related to ESL teaching and learning. She has several publications in these areas in journals such as *Intercultural Pragmatics*, *Journal of Asian Pacific Communication* and *Pragmatics and Language Learning*.

Abbass Eslami-Rasekh is currently the Dean of the Faculty of Foreign Languages at Isfahan University in Iran. His research interests are discourse analysis, development of ESL/EFL learners' language competence and EFL teacher education. He has published in journals such as *TESL EJ*, *EAP Across Cultures* and *Asian EFL* journal.

Marta González-Lloret is a PhD candidate in the Second Language Studies Department at the University of Hawai'i, Manoa, where she has taught Spanish for over 12 years. Her research interests include computer-assisted language learning, second language learning and teaching, conversation analysis and interlanguage pragmatics. Her recent articles include CA for computer-mediated interaction in the Spanish L2 classroom (in *Conversation Analytic Studies of L1 and L2 Interaction, Learning, and Education*, edited by G. Kasper and H. Nguyen (in press).

Tim Hassall teaches Indonesian language and linguistics in the Faculty of Asian Studies at The Australian National University. He has a Masters and a PhD degree in Applied Linguistics. His current research interests are the pragmatics of second language learners and lexical and grammatical change in Indonesian.

Juliane House received her first degree in translation and international law from Heidelberg University and her PhD in linguistics and applied linguistics from the University of Toronto. She is currently Professor of Applied Linguistics at Hamburg University and co-director of the German Science Foundation's Research Centre on Multilingualism, where she co-ordinates the multilingual communication group and directs three projects. Her research interests include contrastive pragmatics, discourse analysis, politeness theory, English as a lingua franca and intercultural communication. Her publications include *A Model for Translation Quality Assessment*, *Translation Quality Assessment: A Model Revisited*, *Interlingual and Intercultural Communication*, *Cross-Cultural Pragmatics*, *Misunderstanding in Social Life* and *Multilingual Communication*.

Gabriele Kasper is Professor of Second Language Studies at the University of Hawai'i at Manoa and currently the North American editor of *Applied Linguistics*. Her books include *Misunderstanding in Social Life* (House, Kasper & Ross, Longman/Pearson Education, 2003),

Pragmatic Development in a Second Language (Kasper & Rose, Blackwell, 2002), and *Pragmatics in Language Teaching* (Rose & Kasper, Cambridge University Press, 2001). Her research has recently focused on applying conversation analysis to the study of second language interaction and learning.

Sachiko Kondo is Associate Professor of Linguistics at the English Department, Sophia Junior College, Japan. She has been doing research in interlanguage pragmatics since 1995, especially on development of pragmatic knowledge in study-abroad and instructional contexts. Her publications include 'The Development of Pragmatic Competence by Japanese Learners of English: Longitudinal Study on Interlanguage Apologies' (*Sophia Linguistica* 41, 1997) and 'Teaching Refusals in an EFL Setting' (in K. Bardovi-Harlig and R. Mahan-Taylor. eds. 2003. *Teaching Pragmatics*. Washington, DC: US Department of State, Office of English Language Programs). She is also one of the authors of *Heart to Heart* (Macmillan Languagehouse, 2000), which is a research-based textbook for teaching pragmatics to Japanese EFL learners.

Alicia Martínez-Flor is a lecturer in the Department of English Studies, Universitat Jaume I of Castellón, Spain, where she teaches both undergraduate and postgraduate courses in EFL teaching methodology. She has co-edited the special issue 'Pragmatics in Instructed Language Learning' in the international journal *System* (2005) with Eva Alcón Soler, as well as the volumes *Pragmatic Competence and Foreign Language Teaching* (Universitat Jaume I, 2003) with Esther Usó-Juan and Ana Fernández-Guerra and *Current Trends in the Development and Teaching of the Four Language Skills* (Mouton de Gruyter, 2006) with Esther Usó-Juan. Her research interests are in second language acquisition and interlanguage pragmatics.

Tarja Nikula, Professor, is the director of the Centre for Applied Language Studies, University of Jyväskylä, Finland. Her research interests include pragmatics of language learning and teaching, classroom interaction in content-based and EFL classrooms, and English–Finnish language contact phenomena. She is also involved in an ethnographic research project on the role of English in Finnish teenagers' everyday lives. Her publications have appeared in *Pragmatics*, *Linguistics and Education*, *Applied Linguistics*, *World Englishes* and *Multilingua*.

Carsten Roever is a Senior Lecturer in Applied Linguistics in the School of Languages & Linguistics at the University of Melbourne. He holds a PhD in Second Language Acquisition from the University of Hawai'i at Manoa. His research interests include second language acquisition, interlanguage pragmatics, research methods and second language testing. He authored the book *Testing ESL Pragmatics* (Peter Lang, 2005) and co-authored *Language Testing: The Social Dimension* (Blackwell, 2006) with Tim McNamara, as well as several book chapters and journal articles.

Yumiko Tateyama is a PhD candidate in the Department of East Asian Languages and Literatures at the University of Hawai'i at Manoa, where she also teaches Japanese. Her research interests include interlanguage pragmatics, second language learning and teaching, conversation analysis, and translation and interpretation. She has published studies on the development of JFL learners' pragmatic competence, including a book chapter that appeared in Rose and Kasper (2001).

Sayoko Yamashita, EdD, is Professor of Applied Linguistics in the Faculty of Languages and Cultures, and Graduate School of Applied Linguistics at Meikai University, Japan. She has carried out cross-cultural pragmatics, interlanguage pragmatics specifically in JSL contexts, and testing research. She is currently working in the field of communication and interaction with particular reference to medical communication. Her previous books include *Six Measures of JSL Pragmatics* (1996) and *Language Testing in Japan* (co-edited with J.D. Brown, 1996). Her recent articles include 'Pragmatic Strategies of Japanese Elderly People' (in *Pragmatics in Language Learning, Theory, & Practice*, edited by D. Tatsuki, 2005).

Preface

AMY SNYDER OHTA

The field of applied linguistics has seen a great deal of change in the last 40 years. In the 1960s and 1970s the business of classroom language instruction was, by and large, teaching grammar. Even when focused on oral production, the emphasis was on producing complete sentences. And, the sentences that were put together in textbooks to serve as models often didn't make good pragmatic sense. I recall one audiolingual text writer stating that she was asked to write a textbook for a language she could hardly speak, Japanese, and one of the dialogues began with a Japanese person asking a Westerner, 'Do you like meat?' Needless to say, pragmatics was not yet on the radar. For foreign language learners worldwide, pragmatics was what students learned in-country if they were fortunate enough to travel or study abroad, or if they emigrated.

In my early days of teaching Japanese, I worked in a program where we used an old-fashioned audiolingual method textbook. Even at the time, in the late 1980s, the text was out of date. We tried to compensate for the poor textbook by making a lot of handouts, but these also focused on sentence-level concerns and nearly always neglected pragmatics. One of my students visited Japan, and when she returned she said 'Boy, they sure don't talk like we were taught in class'. Reflecting on my own experiences living in Japan, I realized that that was true. At the time, I felt that there was little I could do to change how Japanese was taught, but facing the gap between what I was teaching and what students needed to learn inspired me to do research in interlanguage pragmatics. That gap continues to inspire me today.

Fortunately, times have changed. These days, materials developers and textbook writers are informed by the field of interlanguage pragmatics, a subfield of applied linguistics that emerged from cross-cultural pragmatic studies. Moving beyond comparisons of how native and target cultural routines differ, the field of interlanguage pragmatics today grapples with a range of issues faced by language learners and those who teach and assess them. Some of the questions addressed relate to how pragmatics competence develops in classroom contexts, online communities or sojourns abroad. Other studies consider developmental issues and problems related to language transfer. Yet others investigate methods of teaching and assessing pragmatics. Interlanguage pragmatics research has a wide variety of investigative tools at its disposal and draws on diverse theoretical approaches. This diversity continues to grow, enriching the field.

The present volume is devoted to consideration of developmental pragmatics – its learning, teaching and testing – in foreign language contexts. The work gathered reflects the diversity of the field and provides a view of how interlanguage pragmatics research has developed and is growing. The editors and chapter authors bring an impressive range of theoretical perspectives and investigative tools to this endeavor for application to questions related to development of pragmatics in foreign language settings.

Following an overview chapter authored by the editors, the volume has three sections. The first two sections focus on issues related to learning and teaching. The contexts considered include traditional classrooms, context-based instruction, computer- and internet-mediated learning opportunities, translation and interpretation, and teacher training. The third section focuses on how foreign language pragmatics can be assessed using a variety of approaches, including oral and written discourse completion tasks, roleplay, self-assessment, video prompting and conversation analysis.

Along with the diversity of contexts investigated throughout the volume, the chapters also draw upon a range of theoretical approaches: psycholinguistics, language socialization, conversation analysis and sociocultural theory. Data are presented from learners of such languages as Indonesian, German, Korean, Japanese, Spanish, Finnish, Iranian and English. Chapter authors are scholars with reputations for excellence in the field, including those whose early work formed the foundation of inquiry that continues today. I commend the editors for their leadership in the field. Their collaboration as editors has resulted in important forums for the production and dissemination of research. It is a pleasure to see the completion of this volume as it brings the best of the field together to focus on interlanguage pragmatics in foreign language contexts.

Introduction

Chapter 1
Pragmatics in Foreign Language Contexts

EVA ALCÓN SOLER and ALICIA MARTÍNEZ-FLOR

The study of pragmatics deals with areas such as deixis, conversational implicature, presupposition and conversational structure. However, the study of second language pragmatics, also referred to as interlanguage pragmatics (ILP), focuses mainly on the investigation of speech acts, conversational structure and conversational implicature. These research topics have been addressed by comparative and acquisitional studies. While comparative studies are close to research on cross-cultural pragmatics, those conducted from an acquisitional perspective address developmental issues that affect learners' acquisition of pragmatics. In addition, interlanguage pragmatic research has traditionally divided linguistic knowledge from social knowledge. Leech (1983) and Thomas (1983) account for this fact by dividing pragmatics into two components: pragmalinguistics and sociopragmatics. The former refers to the linguistic resources for conveying communicative acts and interpersonal meanings, whereas the latter refers to the social perceptions underlying participants' interpretation and performance of communicative acts. Hence, while dealing with pragmatics attention is paid to consider knowledge of the means to weaken or strengthen the force of an utterance (i.e. pragmalinguistic knowledge) and knowledge of the particular means that are likely to be most successful for a given situation (i.e. sociopragmatic knowledge).

In the field of language learning there has also been a tendency to consider Leech's (1983) and Thomas's (1983) division of pragmatics into pragmalinguistics and sociopragmatics, but one has to accept that this has resulted in an unbalanced focus on the pragmalinguistic component. To date, most of the studies in the field of ILP present a partial view of learners' use of the target language, as either the sociopragmatic component is not taken into account or, when it is considered, general descriptions of the situational context are provided. From this perspective, most research studies have analysed routines and pragmalinguistic realisations (see Kasper & Rose, 2002; Rose & Kasper, 2001). Several studies exist that concentrate on request realisations (Blum-Kulka, 1991; Hassall, 1997; Li, 2000; Rose, 2000, among others), refusals (Félix-Brasdefer, 2004), compliments (Rose & Ng Kwai-fun, 2001) and apologies

(Trosborg, 1995). In addition, although pragmatics has become a focus of attention in language teaching (see Bardovi-Harlig & Mahan-Taylor, 2003, among others), current proposals for pragmatic instruction are also based on routines and strategies associated to particular speech acts, such as requests (Alcón & Codina, 2002; Cook & Liddicoat, 2002; Mach & Ridder, 2003; Martínez-Flor & Usó-Juan, 2006), refusals (Kondo, 2003), complaints (Reynolds, 2003) or suggestions (Martínez-Flor & Usó-Juan, 2006).

In spite of the unbalanced focus on the pragmalinguistic component in investigating pragmatic learning, Alcón (2008) claims that when dealing with pragmatics the relationship between routines and forms of particular speech acts and the contextual factors of particular situations need to be considered. In other words, the author claims that the pragmalinguistic and sociopragmatic components suggested by Leech (1983) and Thomas (1983) should be viewed in interaction, which in turn involves considering politeness as a pragmatic phenomenon. From this point of view, the performance of face-threatening acts (Brown & Levinson, 1987), the universal principle of avoiding friction in conversation (Leech, 1983) and Fraser's (1990) view of politeness as a social norm are key issues to understand why participants use particular linguistic devices, which are triggered by contextual factors. Among the contextual factors, type of interaction is one which may be reflected in language use. For instance, while in transactional discourse, such as doctor–nurse interaction during an emergency, participants focus on task performance and do not need to make use of politeness strategies, in interactional discourse language also has an interpersonal function.

Bearing in mind the above theoretical insights, this chapter reviews research in the field of ILP conducted from an acquisitional perspective. First, we will define the concept of pragmatic competence, taking into account the construct of communicative competence and whether the pragmalinguistic and sociopragmatic components are considered. We will then examine the two theoretical perspectives of understanding pragmatics learning (i.e. cognitive and socially oriented views). After that, three main issues addressed in ILP research, that is to say, learners' production and perception of speech acts, factors influencing pragmatic learning and the teachability of pragmatics, will be presented. Finally, we will take a critical look at some methodological issues related to investigating pragmatic learning in foreign language (FL) classrooms.

Pragmatics Within the Construct of Communicative Competence

Different scholars in the field of applied linguistics have attempted to describe the construct of communicative competence by identifying its various components, one of them being the pragmatic component. In

Canale and Swain's (1980) and Canale's (1983) model, the sociolinguistic component implicitly includes pragmatics, as it refers to rules of discourse and rules of use. While in the case of rules of discourse the authors refer to cohesion and coherence, the rules of use can be seen to fit into pragmatics, that is to say, they relate to the appropriateness of an utterance with respect to a specific speech event. However, Bachman (1990) was the first applied linguist to mention the pragmatic component explicitly. The author distinguished between organisational and pragmatic competence. On the one hand, organisational competence refers to those abilities involved in the production and identification of grammatical and ungrammatical sentences, and also in understanding their meaning and in ordering them to form texts. These abilities are subdivided into grammatical and textual competences. On the other hand, in Bachman's (1990) model, pragmatic competence is understood as dealing with the relationship between utterances and the acts performed through these utterances, as well as with the features of the context that promote appropriate language use. The relationship between utterances and acts concerns the illocutionary force, whereas the context has to do with those sociolinguistic conventions involved in using the language. In the same vein, Celce-Murcia *et al.* (1995) refer to pragmatic competence as actional competence, which comprises knowledge of language functions and knowledge of speech act sets, that is to say, emphasis is paid to the pragmalinguistic aspects of language. In addition, the authors include the sociocultural component as part of their construct of communicative competence. According to them, sociocultural competence refers to knowledge about appropriate use within particular social and cultural contexts of communication. More recently, the models developed by Alcón (2000) and Usó-Juan and Martínez-Flor (2006) also highlight the pragmatic competence as one of its main components.

The common idea underlying the above-mentioned models refers to the fact that communicative competence is not only achieved by improving learners' grammatical knowledge, but it also concerns the development of discourse and pragmatic competences, among others. From this point of view, pragmatic instruction has been based on routines and strategies associated to particular speech acts such as requests, refusals, apologies or complaints. However, in our opinion, when pragmatics is the focus of attention in FL classrooms, the pragmalinguistic and sociopragmatic components suggested by Leech (1983) and Thomas (1983) are not viewed in interaction. In other words, the relationship between routines and forms of particular speech acts are not considered together with the contextual factors of particular situations. This point of view presents new challenges for pragmatics in FL contexts and is also pointed out by Kasper and Roever (2005: 318), for whom becoming pragmatically competent is understood as being '... the process of establishing sociopragmatic and pragmalinguistic competence and the increasing ability to understand and produce sociopragmatic meanings with pragmalinguistic conventions'.

The importance of the role played by pragmatics in the communicative competence framework has led to increased attention paid to the field of ILP, where the main objective is to examine the developmental stages that learners go through when acquiring the pragmatic system of the target language. The two theoretical perspectives in which such a field of research has been framed are addressed in the next section.

Theoretical Perspectives Within ILP Research

Similarly to the way in which the debate in the field of second language acquisition is represented by cognitivists and socioculturalists, ILP research has been framed within two views of understanding pragmatic learning, i.e. as either a cognitive or a socially oriented activity. Following a cognitive theoretical approach, the development of pragmatic competence has been considered as an individual mental process, and, although researchers have paid attention to context, data have been collected under experimental or quasiexperimental conditions by means of written and oral discourse completion and discourse evaluation tasks. In particular, the noticing hypothesis (Schmidt, 1993, 1995, 2001), Bialystok's two-dimensional model of L2 proficiency development (1993) and, more recently, the interactive hypothesis (Long, 1996) have been operationalised in ILP research from a cognitive perspective. Schmidt's (1993, 1995, 2001) noticing hypothesis and his distinction between noticing and understanding have been used as a theoretical construct of the role of awareness in pragmatic learning (see Alcón & Safont, 2008, for a review of pragmatic awareness in language learning). In addition, Schmidt's (1993) consciousness-raising approach, which involves paying conscious attention to relevant forms, their pragmalinguistic functions and the sociopragmatic constraints these particular forms involve, and Sharwood Smith's (1981, 1991) suggestion of input enhancement techniques have motivated cognitive-based research exploring the effects of instruction on the development of learners' pragmatic competence. Up till now, studies on the teachability of pragmatics have been set within a cognitive perspective and have examined a wide range of discourse, pragmatic and sociolinguistic issues (House & Kasper, 1981; Lyster, 1994; Wildner-Bassett, 1994), speech acts (Martínez-Flor & Alcón, 2007 on suggestions; Olshtain & Cohen, 1990 on apologies; Rose & Ng Kwai-Fun, 2001 on compliments and compliment responses; Martínez-Flor, 2007a; Safont, 2005, 2007; Salazar, 2007; Takahashi, 2001; and Usó-Juan, 2007 on requests), pragmatic fluency (House, 1996) and discourse competence (Alcón, 1997).

Although the range of learner characteristics in studies on the effectiveness of instruction is rather narrow (English and Japanese are mainly learners' first language and the university context is the research setting), research findings on the teachability of pragmatics suggest that instruction is both necessary and effective (Jeon & Kaya, 2006; Olshtain & Cohen, 1990; Rose, 2005; Safont, 2005; Wildner-Bassett, 1984, 1986; see also the collection of papers in Rose & Kasper, 2001), and that explicit and deductive instruction is more effective for pragmatic learning than implicit and inductive teaching (Alcón, 2005; House, 1996; Rose & Ng Kwai-Fun, 2001; Takahashi, 2001).

In addition, while much research has been conducted on the teachability of pragmatics with the aim of testing Schmidt's (1993, 1995, 2001) noticing hypothesis, and has provided evidence that high levels of attention-drawing activities are more helpful for pragmatic learning than exposure to positive evidence, Bialystok's (1993) model and Long's (1996) interaction hypothesis have also motivated ILP research from a cognitive perspective. For instance, the studies by Hassall (1997) and Koike (1989) support Bialystok's claim that pragmatic representation is already accomplished for adult second-language learners, and thus the key issue is the development of control over attention in selecting pragmatic knowledge appropriately. Within the framework of Long's (1996) interactive hypothesis, in an attempt to operationalise focus on form versus focus on forms in pragmatics, Kasper (2001a) suggests the need to draw a distinction between language in use versus metalinguistic knowledge, and pragmatics versus metapragmatics.

The study of pragmatic learning from socially oriented perspectives views social interaction as being crucial. Sociocultural and language socialisation work on the development of pragmatic learning has been gaining ground in the last decade. Both theories place great importance on the social and cultural context of learning and they focus on the process of language acquisition by examining language use between experts and novices over time. In other words, they are inherently developmental and thus adequate frameworks for conducting studies with a focus on developmental issues in pragmatics. Examples of research motivated by sociocultural theory are, for instance, those conducted by Hall (1998) and Ohta (2001) showing, respectively, that opportunities for participation affect the development of interactional competence and that pragmatic knowledge may emerge from assisted performance, in both teacher and peer interaction.

In contrast to the interest of sociocultural theory in exploring the mediating role of language in the process of language learning, language socialisation focuses on the integration of culture and language (Schieffelin & Ochs, 1986). Studies conducted within the setting of language socialisation theory have demonstrated that the theory provides an appropriate framework for teaching and researching pragmatics. For instance, Kanagy (1999) illustrates how American children learning Japanese in an immersion programme were learning the routines of greetings, taking attendance and making personal introductions at the same time as they were learning about Japanese values and behaviours. The integration of the acquisition of language and culture is also evident in Duff's (1995, 1996) investigations of language learning at the secondary school level in Hungary after the dissolution of the Soviet Union. In these studies, one can observe how different models of discourse socialisation evolve and may be either in conflict or in harmony with existing cultural practices. However, although the emphasis on integrating culture and language makes the approach suitable for developmental research on pragmatics in second language or immersion contexts, it may present problems when dealing with research in FL contexts.

Finally, following a conversation analysis (CA) approach, research has provided information about how learners' interactional competencies are both resources and objects of learning. For instance, Kasper (2004) examines a dyadic conversation for learning conducted between a learner of German as a FL at beginner level and a native speaker of German, pointing out that the metalingual exchanges stood out for their acquisitional potential. In a similar vein, another example can be found in Young and Miller's (2004) study, focusing on tracking a student's changing participation in revision talk, and revealing how the student takes over tasks which were initially performed by the teacher. In these studies, CA provides a method of observing classroom talk, but, as reported by Kasper (2006), the benefits of CA to explain pragmatic learning are less evident. However, the question is how different theories may be used as a framework to examine different issues that intervene in the process learners go through when acquiring the pragmatic competence of the target language. Those issues are examined in the following section, with particular emphasis on their development in FL contexts.

Issues Addressed in ILP Research in FL Contexts

ILP research has focused on describing and explaining learners' use, perception and acquisition of second language (L2) pragmatic ability both in L2 and FL contexts. Regarding learners' use, most of the studies have been comparative given its closeness to cross-cultural pragmatics, and their main focus of research has been speech acts. In those studies, as reported by Bardovi-Harlig (2001), it has been shown that native speakers (NSs) and non-native speakers (NNSs) appear to differ in the production of speech acts. Bardovi-Harlig (2001) illustrates how NSs and NNSs may use different speech acts (in advising sessions NSs use suggestions while NNSs opt for rejections) and how they also differ in the semantic formulae (explanations versus alternatives for rejecting), content (what they say) and form of the speech acts (whether learners make use of mitigators). In addition, research focused on perception of speech acts suggests that NNSs' judgements are often different from those of NSs. The studies conducted by Bardovi-Harlig and Dörnyei (1998), Bardovi-Harlig and Hartford (1996), Schauer (2006) and Takahashi (1996) illustrate this issue, and variables such as length of residence (Olshtain & Blum-Kulka, 1985), level of proficiency (Koike, 1996) and learning environment (Bardovi-Harlig & Dörnyei, 1998; Niezgoda & Röver, 2001; Schauer, 2006) are reported to be decisive factors with respect to the perception of appropriate speech acts. Finally, in accounting for an acquisitional perspective, scholars have claimed the need to conduct more studies addressing developmental issues (Bardovi-Harlig, 2002; Kasper & Rose, 1999, 2002; Kasper & Schmidt, 1996), and research in second language contexts has provided us with information about the factors that influence the development of learners' pragmatic competence (Barron, 2003). Those factors, which include availability of input, L2 proficiency, length of stay, transfer and instruction, have also been addressed in FL contexts.

Regarding the first of them, Alcón (2005) claims that learners are exposed to pragmatic input through classroom interaction, textbook conversations and films. However, research conducted in FL settings reports that in this language learning context the range of speech acts and realisation strategies is quite narrow, and that the typical interaction patterns restrict pragmatic input and opportunities for practising discourse organisation strategies (Lörscher & Schulze, 1988). Likewise, as illustrated by Crandall and Basturkmen (2004), textbook conversations do not provide adequate pragmatic input. The results from Bardovi-Harlig *et al.*'s (1991) survey on conversational closings, Boxer and Pickering's (1995) analysis of complaints, Gilmore's (2004) study on discourse features and Usó-Juan's (2007) research on request modification devices all illustrate that textbook conversations are not a reliable source of pragmatic input. In contrast to classroom interaction and textbook conversations, the use of audiovisual input has been reported as being useful to address knowledge of a pragmatic system and knowledge of its appropriate use in FL contexts. The studies conducted by Alcón (2005), Grant and Starks (2001), Martínez-Flor (2007a) and Washburn (2001) were motivated by the assumption that both pragmalinguistic and sociopragmatic awareness are particularly difficult for those studying in an English as a foreign language (EFL) context. From this perspective, the authors claim that authentic audiovisual input provides ample opportunities to address all aspects of language use in a variety of contexts. Besides, as reported by Rose (1997, 2001), it offers the possibility of being able to choose the richest and most suitable segments, analysing them in full, and designing software to allow learners to access pragmatic aspects as needed.

The second factor that has also received attention in ILP is the influence of learners' level of target language proficiency on developing pragmatic competence. Bialystok's (1993) suggestion that pragmatic learning is a question of achieving control of processing over already universal features in discourse and pragmatics, such as categories of speech acts and realisation strategies, conversational organisation or turn-taking sequences, could support the need to focus on grammar and let language learners draw on pragmatic universals and first language (L1) transfer of pragmatic knowledge. Along these lines, some studies show that FL learners' pragmatic ability progresses in line with their language proficiency (Rose, 2000, for supportive moves in requests; Takahashi & Beebe, 1987, for refusal realisation strategies), whereas in other studies it appears that, although proficiency has little effect on the range of realisation strategies (Kasper & Schmidt, 1996), it does influence the order and frequency of semantic formulae used by learners (Kasper & Rose, 2002). In addition, most interlanguage studies have found an inverse relationship between negative pragmatic transfer and proficiency (for instance, House & Kasper, 1981; Trosborg, 1987, for modality markers; Maeshiba et al., 1996, for apologies; Kobayashi & Rinnert, 2003; Rossiter & Kondoh, 2001, for requests). Similarly, the influence of the level of L2 proficiency and pragmatic competence may be supported by findings reporting a positive relationship between length of stay, which is likely to result in an improvement in learners' level of proficiency, and pragmatic competence (Bardovi-Harlig & Hartford, 1993; Olshtain & Blum-Kulka, 1985). However, ILP research outcomes provide evidence that even long exposure to the target language does not always result in pragmatic learning (Bardovi-Harlig, 2001).

In addition to these factors, the role of instruction has also received special attention in ILP research, since, as mentioned above, FL contexts provide learners with little access to appropriate pragmatic input (see the volumes by Alcón & Martínez-Flor, 2005; Martínez-Flor et al., 2003; Rose & Kasper, 2001; Tatsuki, 2005 for reviews of research on pragmatic instruction). It has been claimed that this particular factor requires further examination in FL contexts. As suggested by Rose (2005: 386), there seem to be three central questions, i.e. 'whether pragmatics is teachable, whether instruction in pragmatics produces results that outpace exposure alone, and whether different instructional approaches yield different outcomes'. First, with regard to the teachability of pragmatics, there is evidence indicating that pragmatics is teachable and that pedagogical intervention has a facilitative role in learning pragmatics in FL contexts (Liddicoat & Crozet, 2001; Olshtain & Cohen, 1990; Safont, 2003, 2005; Salazar, 2003). Second, focusing on whether instruction is more effective than simple exposure, research seems to indicate that, regardless of the length of the instructional period, learners receiving pragmatic instruction outperformed those who did not (Lyster, 1994; Yoshimi, 2001). Likewise, research on the effect of different teaching approaches reports the advantage of explicit over implicit instruction (Alcón, 2005; House, 1996; Rose & Ng Kwai-Fun, 2001; Takahashi, 2001; Tateyama, 2001; Tateyama *et al.*, 1997). However, recent studies seem to provide evidence for the benefits of both types of instructions, when the implicit treatment is properly operationalised (Koike & Pearson, 2005; Martínez-Flor, 2006; Martínez-Flor & Fukuya, 2005).

The overall outcome of studies on the effect of instruction in pragmatics is particularly relevant for learners in FL contexts. Nevertheless, these results have to be taken as tentative until a larger number of studies on the instructional effect of particular target forms have been conducted in FL classrooms. It may be claimed that the specificity of local classroom setting limits the generalisability of results but, as suggested by Kasper (2001a), it may offer the possibility of combining observational and interventional studies (see Alcón, 2008). Likewise, the research outcomes across different educational settings might help to generalise the effect of different variables on pragmatic learning. However, before conducting studies in FL contexts, it would be wise to examine the operationalisation of language learning theories in the pragmatic realm and whether outcome measures can influence results. By having a thorough knowledge of the two aspects, appropriate decisions can be adopted in classroom research on ILP.

Classroom Research on ILP: Research Decisions

When conducting research on ILP in classroom contexts, some decisions need to be taken so that the study to be carried out is operationalised properly. On the one hand, ILP research needs to be grounded on a particular language learning theory that provides the appropriate theoretical base for the study. On the other hand, the data collection method also needs to be chosen appropriately, taking into account the objectives to be achieved in the study. We dedicate the present section to dealing with these two research decisions.

Regarding the first one, most ILP studies have adopted an observational or interventional approach. On the one hand, the question raised by observational studies has been to examine opportunities for pragmatic input through input sources, such as teachers' talk, classroom interaction, textbook conversations, audiovisual material or, more recently, to study how pragmatic information is conveyed through interaction from a sociocultural (Alcón, 2002; Antón, 1999; Hall, 1998; Ohta, 1995) and socialisation perspective (Falsgraf & Majors, 1995;

Li, 2000). On the other hand, interventional studies have been based on SLA hypotheses. In particular, the noticing hypothesis (Schmidt, 1993, 1995, 2001) and the interactive hypothesis (Long, 1996) have motivated recent ILP research from an acquisitional perspective. Schmidt's (1993, 1995, 2001) noticing hypothesis (which claims that for second language development to take place, learners need to notice the target features in the input) has been taken into account in interventional research to test whether a higher degree of awareness at the noticing and understanding level is ensured by manipulating input, both in explicit and implicit conditions. The problem seems to be that while metapragmatic explanations are used to measure pragmatic learning under explicit conditions (House, 1996), the way implicit conditions are operationalised may vary including input flood (Nikula, 1996), bold or italics as input enhancement techniques (Alcón, 2005; Martínez-Flor & Fukuya, 2005), recasts (Martínez-Flor & Fukuya, 2005) or the use of implicit consciousness-raising tasks (Alcón, 2006). Thus, before ILP research can be applied to pragmatic learning and teaching, first there is a need to provide detailed explanations about the way the concept of awareness and learning under implicit conditions are operationalised. Second, in line with SLA studies that suggest that higher levels of grammatical awareness are ensured by manipulating input (Leow, 1997, 2000; Rosa & Leow, 2004; Rosa & O'Neill, 1999), there seems to be a need to focus on learners' intake of pragmatic issues in classroom settings by enhancing the relationship between pragmalinguistic and sociopragmatic aspects of language.

From the interactive perspective of language learning (Long, 1996), care should be taken to state how focus on form can be operationalised in pragmatics. Considering that pragmatic knowledge requires mapping of form, meaning and context, the operationalisation of focus on form versus focus on forms in classroom research appears to be a difficult task. Empirical research conducted by Martínez-Flor (2007b) illustrates how the focus on form approach can be conceptualised in interventional research on pragmatic learning. By adopting a proactive focus on form in an EFL context, the author analyses the effect of explicit and implicit teaching in developing learners' use of downgraders when making suggestions. Results of her study show that both focus on form (operationalised by the combination of input enhancement and recasts) and focus on forms (teachers' explanation of the speech act of suggesting) treatment conditions were effective, as no significant differences were found when comparing learners' performance after receiving the two types of instruction. However, further research is needed to examine whether a different operationalisation of a focus on form approach in FL classrooms might report differences as far as the potential effect of saliency is concerned.

Moving on to the second decision to be considered in ILP research, attention needs to be paid to whether methods of data collection potentially influence research outcomes. Kasper and Roever (2005) claim that methods of data collection in ILP can be categorised in three groups: recording spoken interaction, questionnaires and self-report data. The method employed in the first group, that is, recording authentic discourse, allows the researcher to observe how participants produce and understand pragmatic information and how they interact in contextual settings, but the researcher has no control over the interaction or over how different variables influence participants' behaviour in conversation (Bardovi-Harlig & Hartford, 1996; Young & He, 1998). In order to gain more control over spoken interaction, observational research resorts to elicited conversations by making use of open and closed roleplays (Liddicoat & Crozet, 2001; Morrow, 1995; Safont, 2005; Tateyama, 2001). In those cases, interactional data are obtained under controlled conditions, but the relationship of elicited conversation to authentic discourse offers problems of validity. Moving on to the second group, different questionnaires have been used to examine FL learners' pragmatic competence. Thus, discourse completion tests have been used to collect pragmatic production of speech act strategies (Rose & Ng Kwai-Fun, 2001; Takahashi, 2001), multiple choice questionnaires serve to measure recognition and interpretation of utterances (Liddicoat & Crozet, 2001) and scaled-response formats have been utilised to evaluate learners' perceptions of pragmatic errors (Bardovi-Harlig & Dörnyei, 1998; Niezgoda & Röver, 2001) or appropriateness of speech act realisation strategies (Martínez-Flor, 2006; Safont, 2005). Finally, in relation to the third group, that of self-report data, although the use of diaries (Cohen, 1997; DuFon, 1999) or verbal protocols (Cohen & Olshtain, 1993; Roever, 2005) may provide information on learners' cognitive processes, this type of data has not often been used in classroom research on ILP. One reason could be that qualitative data is more time consuming than the administration and analysis of questionnaires, and it is also more difficult to generalise the results obtained. However, a qualitative type of methodology is needed if we follow a sociocultural or socialisation perspective in research on pragmatic learning. In this case, CA may be used to examine in detail how opportunities for pragmatic learning arise in different contexts, and interviews and self-report data may be useful assessment measures; we can choose the one that best suits our purposes.

Having addressed the two above-mentioned research decisions, we believe that a key issue is to decide how the types of data match our particular research questions taking into account the theoretical perspective adopted in each study (see Kasper, 2001b, for the theoretical perspectives adopted in ILP research). Once the researcher has adopted a theoretical perspective to investigate a particular pragmatic issue, the context in which learners acquire the target language and the type of research (cross-sectional or longitudinal) will be considered in order to choose the most suitable research methods and types of data collection. This is illustrated in Alcón (2002), Martínez-Flor (2006) and Safont (2005), all of which were conducted in FL classrooms. On the one hand, Alcón (2002) aimed to analyse the effect of collaborative dialogue in constructing learners' pragmatic knowledge of requests. Thus, although classrooms are described as poor laboratories that hinder the generalisation of outcomes, the author adopts a sociocultural perspective which allows classroom interaction to be analysed in detail and examines participants' verbal behaviour in relation to learning outcomes. On the other hand, Martínez-Flor (2006) and Safont (2005) sought to examine the effect of pragmatic instruction on the speech acts of requesting and suggesting, respectively. Thus, following an information processing perspective, issues such as the role of pragmatic awareness, both at the level of noticing and understanding, are discussed and possible pedagogical implications are suggested which might help to further understand pragmatic learning in FL classrooms.

Conclusion

After presenting the two theoretical perspectives in which ILP research has been framed (i.e. cognitive and socially oriented views), this chapter has reviewed this research by focusing on the most important areas that have been examined, namely, (1) learners' production and perception of speech acts; (2) factors influencing pragmatic learning; and (3) the teachability of pragmatics. In addition, we have also argued the need for planning and reflection on important methodological issues in ILP research. More specifically, we have highlighted the importance of exploring the conditions that influence pragmatic learning and teaching in FL classrooms. It has been claimed that learners in a FL setting do not have the same exposure and opportunities for practice as learners who are immersed in the second language community. For this reason, and as illustrated in the following chapters, there is a need to examine those conditions that influence how pragmatics is learned, taught and tested in different formal language learning settings. This requires choosing from among different approaches, research paradigms, methods of data collection and analysis. The task is not easy, but it represents an opportunity to widen the scope of research in the field of ILP in different sociocultural FL contexts.

References

Alcón, E. (1997) Desarrollo de la competencia discursiva oral desde una perspectiva metodológica de autoaprendizaje. In J. Cantero, A. Mendoza and C. Romea (eds) *Didáctica de la Lengua y la Literatura para una Sociedad Plurilingüe del Siglo XXI* (pp. 963–966). Barcelona: Publicacions de la Universitat de Barcelona.

Alcón, E. (2000) Desarrollo de la competencia discursiva oral en el aula de lenguas extranjeras: Perspectivas metodológicas y de investigación. In C. Muñoz (ed.) *Segundas Lenguas: Adquisición en el Aula* (pp. 259–272). Barcelona: Ariel.

Alcón, E. (2002) Relationship between teacher-led versus learners' interaction and the development of pragmatics in the EFL classroom. *International Journal of Educational Research* 37, 359–375.

Alcón, E. (2005) Does instruction work for pragmatic learning in EFL contexts? *System* 33 (3), 417–435.

Alcón, E. (2006) Fostering EFL learners' awareness of requesting through explicit and implicit consciousness-raising tasks. In M.P. García Mayo (ed.) *Investigating Tasks in Formal Language Learning* (pp. 221–241). Clevedon: Multilingual Matters.

Alcón, E. (ed.) (2008) *Learning How to Request in an Instructed Language Learning Context*. Bern: Peter Lang.

Alcón, E. and Codina, V. (2002) Practice opportunities and pragmatic change in a second language context: The case of requests. *Estudios de Lingüística Aplicada* 3, 123–138.

Alcón, E. and Martínez-Flor, A. (2005) Pragmatics in instructed language learning [Special Issue]. *System* 33 (3), 381–536.

Alcón, E. and Safont, M.P. (2008) Pragmatic awareness. In J. Cenoz and N. Hornberger (eds) *Encyclopedia of Language and Education* (Vol. 6, pp. 193–204). New York: Springer.

Antón, M. (1999) The discourse of a learner-centered classroom: Sociocultural perspectives on teacher–learner interaction in second-language classroom. *Modern Language Journal* 83, 303–318.

Bachman, L.F. (1990) *Fundamental Considerations in Language Testing*. Oxford: Oxford University Press.

Bardovi-Harlig, K. (2001) Evaluating the empirical evidence: Grounds for instruction in pragmatics. In K.R. Rose and G. Kasper (eds) *Pragmatics in Language Teaching* (pp. 13–32). Cambridge: Cambridge University Press.

Bardovi-Harlig, K. (2002) Pragmatics and second language acquisition. In R.B. Kaplan (ed.) *The Oxford Handbook of Applied Linguistics* (pp. 182–192). Oxford: Oxford University Press.

Bardovi-Harlig, K. and Dörnyei, Z. (1998) Do language learners recognize pragmatic violations? Pragmatic versus grammatical awareness in instructed L2 learning. *TESOL Quarterly* 32, 233–259.

Bardovi-Harlig, K. and Hartford, B.S. (1993) Learning the rules of academic talk: A longitudinal study of pragmatic development. *Studies in Second Language Acquisition* 15, 279–304.

Bardovi-Harlig, K. and Hartford, B.S. (1996) Input in an institutional setting. *Studies in Second Language Acquisition* 18, 171–190.

Bardovi-Harlig, K. and Mahan-Taylor, R. (2003) *Teaching Pragmatics*. Washington DC: US Department of State Office of English Language Programs.

Bardovi-Harlig, K., Hartford, B.S., Mahan-Taylor, R., Morgan, M.J. and Reynolds, D.W. (1991) Developing pragmatic awareness: Closing the conversation. *ELT Journal* 45, 4–15.

Barron, A. (2003) *Acquisition in Interlanguage Pragmatics: Learning How To Do Things with Words in a Study Abroad Context*. Amsterdam: John Benjamins.

Bialystok, E. (1993) Symbolic representation and attentional control in pragmatic competence. In G. Kasper and S. Blum-Kulka (eds) *Interlanguage Pragmatics* (pp. 43–57). New York: Oxford University Press.

Blum-Kulka, S. (1991) Interlanguage pragmatics: The case of requests. In R. Phillipson, E. Kellerman, L. Selinker, M. Sharwood-Smith and M. Swain (eds) *Foreign/Second Language Pedagogy Research* (pp. 255–272). Clevedon: Multilingual Matters.

Boxer, D. and Pickering, L. (1995) Problems in the presentation of speech acts in ELT materials. The case of complaints. *ELT Journal* 49, 44–58.

Brown, P. and Levinson, S.C. (1987) *Politeness. Some Universals in Language Use*. Cambridge: Cambridge University Press.

Canale, M. (1983) From communicative competence to communicative language pedagogy. In J.C. Richards and R.W. Schmidt (eds) *Language and Communication* (pp. 2–27). London: Longman.

Canale, M. and Swain, M. (1980) Theoretical bases of communicative approaches to second language teaching and testing. *Applied Linguistics* 1, 1–47.

Celce-Murcia, M., Dörnyei, Z. and Thurrell, S. (1995) Communicative competence: A pedagogically motivated model with content specifications. *Issues in Applied Linguistics* 6, 5–35.

Cohen, A. (1997) Developing pragmatic ability: Insights from the accelerated study of Japanese. In H.M. Cook, K. Hijirida and M. Tahara (eds) *New Trends and Issues in Teaching Japanese Language and Culture* (pp. 137–163). Honolulu: University of Hawai'i, Second Language Teaching and Curriculum Center.

Cohen, A. and Olshtain, E. (1993) The production of speech acts by EFL learners. *TESOL Quarterly* 27, 33–56.

Cook, M. and Liddicoat, A.J. (2002) The development of comprehension in interlanguage pragmatics: The case of request strategies in English. *Australian Review of Applied Linguistics* 25 (1), 19–39.

Crandall, E. and Basturkmen, H. (2004) Evaluating pragmatics-focused materials. *ELT Journal* 58 (1), 38–49.

Duff, P.A. (1995) Ethnography in a foreign language immersion context: Language socialization through EFL and history. *TESOL Quarterly* 29, 505–537.

Duff, P.A (1996) Different languages, different practices: Socialization of discourse competence in dual-language school classroom in Hungary. In D. Nunan and K.B. Bailey (eds) *Voices from the Language Classroom* (pp. 407–433). Cambridge: Cambridge University Press.

DuFon, M.A. (1999) The acquisition of linguistic politeness in Indonesian as a second language by sojourners in naturalistic interactions. Unpublished PhD thesis, University of Hawai'i at Manoa.

Falsgraf, C. and Majors, D. (1995) Implicit culture in Japanese immersion classroom discourse. *Journal of the Association of Teachers of Japanese* 29 (2), 1–21.

Félix-Brasdefer, J.C. (2004) Interlanguage refusals: Linguistic politeness and length of residence in the target community. *Language Learning* 54, 587–653.

Fraser, B. (1990) Perspectives on politeness. *Journal of Pragmatics* 14, 219–236.

Gilmore, A. (2004) A comparison of textbooks and authentic interactions. *ELT Journal* 58, 362–374.

Grant, L. and Starks, D. (2001) Screening appropriate teaching materials. Closings from textbooks and television soap operas. *International Review of Applied Linguistics* 39, 39–50.

Hall, J.K. (1998) Differential teacher attention to student utterances: The construction of different opportunities for learning in the IRF. *Linguistics and Education* 9, 287–311.

Hassall, T. (1997) Requests by Australian learners of Indonesian. Unpublished doctoral dissertation, Australian National University, Canberra.

House, J. (1996) Developing pragmatic fluency in English as a foreign language. *Studies in Second Language Acquisition* 18, 225–253.

House, J. and Kasper, G. (1981) Politeness markers in English and German. In F. Coulmas (ed.) *Conversational Routine* (pp. 157–185). The Hague: Mouton de Gruyter.

Jeon, E.H. and Kaya, T. (2006) Effects of L2 instruction on interlanguage pragmatic development. In J.M. Norris and L. Ortega (eds) *Synthesizing Research on Language Learning and Teaching* (pp. 165–211). Amsterdam: John Benjamins.

Kanagy, R. (1999) Interactional routines as a mechanism for L2 acquisition and socialization in an immersion context. *Journal of Pragmatics* 31, 1467–1492.

Kasper, G. (2001a) Classroom research on interlanguage pragmatics. In K.R. Rose and G. Kasper (eds) *Pragmatics in Language Teaching* (pp. 33–60). Cambridge: Cambridge University Press.

Kasper, G. (2001b) Four perspectives on L2 pragmatic development. *Applied Linguistics* 22 (4), 502–530.

Kasper, G. (2004) Participant orientation in German conversation-for-learning. *The Modern Language Journal* 88, 551–567.

Kasper, G. (2006) Beyond repair. Conversation analysis as an approach to SLA. *AILA Review* 19, 83–99.

Kasper, G. and Roever, C. (2005) Pragmatics in second language learning. In E. Hinkel (ed.) *Handbook of Research in Second Language Teaching and Learning* (pp. 317–334). Mahwah, NJ: Lawrence Erlbaum Associates.

Kasper, G. and Rose, K.R. (1999) Pragmatics and SLA. *Annual Review of Applied Linguistics* 19, 81–104.

Kasper, G. and Rose, K.R. (2002) *Pragmatic Development in a Second Language*. Malden: Blackwell Publishers.

Kasper, G. and Schmidt, R. (1996) Developmental issues in interlanguage pragmatics. *Studies in Second Language Acquisition* 18, 149–169.

Kobayashi, H. and Rinnert, C. (2003) Coping with high imposition requests: High vs. low proficiency EFL students in Japan. In A. Martínez-Flor, E. Usó-Juan and A. Fernández-Guerra (eds) *Pragmatic Competence in Foreign Language Teaching* (pp. 161–184). Castelló: Servei de Publicacions de la Universitat Jaume I.

Koike, D.A. (1989) Pragmatic competence and adult L2 acquisition. Speech acts in interlanguage. *Modern Language Journal* 73 (3), 79–89.

Koike, D.A. (1996) Transfer of pragmatic competence and suggestions in Spanish foreign language learning. In S. Gass and J. Neu (eds) *Speech Acts across Cultures* (pp. 257–281). Berlin: Mouton de Gruyter.

Koike, D.A. and Pearson, L. (2005) The effect of instruction and feedback in the development of pragmatic competence. *System* 33 (3), 481–501.

Kondo, S. (2003) Teaching refusals in an EFL setting. In K. Bardovi-Harlig and R. Mahan-Taylor (eds) *Teaching Pragmatics*. Washington DC: US Department of

State Office of English Language Programs. On WWW at http://exchanges. state.gov/education/engteaching/pragmatics/kondo.htm. Accessed 25.2.08.
Leech, G. (1983) *The Principles of Pragmatics*. London: Longman.
Leow, R.P. (1997) Attention, awareness, and foreign language behaviour. *Language Learning* 47, 467–505.
Leow, R.P. (2000) A study of the role of awareness in foreign language behaviour. *Studies in Second language Acquisition* 22, 557–584.
Li, D. (2000) The pragmatics of making requests in the L2 workplace: A case study of language socialization. *The Canadian Modern Language Review* 57, 58–87.
Liddicoat, A.J. and Crozet, C. (2001) Acquiring French interactional norms through instruction. In K.R. Rose and G. Kasper (eds) *Pragmatics in Language Teaching* (pp. 125–144). Cambridge: Cambridge University Press.
Long, M.H. (1996) The role of linguistic environment in second language acquisition. In W.C. Ritchie and T.K. Bhatia (eds) *Handbook of Second language Acquisition* (pp. 413–468). San Diego: Academic Press.
Lörscher, W. and Schulze, R. (1988) On polite speaking and foreign language classroom discourse. *International Review of Applied Linguistics in Language Teaching* 26, 183–199.
Lyster, R. (1994) The effect of functional-analytical teaching on aspects of French immersion students' sociolinguistic competence. *Applied Linguistics* 15 (3), 263–287.
Mach, T. and Ridder, S. (2003) E-mail requests. In K. Bardovi-Harlig and R. Mahan-Taylor (eds) *Teaching Pragmatics*. Washington DC: US Department of State Office of English Language Programs. On WWW at http://exchanges. state.gov/education/engteaching/pragmatics/mach.htm. Accessed 25.2.08.
Maeshiba, N., Yoshinaga, N., Kasper, G. and Ross, S. (1996) Transfer and proficiency in interlanguage apologizing. In S.M. Gass and J. Neu (eds) *Speech Acts across Cultures* (pp. 155–187). Berlin: Mouton de Gruyter.
Martínez-Flor, A. (2006) The effectiveness of explicit and implicit treatments on EFL learners' confidence in recognising appropriate suggestions. In K. Bardovi-Harlig, C. Félix-Brasdefer and A.S. Omar (eds) *Pragmatics and Language Learning* (Vol. 11, pp. 199–225). Honolulu: University of Hawai'i at Manoa, National Foreign Language Resource Center.
Martínez-Flor, A. (2007a) Analysing request modification devices in films: Implications for pragmatic learning in instructed foreign language contexts. In E. Alcón and M.P. Safont (eds) *Intercultural Language Use and Language Learning* (pp. 245–280). Amsterdam: Springer.
Martínez-Flor, A. (2007b) Learners' use of downgraders in suggestions under Focus on FormS and focus on form treatment conditions. *Revista Canaria de Estudios Ingleses* (55), 167–180.
Martínez-Flor, A. and Alcón, E. (2007) Developing pragmatic awareness of suggestions in the EFL classroom: A focus on instructional effects. *Canadian Journal of Applied Linguistics* 10 (1), 47–76.
Martínez-Flor, A. and Fukuya, Y.J. (2005) The effects of instruction on learners' production of appropriate and accurate suggestions. *System* 33 (3), 463–480.
Martínez-Flor, A. and Usó-Juan, E. (2006) A comprehensive pedagogical framework to develop pragmatics in the foreign language classroom: The 6Rs approach. *Applied Language Learning* 16 (2), 39–64.
Martínez-Flor, A., Usó-Juan, E. and Fernández-Guerra, A. (eds) (2003) *Pragmatic Competence and Foreign Language Teaching*. Castellón: Servei de Publicacions de la Universitat Jaume I.

Morrow, C.K. (1995) The pragmatic effects of instruction on ESL learners' production of complaint and refusal speech acts. Unpublished PhD thesis, State University of New York.

Niezgoda, K. and Röver, C. (2001) Pragmatic and grammatical awareness. In K.R. Rose and G. Kasper (eds) *Pragmatics in Language Teaching* (pp. 63–79). Cambridge: Cambridge University Press.

Nikula, T. (1996) *Pragmatic Force Modifiers. A Study in Interlanguage Pragmatics.* Jyväskylä: University of Jyväskylä.

Ohta, A.S. (1995) Applying sociocultural theory to an analysis of learner discourse: Learner–learner collaborative interaction in the zone of proximal development. *Issues in Applied Linguistics* 6, 93–121.

Ohta, A.S. (2001) *Second Language Processes in the Classroom: Learning Japanese.* Mahwah, NJ: Lawrence Erlbaum Associates.

Olshtain, E. and Blum-Kulka, S. (1985) Degree of approximation: Non-native reactions to native speech act behaviour. In S. Gass and C. Madden (eds) *Input in Second Language Acquisition* (pp. 303–325). Rowley, MA: Newbury House.

Olshtain, E. and Cohen, A.D. (1990) The learning of complex speech act behavior. *TESL Canada Journal* 7, 45–65.

Reynolds, D. (2003) Complaining successfully. In K. Bardovi-Harlig and R. Mahan-Taylor (eds) *Teaching Pragmatics.* Washington, DC: US Department of State Office of English Language Programs. On WWW at http://exchanges.state.gov/education/engteaching/pragmatics/reynolds.htm. Accessed 25.2.08.

Roever, C. (2005) *Testing ESL Pragmatics: Development and Validation of a Web-based Assessment Battery.* Frankfurt: Peter Lang.

Rosa, E. and Leow, R. (2004) Computerized task-based exposure, explicitness, type of feedback, and Spanish L2 development. *The Modern Language Journal* 88, 192–216.

Rosa, E. and O'Neill, M.D. (1999) Explicitness, intake, and the issue of awareness. *Studies in Second language Acquisition* 21, 511–556.

Rose, K.R. (1997) Pragmatics in the classroom: Theoretical concerns and practical possibilities. In L.F. Bouton (ed.) *Pragmatics and Language Learning* (Vol. 8, pp. 267–295). Urbana, IL: University of Illinois at Urbana-Champaign.

Rose, K.R. (2000) An exploratory cross-sectional study of interlanguage pragmatic development. *Studies in Second Language Acquisition* 22, 27–67.

Rose, K.R. (2001) Compliments and compliment responses in film: Implications for pragmatics research and language teaching. *International Review of Applied Linguistics* 39, 309–326.

Rose, K.R. (2005) On the effects of instruction in second language pragmatics. *System* 33 (3), 385–399.

Rose, K.R. and Kasper, G. (eds) (2001) *Pragmatics in Language Teaching.* Cambridge: Cambridge University Press.

Rose, K.R. and Ng Kwai-fun, C. (2001) Inductive and deductive approaches to teaching compliments and compliment responses. In K.R. Rose and G. Kasper (eds) *Pragmatics in Language Teaching* (pp. 145–170). Cambridge: Cambridge University Press.

Rossiter, P. and Kondoh, A.S. (2001) Pragmatic transfer in making requests. In K. Matsuno and S. Yoshijima (eds) *Foreign Language Theory: From Theory to Practice* (pp. 107–154). Tokyo: Asahi Shuppan.

Safont, M.P. (2003) Instructional effects on the use of request acts modification devices by EFL learners. In A. Martínez-Flor, E. Usó-Juan and A. Fernández-Guerra (eds) *Pragmatic Competence and Foreign Language Teaching* (pp. 211–232). Castelló: Publicacions de la Universitat Jaume I.

Safont, M.P. (2005) *Third Language Learners. Pragmatic Production and Awareness.* Clevedon: Multilingual Matters.

Safont, M.P. (2007) Pragmatic production of third language learners: A focus on request external modifications. In E. Alcón and M.P. Safont (eds) *Intercultural Language Use and Language Learning* (pp. 167–189). Amsterdam: Springer.

Salazar, P. (2003) Pragmatic instruction in the EFL context. In A. Martínez-Flor, E. Usó-Juan and A. Fernández-Guerra (eds) *Pragmatic Competence and Foreign Language Teaching* (pp. 233–246). Castelló: Publicacions de la Universitat Jaume I.

Salazar, P. (2007) Examining mitigation in requests: A focus on transcripts in ELT coursebooks. In E. Alcón and M.P. Safont (eds) *Intercultural Language Use and Language Learning* (pp. 207–222). Amsterdam: Springer.

Schauer, G.A. (2006) Pragmatic awareness in ESL and EFL contexts: Contrast and development. *Language Learning* 56 (2), 269–318.

Schieffelin, B. and Ochs, E. (1986) Language socialization. *Annual Review of Anthropology* 15, 163–191.

Schmidt, R. (1993) Consciousness, learning and interlanguage pragmatics. In G. Kasper and S. Blum-Kulka (eds) *Interlanguage Pragmatics* (pp. 21–42). New York: Oxford University Press.

Schmidt, R. (1995) Consciousness and foreign language learning: A tutorial on the role of attention and awareness in learning. In R. Schmidt (ed.) *Attention and Awareness in Foreign Language Learning* (pp. 1–63). Honolulu: University of Hawai'i at Manoa, National Foreign Language Resource Center.

Schmidt, R. (2001) Attention. In P. Robinson (ed.) *Cognition and Second Language Instruction* (pp. 3–33). New York: Cambridge University Press.

Sharwood Smith, M. (1981) Consciousness-raising and the second language learner. *Applied Linguistics* 11, 159–168.

Sharwood Smith, M. (1991) Speaking to many minds: On the relevance of different types of language information for the L2 learner. *Second Language Research* 7, 118–132.

Takahashi, S. (1996) Pragmatic transferability. *Studies in Second Language Acquisition* 18, 189–223.

Takahashi, S. (2001) The role of input enhancement in developing pragmatic competence. In K.R. Rose and G. Kasper (eds) *Pragmatics in Language Teaching* (pp. 171–199). Cambridge: Cambridge University Press.

Takahashi, T. and Beebe, L.M. (1987) The development of pragmatic competence by Japanese learners of English. *JALT Journal* 8, 131–155.

Tateyama, Y. (2001) Explicit and implicit teaching of pragmatic routines. In K.R. Rose and G. Kasper (eds) *Pragmatics in Language Teaching* (pp. 200–222). Cambridge: Cambridge University Press.

Tateyama, Y., Kasper, G., Mui, L., Tay, H. and Thananart, O. (1997) Explicit and implicit teaching of pragmatics routines. In L.F. Bouton (ed.) *Pragmatics and Language Learning* (Vol. 8, pp. 163–177). Urbana, IL: University of Illinois at Urbana-Champaign.

Tatsuki, D. (ed.) (2005) *Pragmatics in Language Learning, Theory and Practice.* Tokyo: JALT, The Japan Association for Language Teaching, Pragmatics Special Interest Group.

Thomas, J. (1983) Cross-cultural pragmatic failure. *Applied Linguistics* 4, 91–112.

Trosborg, A. (1987) Apology strategies in natives/non-natives. *Journal of Pragmatics* 11, 147–167.

Trosborg, A. (1995) *Interlanguage Pragmatics: Requests, Complaints and Apologies.* Berlin/New York: Mouton de Gruyter.

Usó-Juan, E. (2007) The presentation and practice of the communicative act of requesting in textbooks: Focusing on modifiers. In E. Alcón and M.P. Safont (eds) *Intercultural Language Use and Language Learning* (pp. 223–244). Amsterdam: Springer.

Usó-Juan, E. and Martínez-Flor, A. (2006) Approaches to language learning and teaching: Towards acquiring communicative competence through the four skills. In E. Usó-Juan and A. Martínez-Flor (eds) *Current Trends in the Development and Teaching of the Four Language Skills* (pp. 3–25). Berlin: Mouton de Gruyter.

Washburn, G.N. (2001) Using situation comedies for pragmatic language teaching and learning. *TESOL Journal* 10 (4), 21–26

Wildner-Bassett, M. (1984) *Improving Pragmatic Aspects of Learners' Interlanguage.* Tübingen: Narr.

Wildner-Bassett, M. (1986) Teaching and learning 'polite noises': Improving pragmatic aspects of advanced adult learners' interlanguage. In G. Kasper (ed.) *Learning, Teaching and Communication in the Foreign Language Classroom* (pp. 163–178). Aarthus: Aarthus University Press.

Wildner-Bassett, M. (1994) Intercultural pragmatics and proficiency: 'Polite noises for cultural appropriateness. *International Review of Applied Linguistics* 32, 3–17.

Yoshimi, D.R. (2001) Explicit instruction and the use of interactional discourse markers. In K.R. Rose and G. Kasper (eds) *Pragmatics in Language Teaching* (pp. 223–244). Cambridge: Cambridge University Press.

Young, R. and He, A.W. (1998) *Talking and Testing: Discourse Approaches to the Assessment of Oral Proficiency.* Philadelphia: John Benjamins.

Young, R. and Miller, E.R. (2004) Learning as changing participation: Discourse roles in ESL writing conferences. *The Modern Language Journal* 88, 519–535.

Part 1
Investigating How Pragmatics Can Be Learned in Foreign Language Contexts

Chapter 2
Language Socialization Theory and the Acquisition of Pragmatics in the Foreign Language Classroom

MARGARET A. DUFON

Interlanguage Pragmatics and Language Socialization

The field of second language acquisition (SLA) and its subdisciplines of cross-cultural pragmatics (CCP) and interlanguage pragmatics (ILP) have been dominated since their inception by cognitive approaches to language acquisition theory. These theories view language learning as an individual, mental process, which functions independently of context of use (Davis, 1995; Zuengler & Miller, 2006). While research on pragmatics in SLA has given attention to context, data have typically been collected under controlled experimental or quasi-experimental conditions, most often using discourse completion tasks (Bardovi-Harlig & Hartford, 2005a), in which learners only imagine what they would say in a given context. In relatively few studies (e.g. Bardovi-Harlig & Hartford, 2005b; DuFon, 2000, 2003, 2006; Siegal, 1995a, 1995b) have pragmatic data been collected within the actual context itself. However, in the last decade or so, sociocultural theories, which 'foreground the social and cultural contexts of learning' (Zuengler & Miller, 2006: 37) such as language socialization (LS) theory, have been gaining ground within SLA in general and in ILP in particular. In fact, LS theory has accumulated such force that in her article on *Mind, Language, and Epistemology: Toward a Language Socialization Paradigm for SLA*, Watson-Gegeo (2004) indicates that we are in the process of a paradigm shift, one in which LS theory will emerge as central in SLA research and practice.

Language Socialization Theory

LS theory is particularly useful to the study of ILP because it focuses on language use in social interaction or the pragmatic aspects of linguistic behavior; however, its scope and perspective are broader (Davis & Henze, 1998; Kasper & Rose, 2002). In LS theory, the language learner is viewed more holistically (Watson-Gegeo, 1988; Watson-Gegeo & Nielsen, 2003), a trend which is not isolated to language acquisition but can also be seen in other fields such as the health care industry (e.g. Benor, 2001,

2004; Duff *et al.*, 2002) and education (Miller, 1996). With a holistic view, greater emphasis is placed on the human being as a social, emotional, mental and spiritual being embodied in a physical form (Watson-Gegeo, 2004) and the sociocultural, political, economic and educational environment in which they live (cf. Johnson, 2006; Watson-Gegeo, 1992). All of these aspects need to be taken into consideration in the study of SLA.

Much of the current theoretical debate in SLA seems to center around which view of the learner – as an individual mind or a social being – and which general theoretical approach – cognitive or sociocultural – should dominate in SLA (e.g. Zuengler & Miller, 2006). However, theoretical approaches that focus only on the mental or only on the social aspects of acquisition can just tell a part of the story. We need to view SLA theory more like light, which is *both* wave *and* particle. Language acquisition is *both* social *and* mental; both are required and both depend on the other. However, Watson-Gegeo (2004) challenges us to expand its domain even further to include greater emphasis on the *mind* in general, not just cognition or higher level mental functions (e.g. language, voluntary memory, logical reasoning, etc.), but also lower level functions such as emotions (cf. Pavlenko, 2006), as higher level processes cannot operate independently of them. She also challenges us to consider the spiritual and physical aspects as well, which so far have been given little attention in SLA (however see Christison *et al.*, 2002; Crozet, 2006; Goulah, 2006a, 2006b; Hong, 2005 for some exceptions). Moreover, LS theory, as conceived and developed by Ochs and Schieffelin (1984) and Schieffelin and Ochs (1986a, 1986b), is inherently developmental. It focuses on the process of language acquisition over time by examining language use between experts and novices in naturalistic interactive contexts. Microanalyses of this language use are then linked to macrolevel analyses of cultural values, beliefs and practices in informal and institutional contexts (Kasper, 1997; Watson-Gegeo, 1992). As Western dualistic thinking – which separates mind from body, mental processes from social ones, language acquisition from language use – is increasingly questioned by scientists across a range of disciplines (Watson-Gegeo, 2004), we ultimately need a theory that is holistic in nature, taking all aspects of our human beingness and our interconnectedness with other human beings and the rest of the world into consideration. With its holistic orientation, LS theory is ideally positioned to take on such a task.

LS theory is an interactionist theory; it views social interaction as crucial to the acquisition of language. According to LS theory, the relationship between language and socialization is two-fold: *socialization to use language* and *socialization through the use of language* (Ochs & Schieffelin, 1984; Schieffelin & Ochs, 1986a, 1986b). *Socialization to use language* refers to those instances when learners are taught what to say in a given context. In naturalistic contexts, this teaching can be either direct or indirect (DuFon, 1994). Direct teaching might occur when, for example, a caregiver tells a child who has been greeted by an adult to, 'Say, *hello*'. Indirect teaching can occur through prompts such as when the caregiver asks the child in the same situation, 'What do you say'? In the foreign language classroom, teachers often socialize their students to use language by informing them of how a particular speech act could be realized appropriately in a given context. For example, in an Indonesian language classroom an instructor might tell the class, 'When passing an older person on the street, it is not sufficiently polite to just say "Selamat pagi" [Good morning]; you should say "Selamat pagi, Pak" [Good morning, Sir] or "Selamat pagi, Bu" [Good morning, ma'am] in order to show proper respect'.

Socialization through the use of language refers to the process by which learners acquire knowledge of the culture in question as well as of their status and role and their associated rights and obligations as they learn the language. That is, the ways in which discourse is structured, the linguistic forms that are chosen, the functions of these forms and the contexts in which they occur carry implicit messages regarding the values, beliefs, attitudes and world view of the speech community in question toward the situation and participants in any given interaction. For example, in classrooms and seminars in a state university in Indonesia, professors often greeted their students only with the Muslim greeting *assalamu'alaikum*. In other cases, they greeted Moslems first with *assalamu'alaikum* and followed with a second more general greeting, *'dan untuk yang bukan muslim, selamat pagi'* [And for those of you who are not Muslim, good morning]. The content and information structuring of these greetings socialize foreign language learners into several cultural values and realities: (1) religion is a very important part of everyday life in Indonesia (indicated by the use of a religious greeting, *assalamu'alaikum*); (2) Islam is the dominant religion and those who are Muslims are privileged over those who are not (indicated by the use of the Muslim greeting first followed by a more generic greeting second); and (3) although Indonesia is not an Islamic state, religion and government are not kept separate to the extent they are in the USA (indicated by the use of a religious greeting in a government institution). In other words, the way these greetings are used in this context socializes learners regarding mainstream societal values at the same time that language use is being acquired. As such, LS can be viewed in part as 'a process of assigning situational, ie, indexical meanings...to particular forms' (Ochs, 1996: 410–411). Thus LS theory draws upon but modifies the ideas of Whorf (1941) that the way in which language is used shapes our world view (Ochs, 1988).

LS Theory in First Language Acquisition

LS theory was first developed in the study of first language and culture acquisition within the field of anthropology and many studies began to appear in the mid to late 1980s. Because of its anthropological roots, the cultures and languages under study tended to be non-Western such as Basotho (Demuth, 1986), Japanese (Clancy, 1986, 1989; Cook, 1990), Javanese (Smith-Hefner, 1988); Kaluli (Schieffelin, 1986, 1990), Kwara'ae (Watson-Gegeo & Gegeo, 1986) and Samoan (Ochs, 1986, 1988; Platt, 1986), and the method of investigation, ethnography, viewed language acquisition holistically. With a holistic approach, the structural components of language cannot be separated from their functions or from the context in which they exist. Consequently, the process of acquisition is as important as the product, attention is focused not only on the language of the child and caregivers, but also on the built environment (e.g. the influence of the spatial arrangement of houses within a community as well as their interior design on social interaction), the structure of caregiving (the family structure and the roles, rights and obligations of the various members with respect to the child), the society's view of the child (e.g. as a conversation partner/information giver or as someone who should listen respectfully to wiser elders) and its beliefs about language acquisition (e.g. whether modified speech is necessary, whether unintelligible utterances are nevertheless meaningful). Thus, as children learn their mother tongue, they also acquire the culture of its members (Ochs & Schieffelin, 1984).

This is not to say that all persons in a speech community are identical in their values and beliefs. There is, of course, some degree of individual variation. Moreover, caregivers are not always totally successful in socializing their children exactly the way they would like them to be. LS theory, in fact, argues that socialization is a two-way process. The child also socializes the caregivers, who need to adjust their ways of thinking, believing and behaving to accommodate the child to some extent. While most of the socialization is from expert to novice, some portion is also novice to expert socialization in both first (e.g. Ochs, 1988, 1996; Pease-Alvarez & Vasquez, 1994; Schieffelin, 1990) and second (e.g. Cook, 2006) LS. While some individual variation exists, there are, nevertheless, predominant cultural patterns. Thus, as part of the process of socialization, each person develops both individual and cultural identities, which are associated with his or her beliefs and values, and which manifest themselves in the ways in which language is used and social roles are enacted; likewise the ways in which language is used and social roles are enacted reinforce those identities and their associated values and beliefs. Thus as children are socialized through the use of language in their mother tongue, they develop not only a *language for communication* but also *a language for identification* (Hüllen, 1992 as cited by House, 2003).

LS Theory and SLA

During the 1990s, studies of second language socialization began to appear. Because LS theory focuses on interaction with competent native speakers, most of these have investigated language acquisition in second language contexts at home (Schecter & Bayley, 1997), school (Duff, 2002; Poole, 1992; Willett, 1995) or both (Crago, 1992; Findlay, 1995; Pease-Alvarez & Vasquez, 1994; Watson-Gegeo, 1992). Studies of the socialization of foreign language learners in either study abroad contexts (Cook, 2006; DuFon, 2000, 2006; Siegal, 1995a, 1995b, 1996; Yoshimi, 1999) or foreign language classrooms at home (e.g. Duff, 1995, 1996; Ohta, 1994, 1999) have so far been small in number. Nevertheless, these studies demonstrate that LS theory can be an appropriate framework for teaching and researching pragmatics in the foreign language classroom (cf. Kasper, 2001).

However, the process of second and foreign language socialization rests on a different set of assumptions than that of L1 socialization (Duff, 2003). First, in the case of first language socialization, children have ready access to competent members of their target community, who provide them with many opportunities for the input and interaction needed to acquire language forms and appropriate ways of speaking. Second language learners, in contrast, frequently find themselves outside the target culture without ready access to native speakers of the target language even when they are surrounded by them (Hoffman-Hicks, 2000; Isabelli-García, 2003, 2006; Kinginger & Whitworth, 2005).

Second, while L1 acquisition studies have focused on monolingual acquisition and membership in a single speech community, no such assumption can be taken for granted in foreign language contexts (Duff, 2003). In foreign language contexts, learners are by definition becoming bilingual. They might be interested in integrating into a particular culture whose members speak the particular language they are studying but without losing their own native linguistic and cultural identities. Consequently, they will aim to be bilingual–bicultural persons who can dance back and forth between their native and foreign languages and cultures. However, particularly in the case of English, which is the current international lingua franca, foreign language learners do not necessarily want to integrate into British, North American, Australian or other *inner circle* (Kachru, 1985) groups. Their goal may be one of bilingual or multilingual competence, which would enable them to participate in international discourse and to interact with people from a range of cultures for the purpose of business, education or diplomacy. In other words, they are interested in English as a *language for communication* but not as a *language for identification* (House, 2003).

Because English is not always a language of identification, we need then to ask the questions: Who are the experts that will socialize the novice? To which norms (i.e. to whose values, beliefs and behaviors) will they be socialized? Investigations into the use of English in international business settings (House, 2003) have revealed that the norms of interaction are more fluid when the interaction is between those who speak English as a foreign language than when it includes native English speakers. For example, although significantly fewer politeness markers and conversational management features were found in non-native interactions, the interactions appeared to have gone rather smoothly; as long as a certain minimum of understanding was maintained, unclear talk tended to be tolerated and EFL interlocutors waited for ensuing discourse to clear up misunderstandings rather than initiate repair sequences. Thus communication between EFL speakers can often be successful in its outcome in spite of many non-native qualities and 'pragmatic violations'.

Consequently House suggests that in EFL classrooms in which we are preparing students to use English as a lingua franca in international discourse, native speaker norms should not be the standard; instead we should look to expert EFL users, who have been successful communicators in international discourse, an approach that is in line with recent work in English for Specific Purposes with respect to pragmatics (Gibbs, 2005; Tarone, 2005). That is, rather than a generic native speaker as a model of what is appropriate use of language, we need to look for expert speakers, whether native or non-native, in a particular context to be the language socializers.

As we socialize learners into the foreign language, classroom teachers need to be mindful of the current and possible future goals of the students they teach. Is their goal to gain literacy in the foreign language in order to access material published in that language? Is it to acquire communicative competence in order to interact with native members of the target language community while studying or working abroad? Is it to acquire communicative competence in order to interact in an international environment with other non-native speakers of the target language? The answers to these questions will help determine what the learners need to be socialized to, who might be most appropriate to socialize them and how it might be appropriate to socialize them in the academic environment.

One study that illustrates this in practice is a second language study by Duff *et al.* (2002), which investigated the LS of Canadian immigrants training to be health-care aids in residential facilities and private homes. The training program itself placed an emphasis on the whole person (i.e. the mental, physical, emotional, spiritual, social aspects). While this study deals with pragmatics in only a very general way (as opposed to focusing on the linguistic details of speech acts for example), it does deal with the learners in a more holistic way, examining their communication needs and abilities in the classroom, in their two practicum settings, in their job settings, at home and in their community. In the classroom, emphasis was placed on nursing skills and English proficiency. However, at one practicum site, few patients spoke English and many suffered from Alzheimer's and dementia as well. Consequently proficiency in nursing skills and English was not sufficient; rather the L1 was sometimes a valuable resource as was the ability to communicate using foreigner talk and by 'reading' and 'writing' body language. At the second practicum sight, patients socialized the health care workers in training by letting them know their wants and needs and how they wanted to be treated. Duff *et al.* also document the social consequences that LS had on the trainees' social and emotional lives as they raised their status within their families and neighborhoods, and began to feel part of mainstream Canadian life. Consequently, this kind of study, while not providing us with information on the use of specific pragmatic forms, does give a more complete picture of the life of the learner and the forces and factors that facilitate or inhibit language acquisition and socialization. Another example can be found in a series of articles on ILP by Kerekes (2005, 2006, 2007), who investigated success in job interviews. While she examined language use in the job interviews, she also went beyond the interview itself to examine personal traits and other conditions that affected success in obtaining job placements. Although her studies were not LS studies, they were in many ways similar to them in that they involved microanalysis of naturalistic data, which was then analyzed with respect to the larger macrolevel context. Studies such as these are evidence that the fields of ILP and LS are moving closer together.

Another point that must be kept in mind in foreign language classrooms is that even in situations where one might socialize students into a specific culture as they teach language, it will likely not be possible to replicate the native classroom conditions in the target language classroom except possibly in very closely related cultures due to cultural, institutional and legal constraints. For example, as an American foreign student in Indonesia, I was shocked when one of my instructors returned our examinations in order by grade from highest to lowest, reading out the names and the grades as he did so. This did not occur in every class; nevertheless one's grade in Indonesia does not have the same legal privacy protection it does in America. In America, one's grade can only be conveyed to the student who earned it. Public postings of grades must use student ID numbers rather than names so that only the student will know which grade is his or hers. Later, when I became an instructor of Indonesian in the USA, theoretically I could have socialized them into this practice by returning examinations in that manner. However, as I was not comfortable with violating this American social norm and did not want any legal risks, I opted to merely tell them about this practice.

Davies and Tyler (2005) demonstrate the difficulty of transferring strategies across cultures. They examined an incident in which a Korean international teaching assistant (ITA) at an American university accused a student of cheating. Under normal circumstances, Americans typically use a deductive/assertive style when communicating with students while Koreans use an inductive/collaborative style. With a heavily face-threatening topic such as cheating, however, Americans would most likely switch to an inductive/collaborative style. In this particular cheating incident, interestingly, the Korean ITA switched to a deductive/assertive style. While this behavior was outside native English speaker norms, it was also outside Korean norms and could not be attributed to negative transfer. Rather such a situation was not likely to occur in Korea in the first place because of differences in teacher–student relationships, and in pedagogical, assessment and classroom management practices. Therefore the Korean had no experience or schema for handling the problem as it presented itself. In fact, to some extent, his behavior was the result of his attempting to accommodate to American norms; however, he was not totally clear on what those norms were nor had he mastered some of the finer points of the pragmatics of English such that his language use unwittingly contributed to the problematic communication between him and the student. Although this study was conducted in an ESL context and did not examine the incident from a LS perspective, it does provide empirical evidence that certain cultural and institutional constraints limit the extent to which classroom discourse practices that socialize the learner to the target culture can be transferred from a native to a foreign classroom setting.

Studies of Language Socialization in the Foreign Language Classroom

In this section, key studies of LS in the foreign language classroom will be reviewed. Not all of these studies were necessarily done within a LS framework, but could be interpreted within that frame. These studies examine the socialization of participants ranging in age from children to adults. The approach taken has been somewhat different depending on the age group.

Kanagy (1999) conducted a study of American kindergarten children learning Japanese in an immersion program while focusing on three routines: greetings, taking attendance and making personal introductions, with greetings being the simplest and most formulaic and personal introductions being the most complex and creative. At the same time the children were learning these forms, they were also tacitly learning about Japanese values and behaviors. Japanese culture places a high value on form and outward appearance. This value is evident in pragmatic routines as well as other aspects of the culture. For example, the greeting involved a bow. Before cueing the bow or the verbal words of the greeting, however, the teacher made sure that all students were standing properly – erect with hands folded, heels together and eyes gazing toward the teacher – through the use of modeling, repetition, verbal prompts, non-verbal demonstrations and feedback. In addition, the teacher placed greater emphasis on accurate pronunciation of the words involved over understanding the meaning of each and every one of them. In these ways, then, she scaffolded the children's acquisition of the verbal and non-verbal forms necessary to participate competently in these routines while at the same time sending them implicit messages about the importance of attention to form and personal appearance in Japanese culture. Likewise, this pedagogical approach socialized the children into the value placed on observation and imitation as tools for learning.

Similar patterns can be seen in Bell's (1995) account of her attempts to acquire literacy in Chinese while a student at the college level. As in Kanagy's study, Bell's tutor placed a heavy emphasis on form, and on observation and imitation as key pedagogical tools. Unlike the more open and malleable kindergarteners that Kanagy studied, Bell was older and more resistant to the approach and tried to learn her L2 literacy in the same way that she had learned her L1 literacy. She and her Chinese tutor held different unconscious assumptions regarding the qualities of self displayed by literacy skills, what constitutes a good language learner, the relationship between content and form, and the values placed upon them as well as different values regarding analytic versus holistic approaches to literacy learning, which created a certain degree of tension in the learning environment. Consequently, Bell did not progress as she would have liked. Although Bell did not conduct this study within a LS framework, she does address issues of the connection between language teaching, learning, identity and the cultural values of teacher and learner. Furthermore, her conclusions are very much in line with LS theory.

> It is no doubt possible to learn to read and write in Chinese by methods which essentially allow one to transcribe English thinking via Chinese characters. Such an ability should not be confused, however, with developing Chinese literacy. In the same way, ESL literacy teachers have to recognize that they are teaching far more than the letters of the alphabet. I have suggested above that we need to think about the relationship between form and content and that

between part and whole. We need to become conscious of our notions of how progress is measured and how it is rewarded. We need to consider the human qualities which are valued in our society and explore how these are made manifest in our preferred literacy practices. We need to explore our own assumptions and recognize that much of what we used to consider an inherent part of literacy is actually culturally imposed. (Bell, 1995: 702)

Although Bell did not seem to be aware of LS theory at the time she conducted her research, her own experience as a language learner led her to conclude that language and literacy learning could not be separated from the culture in which language and literacy use are embedded.

The importance of culture is evident as well in Duff's (1995, 1996, 2003) investigations of second language socialization at the secondary level in Hungary during the year following the dissolution of the Soviet Union. These studies are interesting because Hungary was, at that time, in a state of rapid change. Values, attitudes, behaviors and classroom norms of interaction, particularly in English-medium classes, were changing at an accelerated rate. Teachers who taught in English had recently been socialized into the values of democracy and critical thinking and felt compelled to alter their teaching and assessment practices to be more in line with those values. The focus of Duff's investigation was a traditional Hungarian assessment method called *felelés*, which required a fluent and accurate summary of the previous day's history lesson given by a student on demand and graded on a five-point scale. While this method continued in non-dual language (Hungarian) programs, it was modified or replaced in dual language (DL), Hungarian–English, programs. Duff (1996: 409) describes the *felelés* as 'a micro-level crystallization of macro-level changes and tensions pervasive in the school community and beyond'. For example, with the movement toward a more democratic ideology in the larger society, DL teachers felt compelled to replace summarizing the previous lesson by a teacher-selected student with voluntary, pre-planned presentations. While the students initially enjoyed and appreciated these new means of assessment, they were problematic for a number of reasons. First, it was difficult to balance democracy with respect and discipline as increased democracy affected these values. For example, the students had better English than some of their teachers and therefore corrected them; the teachers, in order to maintain their status, had to be very secure with the content, which was often difficult, particularly for new teachers. Second, the DL students tried to *resocialize* the teachers of their more traditionally run classrooms, pushing them away from traditional practices and toward Western pedagogical practices. This was not in every way productive. In a traditional assessment, students were more likely to be given specific, if harsh, feedback on what was problematic with their performance whereas in the more Westernized classes, they were likely to be praised and receive full credit for a weak performance, (e.g. a memorized rendition of an Encyclopedia Britannica entry, which was not comprehensible to their classmates). Thus grade inflation and overuse of praise (so typical and counterproductive in American schools) became a problem with the introduction of more democratic assessments. A third problem was that the students who only had had experiences with the Westernized pedagogical assessments were at a disadvantage for final examinations, which still relied on the *felelés*. Duff (1996: 428) likened the situation at one school to the metaphor of 'new wine in old wineskins' because although a new model of education, new pedagogical practices, new teachers and new technologies had emerged in the DL schools, the infrastructure (including assessment practices), discourse and leadership apparatus were still old. Such incongruency between assessment practices and current values and beliefs about SLA is not isolated to nations like Hungary but is prevalent in first-world nations as well (Jenkins, 2006). Ultimately, many of the more progressive teachers ended up leaving the schools in dismay, and in one school, the *felelés* had been reintroduced. Duff (1996: 431) concluded that 'different models of discourse socialization prevail and evolve in ways that may be in greater or lesser harmony with existing cultural and government-mandated assessment practices'.

Ohta (1999) investigated the socialization of college level learners of Japanese, focusing on interactional style in a Japanese language classroom at an American university. She investigated the acquisition of *extended assessments* and the Initiation-Response-Follow-up (IRF) routine in both learner–learner and teacher-fronted interactive contexts. The assessment typically occurs in the third slot of an exchange, the Follow-up portion of the routine. In teacher-fronted discourse, students had little opportunity to produce assessments. However, through peripheral participation, they were able to observe the teachers' use of assessments and through scripted activities they had the opportunity to produce and practice making assessments, which enabled them to align themselves with their interlocutor. The scripted activities also allowed for greater extension of the assessment when the teacher aligned herself with the students and produced an assessment that agreed with theirs, thus increasing the salience of the assessments. Ohta found that on those occasions in teacher-fronted discourse when the learners did produce an assessment, the effect was powerful. When a learner produced an assessment, all four teachers in the study broke out of their evaluative use of language in order to produce an affective response which aligned them with the learner, and thus produced alignment sequences that more closely resemble those of discourse outside the classroom. This particular study demonstrates how LS theory can be applied to foreign language classroom research to investigate how routines and participation structures affect opportunities for practice of pragmatic forms, how the students' successful use of pragmatic routines affect social interaction in the classroom, and which kinds of activities provide richer opportunities for learning a particular pragmatic act or form.

For her investigation into learner–learner activity, Ohta focused on a single classroom learner, Candace, and her ability to produce the *ne* particle in assessments over the course of the academic year. As the year progressed, she demonstrated increased frequency and greater variety in her assessments even though she was not explicitly guided in the use of the *ne* particle, nor were these assessment turns scripted into the activities that she performed. Thus, even in this foreign language classroom setting, learners could develop greater sensitivity to the function of the Japanese particle *ne* in assessments, provided that appropriate scaffolding and participant-observation were made available along with opportunities for pair work, which afforded her practice in producing spontaneous assessments.

It is interesting to note that in the examples Ohta presented of a scripted activity, the pedagogical purpose was grammatical (to practice producing adversative passives), not pragmatic (appropriate use of assessments and of the particle *ne* to show alignment with one's interlocutor). LS was occurring even though it was not the intent of the lesson. In fact, LS is always occurring in the classroom. Whatever the instructor does or does not do or say and the way in which this is accomplished send implicit messages about the values of the instructor, the institution and the society in general as well as the roles and statuses of the teacher and the students and the rights and obligations associated with them. One cannot avoid socializing students. What any instructor needs to be aware of is how his or her behavior is socializing the students.

From this it follows that another important area of investigation is LS of and from the point of view of foreign language teachers. Duff and Uchida (1997) examined the role of culture in EFL classrooms in Japan by exploring the implicit messages sent by four different teachers (two L1 English, two L1 Japanese) through their choice of materials and use of audiovisual equipment, seating arrangements, lesson plan organization and activities, and the issues, viewpoints and beliefs presented, which were in turn based on their own perceived sociocultural identities and rooted in their personal histories. They found that none of the four teachers perceived themselves as teaching cultural content explicitly, yet whether they were aware of it or not, all of them did nevertheless teach culture. It cannot be avoided. Teachers must react in some way to the course materials, which convey a particular representation of the target culture, identifying or disidentifying with the characters and themes presented. They engage in particular classroom practices, which might or might not align with those of the target culture. For example, Carol initially resisted the identities expected of foreign teachers – entertainer, guidance counselor and informant regarding Western culture – in part because she did not want to impose her viewpoints on her students. However, she discovered that her stance created too much social distance. Consequently, as the year progressed, she incorporated more discussion topics, storytelling and other interactive activities. Such studies invite teachers in the foreign language classroom to examine how their own personal histories, including their primary LS experiences and their cultural assumptions, affect their classroom practices, and their expectations of themselves and their students. Likewise, they invite them to critically reflect on their own ways of speaking, that is, to become more aware of the ways they speak in the classroom and why.

Pedagogical Implications

The research that has been conducted within a LS framework provides us with some insights regarding teaching in the classroom. First, teachers should be aware that LS is always occurring in the classroom. What the teacher says or does not say and how he or she says it send implicit messages about the learners' status and role in the classroom, their rights and obligations, what is and is not valued or believed, and/or what kinds of behaviors are or are not acceptable. We cannot teach in a value vacuum. Therefore, it is best to be aware of our own values and beliefs concerning the nature of language, language acquisition and the language learners we teach (cf. Johnson, 2006). A LS approach can be useful in helping teachers to become more aware of the values, attitudes and beliefs that they project by the way in which they use language. They could examine their own language use in order to identify places where what they say explicitly might differ from their implicit messages, perhaps due to conflicts in norms either within themselves or between themselves and the target culture or between themselves and the institution for which they teach. LS theory can also be used to examine how a lack of congruity between the norms and goals of the foreign language classroom and the institution or government might have negative consequences for the students even when they are successful in the classroom, as was the case in Duff's (1995, 1996, 2003) studies, where even those who succeeded in the English classroom were not prepared for the *felelés* type of assessment required by the national curriculum for graduation. LS theory can also be particularly useful in studying classroom language use and acquisition during times of rapid societal change when the values of society shift resulting in new norms of interaction that do not impact all areas to the same extent. LS theory can provide insights into how teachers and schools handle these changes as well as the consequences of those changes and the strategies used to deal with them.

Second, because this paradigm focuses on linking linguistic behaviors to cultural values and socializing one into a particular cultural group, we need to consider the following questions: What is the cultural group that students need to be socialized into? What are its norms regarding communicative behavior? Who would be the experts to do the socializing? In some cases, students may be preparing to study abroad in a country where the target language is the language of the mainstream society. In this case, the norms of that society might generally be appropriate and native, near-native and even advanced level speakers might be appropriate socializers. In other cases, learners might be studying the language in order to use it as a lingua franca in international discourse. In this case, inner circle native speaker norms would not necessarily be most appropriate; rather the norms used in the situations in question (e.g. business, diplomacy) would be more appropriate and those who successfully communicate within those norms would be the appropriate experts to be used in the socialization process (Snow et al., 2006). In still other cases, particularly with younger students, their ultimate goals may remain unclear. This will make choosing the appropriate norms more difficult. In any case, however, where the target language is likely to be used as a lingua franca, it might be most appropriate to socialize the learners on several different levels. First they need to be socialized into pluralism and tolerance, that is, they need to be taught that different languages and cultures have different preferences regarding general communicative goals and specific grammatical, phonological and pragmatic behaviors. One variety is not inherently better than another; they are just different (Jenkins, 2006; Snow et al., 2006). Second, they need to be socialized to accommodate (Jenkins, 2006). In order to do this, they need to learn about the pragmatics of different varieties of the target language, not necessarily to the point of mastery but enough to become aware that unconscious assumptions might be operating that hinder full communication and learning. Third, they need to learn about the connections between language and identity, and how a change in one accompanies a change in the other. Consequently interlocutors might not want to accommodate to a given norm because it represents a threat to their identity. They also need to learn about the outcomes of their choices to accommodate or not (cf. Siegal, 1995a, 1995b, 1996).

In some cases, LS is not 'successful' (Zuengler & Cole, 2005), that is, the learners either intentionally or unintentionally fail to conform to the target norms, whatever that target may be. At times, they may actively resist the norms imposed upon them or even socialize their teacher to accept new norms. LS theory invites investigation into this area also. It recognizes that socialization is bidirectional, that novices also socialize experts. Students socialize their teachers. Teachers working within this framework can examine the ways in which their own classroom goals and attitudes change and their behaviors shift as a result, and then evaluate the extent to which these changes have had positive and negative effects on the students.

The classroom context is limited compared to naturalistic contexts in terms of the learners' opportunities to genuinely take on different conversational roles in a wide range of situations and engage with a range of fluent competent speakers of the language who provide them with expert input and opportunities for practice. However, there are ways that creative teachers can enhance the socialization experience through their teaching approach and materials. For example, in a pre-experimental study, Narzieva (2005) examined the teaching of pragmatics in a Russian language classroom under two conditions, context-reduced and context-enriched instruction. The context-reduced condition included the provision of specific linguistic forms, semantic formulas and strategies, and verbal explanations regarding contextual variables for the realization of apologies as well as roleplays whose situations were not only explained but enhanced with line drawings. The context-enriched instruction, which equaled the time of context-reduced instruction, included video clips, which enhanced the explanations of request realization, and the roleplays were enhanced with authentic photos rather than simple line drawings. Learning appeared to be more effective under the context-enriched situation. What is particularly interesting from a LS perspective is the socializing effect of the authentic videos as described by the students. One student, Alex, explained the importance of the non-verbal information that was crucial to effective communication:

> If I see videos of Russians interacting, it's gonna be better than somebody drawing out a picture...All those millions of little cues such as movement of the shoulder or the wince, or a smile, or a blush; all those millions of things that are language. (Narzieva, 2005: 70)

As Duff (2003) has pointed out and Narzieva (2005) has demonstrated, the use of body language is extremely important in the LS process. Incorporating this dimension through video clips and photographs into the teaching of pragmatics in the foreign language classroom can enhance the learners' ability to communicate appropriately on both the receptive and productive levels.

Conclusions

LS theory has expanded to include second as well as first language acquisition. This requires us to examine the assumptions underlying L1 socialization and their applicability to L2 socialization and to adjust the theory accordingly. Moreover, LS theory is seeking to push itself beyond a focus almost solely on social interaction to include the cognitive, emotional, physical and spiritual aspects of language learning as well. Classroom research that has been conducted within a LS framework to date demonstrates how learners are simultaneously socialized into both cultural values and verbal and non-verbal language use (Kanagy, 1999), how differing patterns of L1 language and literacy socialization and the unconscious assumptions associated with them can lead to tension between teachers and students (Bell, 1995), how routines and participation structures affect social interaction and opportunities for practice of pragmatic forms (Ohta, 1999) and how students socialize teachers to modify their pedagogical practices (Duff, 1996; Duff & Uchida, 1997). Moreover, a LS framework can provide insights into the interconnection between local level classroom interaction and macrolevel institutional and national constraints, making us more aware that the successful socialization of the language learner does not depend entirely on the teacher and the students. Recent research on foreign language classroom acquisition also raises some questions regarding who the socializers are or should be, into what cultural values students are being socialized and how this process is occurring. LS theory can provide tools for further exploration into these issues.

References

Bardovi-Harlig, K. and Hartford, B.S. (2005a) Institutional discourse and interlanguage pragmatics research. In K. Bardovi-Harlig and B.S. Hartford (eds) *Interlanguage Pragmatics: Exploring Institutional Talk* (pp. 7–36). Mahwah, NJ: Lawrence Erlbaum Associates.

Bardovi-Harlig, K. and Hartford, B.S. (eds) (2005b) *Interlanguage Pragmatics: Exploring Institutional Talk*. Mahwah, NJ: Lawrence Erlbaum Associates.

Bell, J.S. (1995) The relationship between L1 and L2 literacy: Some complicating factors. *TESOL Quarterly* 29 (4), 687–704.

Benor, D.J. (2001) *Spiritual Healing: Scientific Validation of A Healing Revolution*. Southfield, MI: Vision Publications.

Benor, D.J. (2004) *Consciousness, Bioenergy and Healing: Self-Healing and Energy Medicine for the 21st Century*. Bellmawr, NJ: Wholistic Healing Publications.

Christison, M.A., Stevick, E., Shaaban, K., Mendelsohn, D., Scovel, T. and Widdowson, H. (2002) Faith, values and language teaching. Invited colloquium at TESOL, Salt Lake City, Utah, USA, March, 2002.

Clancy, P. (1986) Acquiring communicative style in Japanese. In B.B. Schieffelin and E. Ochs (eds) *Language Socialization across Cultures* (pp. 213–250). Cambridge: Cambridge University Press.

Clancy, P. (1989) A case study in language socialization: Korean wh-questions. *Discourse Processes* 12 (2), 169–191.

Cook, H.M. (1990) The role of Japanese sentence-final particle *no* in the socialization of children. *Multilingua* 9 (40), 377–395.

Cook, H.M. (2006) Joint construction of folk beliefs by JFL learners and Japanese host families. In M.A. DuFon and E. Churchill (eds) *Language Learners in Study Abroad Contexts* (pp. 120–150). Clevedon: Multilingual Matters.

Crago, M.B. (1992) Communicative interaction and second language acquisition: An Inuit example. *TESOL Quarterly* 26 (3), 487–505.

Crozet, C. (2006) The spiritual dimension of intercultural language education. *International Journal of the Humanities* 4 (3), 119–124.

Davies, C.E. and Tyler, A.E. (2005) Discourse strategies in the context of crosscultural institutional talk: Uncovering interlanguage pragmatics in the university classroom. In K. Bardovi-Harlig and B.S. Hartford (eds) *Interlanguage Pragmatics: Exploring Institutional Talk* (pp. 133–156). Mahwah, NJ: Lawrence Erlbaum Associates.

Davis, K.A. (1995) Qualitative theory and methods in applied linguistics research. *TESOL Quarterly* 29 (3), 427–453.

Davis, K.A. and Henze, R.C. (1998) Applying ethnographic perspectives to issues in cross-cultural pragmatics. *Journal of Pragmatics* 30 (4), 399–419.

Demuth, K. (1986) Prompting routines in the language socialization of Basotho children. In B.B. Schieffelin and E. Ochs (eds) *Language Socialization across Cultures* (pp. 51–79). Cambridge: Cambridge University Press.

Duff, P.A. (1995) Ethnography in a foreign language immersion context: Language socialization through EFL and history. *TESOL Quarterly* 29 (3), 505–537.

Duff, P.A. (1996) Different languages, differing practices: Socialization of discourse competence in dual-language school classrooms in Hungary. In D. Nunan and K.M. Bailey (eds) *Voices from the Language Classroom* (pp. 407–433). Cambridge: Cambridge University Press.

Duff, P.A. (2002) The discursive co-construction of knowledge, identity, and difference: An ethnography of communication in the high school mainstream. *Applied Linguistics* 23 (3), 289–322.

Duff, P.A. (2003) New directions in second language socialization research. *Korean Journal of English Language and Linguistics* 3, 309–339.

Duff, P.A. and Uchida, Y. (1997) The negotiation of teachers' sociocultural identities and practices in postsecondary EFL classrooms. *TESOL Quarterly* 31 (3), 451–486.

Duff, P.A., Wong, P and Early, M. (2002) Learning language for work and life: The linguistic socialization of immigrant Canadians seeking careers in healthcare. *The Canadian Modern Language Review* 57 (1), 9–57.

DuFon, M.A. (1994) Input and interaction in the acquisition of L1 pragmatic routines: Implications for SLA. *University of Hawai'i Working Papers in ESL* 12 (2), 39–79.

DuFon, M.A. (2000) The acquisition of linguistic politeness in Indonesian by sojourners in naturalistic interactions. PhD thesis, University of Hawai'i, 1999. *Dissertation Abstracts International-A* 60 (11), 3985.

DuFon, M.A. (2003) Gift giving in Indonesian: A model for teaching pragmatic routines in the foreign language classroom with the less commonly taught languages. In A. Martínez-Flor, E. Usó-Juan and A. Fernández-Guerra (eds) *Pragmatic Competence and Foreign Language Teaching* (pp. 109–131). Castelló: Publicacions de la Universitat Jaume I.

DuFon, M.A. (2006) The socialization of taste during study abroad in Indonesia. In M.A. DuFon and E. Churchill (eds) *Language Learners in Study Abroad Contexts* (pp. 91–119). Clevedon: Multilingual Matters.

Findlay, M.S. (1995) Who has the right answer? Differential cultural emphasis in question/answer structures and the case of Hmong students at a Northern California high school. *Issues in Applied Linguistics* 6 (1), 23–38.

Gibbs, T.L. (2005) Using moves in the opening sequence to identify callers in institutional settings. In K. Bardovi-Harlig and B.S. Hartford (eds) *Interlanguage Pragmatics: Exploring Institutional Talk* (pp. 175–199). Mahwah, NJ: Lawrence Erlbaum Associates.

Goulah, J. (2006a). Transformative second and foreign language learning: Cultivating a deep culture of global citizenship and global literacy for the 21st century. *Dissertation Abstracts International*-A 66 (8), 2819.

Goulah, J. (2006b). Transformative second and foreign language learning for the 21st century. *Critical Inquiry in Language Studies* 3 (4), 201–221.

Hoffman-Hicks, S.D. (2000) The longitudinal development of French foreign language pragmatic competence: Evidence from study abroad. PhD thesis, Indiana University, 1999. *Dissertation Abstracts International*-A, 61 (2), 591.

Hong, M. (2005) Spirituality and second language acquisition: Is there a connection? Paper presented at AILA, Madison, Wisconsin, USA, July 2005.

House, J. (2003) Teaching and learning pragmatic fluency in a foreign language: The case of English as a lingua franca. In A. Martínez-Flor, E. Usó-Juan and A. Fernández-Guerra (eds) *Pragmatic Competence and Foreign Language Teaching* (pp. 133–159). Castelló: Publicacions de la Universitat Jaume I.

Hüllen, W. (1992) Identifikationssprachen und Kommunikationssprachen. *Zeitschrift für Germanistische Linguistik* 20, 298–317.

Isabelli-García, C.L. (2003) Development of oral communication skills abroad. *Frontiers: The Interdisciplinary Journal of Study Abroad*, 9, 149–173. On WWW at http://www.frontiersjournal.com/issues/vol9/vol9-07_isabelligarcia.htm.

Isabelli-García, C. (2006) Study abroad social networks, motivation and attitudes: Implications for second language acquisition. In M.A. DuFon and E. Churchill (eds) *Language Learners in Study Abroad Contexts* (pp. 231–258). Clevedon: Multilingual Matters.

Jenkins, J. (2006) Current perspectives on teaching World Englishes and English as a lingua franca. *TESOL Quarterly* 40 (1), 157–181.

Johnson, K.E. (2006) The sociocultural turn and its challenges for second language teacher education. *TESOL Quarterly* 40 (1), 235–257.

Kachru, B.B. (1985) Standards, codification and sociolinguistic realism: The English language in the outer circle. In R. Quirk and H.G. Widdowson (eds) *English in the World* (pp. 11–34). Cambridge: Cambridge University Press.

Kanagy, R. (1999) Interactional routines as a mechanism for L2 acquisition and socialization in an immersion context. *Journal of Pragmatics* 31 (11), 1467–1492.

Kasper, G. (1997) 'A' stands for acquisition: A response to Firth and Wagner. *Modern Language Journal* 81 (3), 307–312.

Kasper, G. (2001) Four perspectives on L2 pragmatic development. *Applied Linguistics* 22 (4), 502–530.

Kasper, G. and Rose, K.R. (2002) *Pragmatic Development in a Second Language*. Malden, MA: Blackwell.

Kerekes, J. (2005) Before, during, and after the event: Getting the job (or not) in an employment interview. In K. Bardovi-Harlig and B.S. Hartford (eds) *Interlanguage Pragmatics: Exploring Institutional Talk* (pp. 99–131). Mahwah, NJ: Lawrence Erlbaum Associates.

Kerekes, J.A. (2006) Winning an interviewer's trust in a gatekeeping encounter. *Language in Society* 35 (1), 27–57.

Kerekes, J.A. (2007) The co-construction of a gatekeeping encounter: An inventory of verbal actions. *Journal of Pragmatics* special issue on High Stakes Gatekeeping Encounters and their Consequences: Discourses in Intercultural Institutional Settings 39 (11), 1942–1973.

Kinginger, C. and Whitworth, K.F. (2005) Assessing development of metapragmatic awareness in study abroad. *Frontiers: The Interdisciplinary Journal of Study Abroad* 10, 19–42. On WWW at www.frontiersjournal.com/issues/.

Miller, J. (1996) *The Holistic Curriculum*. Toronto: OISE Press.

Narzieva, L. (2005) The role of context in learning foreign language pragmatics. Master's thesis, California State University-Chico.

Ochs, E. (1986) From feelings to grammar: A Samoan case study. In B.B. Schieffelin and E. Ochs (eds) *Language Socialization across Cultures* (pp. 251–272). Cambridge: Cambridge University Press.

Ochs, E. (1988) *Culture and Language Development: Language Acquisition and Language Socialization in a Samoan Village*. Cambridge: Cambridge University Press.

Ochs, E. (1996) Linguistic resources for socializing humanity. In J. Gumperz and S. Levinson (eds) *Rethinking Linguistic Relativity* (pp. 407–437). Cambridge: Cambridge University Press.

Ochs, E. and Schieffelin, B.B. (1984) Language acquisition and socialization: Three developmental stories and their implications. In R.A Shwedar and R.A. Levine (eds) *Culture Theory: Essays on Mind, Self, and Emotion* (pp. 276–320). Cambridge: Cambridge University Press.

Ohta, A.S. (1994) Socializing the expression of affect: An overview of affective particle use in the Japanese as a foreign language classroom. *Issues in Applied Linguistics* 5 (2), 303–326.

Ohta, A.S. (1999) Interactional routines and the socialization of interactional style in adult learners of Japanese. *Journal of Pragmatics* 31 (11), 1493–1512.

Pavlenko, A. (2006) *Emotions and Multilingualism*. Cambridge: Cambridge University Press.

Pease-Alvarez, C. and Vasquez, O. (1994) Language socialization in ethnic minority communities. In F. Genesee (ed.) *Educating Second Language Children* (pp. 82–102). Cambridge: Cambridge University Press.

Platt, M. (1986) Social norms and lexical acquisition: A study of deictic verbs in Samoan child language. In B.B. Schieffelin and E. Ochs (eds) *Language Socialization across Cultures* (pp. 127–152). Cambridge: Cambridge University Press.

Poole, D. (1992) Language socialization in the second language classroom. *Language Learning* 42 (4), 593–616.

Schecter, S.R. and Bayley, R. (1997) Language socialization practices and cultural identity: Case studies of Mexican-descent families in California and Texas. *TESOL Quarterly* 31 (3), 513–541.

Schieffelin, B.B. (1986) Teasing and shaming in Kaluli children's interactions. In B.B. Schieffelin and E. Ochs (eds) *Language Socialization across Cultures* (pp. 165–181). Cambridge: Cambridge University Press.

Schieffelin, B.B. (1990) *The Give and Take of Everyday Life: Language Socialization of Kaluli Children*. Cambridge: Cambridge University Press.

Schieffelin, B.B. and Ochs, E. (1986a) Introduction. In B.B. Schieffelin and E. Ochs (eds) *Language Socialization across Cultures* (pp. 1–13). Cambridge: Cambridge University Press.

Schieffelin, B.B. and Ochs, E. (1986b) Language socialization. *Annual Review of Anthropology* 15, 163–191.

Siegal, M. (1995a) Individual differences and study abroad: Women learning Japanese in Japan. In B.F. Freed (ed.) *Second Language Acquisition in a Study Abroad Context* (pp. 225–244). Amsterdam: John Benjamins.

Siegal, M. (1995b) Looking east: Learning Japanese as a second language in Japan and the interaction of race, gender and social context. PhD thesis, University of California, Berkeley, 1994. *Dissertation Abstracts International*-A 56 (5), 1692.

Siegal, M. (1996) The role of subjectivity in second language sociolinguistic competency: Western women learning Japanese. *Applied Linguistics* 17 (3), 356–382.

Smith-Hefner, N.J. (1988) The linguistic socialization of Javanese children in two communities. *Anthropological Linguistics* 30 (2), 166–198.

Snow, M.A., Kamhi-Stein, L.D. and Brinton, D.M. (2006) Teacher training for English as a lingua franca. *Annual Review of Applied Linguistics* 26, 261–281.

Tarone, E. (2005) English for specific purposes and interlanguage pragmatics. In K. Bardovi-Harlig and B.S. Hartford (eds) *Interlanguage Pragmatics: Exploring Institutional Talk* (pp. 157–173). Mahwah, NJ: Lawrence Erlbaum Associates.

Watson-Gegeo, K.A. (1988) Ethnography in ESL: Defining the essentials. *TESOL Quarterly* 22 (4), 575–592.

Watson-Gegeo, K.A. (1992) Thick explanation in the ethnographic study of child socialization: A longitudinal study of the problem of schooling for Kwara'ae (Solomon Islands) children. In W.A. Corsaro and P.J. Miller (eds) *New Directions for Child Development, Vol. 58. The Production and Reproduction of Children's Worlds: Interpretive Methodologies for the Study of Childhood Socialization* (pp. 51–66). San Francisco: Jossey-Bass.

Watson-Gegeo, K.A. (2004) Mind, language, and epistemology: Toward a language socialization paradigm for SLA. *The Modern Language Journal* 88 (3), 331–350.

Watson-Gegeo, K.A. and Gegeo, D.W. (1986) Calling out and repeating routines in Kwara'ae children's language socialization. In B.B. Schieffelin and E. Ochs (eds) *Language Socialization across Cultures* (pp. 17–50). Cambridge: Cambridge University Press.

Watson-Gegeo, K.A. and Nielsen, S. (2003) Language socialization in SLA. In C.J. Doughty and M.H. Long (eds) *The Handbook of Second Language Acquisition* (pp. 155–177). Malden, MA: Blackwell.

Whorf, B.L. (1941) The relations of habitual thought and behavior to language. In L. Spier, A.I. Hallowell and S.S. Newman (eds) *Language, Culture, and Personality: Essays in Honor of Edward Sapir* (pp. 75–93). Menasha, WI: Sapir Memorial Publication.

Willett, J. (1995) Becoming first graders in a second language: An ethnographic study of second language socialization. *TESOL Quarterly* 29 (3), 473–503.

Yoshimi, D.R. (1999) L1 language socialization as a variable in the use of *ne* by L2 learners of Japanese. *Journal of Pragmatics* 31 (11), 1513–1525.

Zuengler, J. and Cole, K. (2005) Language socialization and second language learning. In E. Hinkel (ed.) *Handbook of Research in Second Language Teaching and Learning* (pp. 301–316). Mahwah, NJ: Lawrence Erlbaum.

Zuengler, J. and Miller, E.R. (2006) Cognitive and sociocultural perspectives: Two parallel SLA worlds? *TESOL Quarterly* 40 (1), 35–58.

Chapter 3
Talking with a Classroom Guest: Opportunities for Learning Japanese Pragmatics

YUMIKO TATEYAMA and GABRIELE KASPER

Introduction

A critical question that foreign language teachers have to confront is how to provide students with opportunities to develop pragmatic abilities in a second language (L2). In order to be academically successful, students have to become competent members of their classroom community, and such membership critically involves classroom-specific ways of participation. An increasing number of studies investigate how students of all ages, from pre-schoolers to graduate students, come to master, with varying success, the pragmatic and discourse practices of educational institutions (Duff, 1995; He, 2000, 2003; Kanagy, 1999; Lo, 2004; Morita, 2000; Willet, 1995). But to the extent that foreign language curricula aim to enable students to participate in a range of activities outside of classrooms, language educators must also create the conditions for achieving that goal. This is a difficult call because the speech exchange system predominant in instructional discourse, the initiation-response-feedback (IRF) sequence[1] (Mehan, 1979; Sinclair & Coulthard, 1975), rather limits the discursive options for students and teachers (Ellis, 1994; Kasper, 1997).

As a measure to overcome the discourse-structural limitations of the IRF and the asymmetrical power relations between teacher and students that the IRF (re)produces, peer activities have become a regular instructional practice. Peer interactions among foreign language students in task-structured activities (e.g. Long *et al.*, 1976; Ohta, 2001; Tateyama, 2001; Yoshimi, 1999) and roleplays (Ohta, 1995, 1997) have been shown to offer productive environments for developing L2 pragmatic and interactional competence. In peer interaction, students assist each other to jointly work through an activity, achieving together what they would not be able to accomplish individually. By virtue of being participant-managed, peer interactions empower students to transform the task or roleplay set by the teacher, take advantage of learning opportunities and create such opportunities for themselves and each other (Mori, 2004).

Another type of environment that charges foreign language learners with more interactional control than teacher-managed discourse is computer-mediated communication with target language speaking peers. In a series of studies, Belz and Kinginger (Belz & Kinginger, 2002; Kinginger, 2000; Kinginger & Belz, 2005) found that through telecollaboration in email and synchronous chat over extended periods, the students came to develop interactional competence in the use of address terms in French and German. The first language (L1) co-participants actively helped students sort out the sociopragmatic complexities of target address term use through feedback, modeling, and metapragmatic comments (see González-Lloret, this volume). Yet a third possibility for expanding the discursive environment of the classroom is to invite a target language speaker as a classroom guest, as Bardovi-Harlig *et al.* (1991) recommended. Although it would be important to know how interactions with an outsider to the classroom community may enhance students' learning of L2 pragmatics, as far as we know, only Mori (2002) has examined classroom guest interactions. Her findings were not encouraging. Instead of conducting a discussion with the guest as planned, the students reconfigured the activity with the visitor as an interview, working through a list of topics in a question–answer format. Mori's findings raise the question of whether other classroom arrangements in which a guest participates may afford more productive contexts for L2 pragmatic learning. The study reported in this chapter was conducted to provide some answers to this question.

Our view of how pragmatics is learned in the classroom builds on theories of learning as a social–interactional process. In this study, we are particularly interested in seeing how interactions between participants in different social roles (student, teacher, classroom guest) may enable different participation frameworks (Goffman, 1981; He, 2003). In turn, we wonder how differently configured participation frameworks might enable various kinds of assisted performance (Tharp & Gallimore, 1988). The idea of assisted performance has its origin in Vygotskyan sociocultural theory (Lantolf & Thorne, 2006; Ohta, 2001), specifically the notion that development occurs when learners are faced with a task that they cannot solve on the strength of their individual current competencies but that becomes possible to accomplish through various forms of mediational tools – teachers, peers, target language speakers, texts, the internet, and other cultural artifacts (Ohta, 2005). Vygotsky (1978) called the distance between actual individual development and potential development through assistance the 'Zone of Proximal Development' (ZPD). The notion has seen various transformations and current interpretations vary (Lantolf & Thorne, 2006; Ohta, 2001, 2005). As our study is interested in the affordances (van Lier, 2000) of different participation frameworks for pragmatic development, the most relevant version of the ZPD is the one proposed by Ohta (2001: 9): 'the ZPD is the distance between the actual developmental level as determined by individual linguistic production, and the language produced collaboratively with a teacher or peer'. Our goal in this study, however, is not to determine the students' ZPD. Rather the ZPD supplies the theoretical rationale for analyzing forms of assisted performance in a range of participation frameworks. In particular, we address the following questions:

(1) What opportunities for learning how to request in Japanese arise when a classroom guest participates in request episodes? In what ways do request episodes with a classroom guest differ from requests made by the teacher to class?
(2) What participation frameworks emerge during request episodes with a classroom guest?
(3) What kinds of assistance are made available to the students during request episodes with a classroom guest?

The Study

Data and analysis

An intact second-year class in Japanese as a Foreign Language (JFL) at the University of Hawai'i at Manoa (UH) participated in the study. The students, six women and five men, were speakers of English as their first language, except for one student whose L1 was Korean. The class was taught by the first author of this chapter, a female L1 speaker of Japanese who had been teaching Japanese in the USA for nine years. Another speaker of Japanese as a first language was visiting the class as a guest. Aya (all personal names are pseudonyms) was born and raised in Japan, and she was a student at the local campus of a Japanese college. As the entire student population at her college was from Japan, Aya had taken the initiative to meet English-speaking peers at UH and participate in an informal language exchange. By the time the data for the present study were collected, Aya had been visiting the JFL class at UH for two months and she and the students had become friends.[2]

As part of a larger study, class sessions were video- and audio-recorded at regular intervals. For the present study, we analyzed request episodes from three 50-minutes class sessions, filmed at an approximately one week interval from early to mid April of a spring semester. In the class sessions prior to the request episodes, requesting in Japanese had been a topic of instruction. The class learned about the factors that people take into account when making requests, watched a video clip of a Japanese request event, and engaged in consciousness-raising activities. In subsequent class sessions, the request episodes below were recorded in the order indicated.

(1) Request episode 1: Requests from the teacher to class
(2) Request episode 2: Requests from the teacher to the classroom guest
(3) Request episode 3: Request from the classroom guest to the teacher
(4) Request episode 4: Request from the classroom guest to a student

Data were transcribed following simplified conversation-analytic conventions (see Appendix 3.1). The analysis of Request episodes 2, 3, and 4 follows their chronological order. In order to examine the interactional organization of the request episodes in detail, the analysis is conducted primarily from a conversation-analytic perspective and draws on Goffman's (1981) notion of participation framework as a further concept for analysis.

Request Episodes

Requests from the teacher to class

As we noted initially, arrangements that break the institutional mold of IRF-structured classroom discourse aim to broaden the range of affordances for student learning. When it comes to learning how to request in a target language, the learning opportunities in teacher-fronted interaction are better than in the case of many other pragmatic and discourse aspects because teachers issue requests to organize class activities and direct students as a matter of regular classroom management (Chaudron, 1988; Falsgraf & Majors, 1995; Kanagy, 1999; Poole, 1992). Provided that classroom business is predominantly conducted in the target language – a condition in place in the first author's classrooms – the issue is therefore how request sequences are organized in teacher-fronted interaction and by what linguistic and other semiotic resources they are implemented. To this end, we examined the teacher's requests to class in the same three 50-minute class sessions that also housed the remaining request episodes.

The teacher issued the following requests to class immediately after students watched a video clip.

Excerpt 1a

```
1→   T: hai jaa ne kinoo sukuriputo o agemashita yo ne. motte masu?
         alright well P yesterday script  P gave            P P   have
         "alright well I gave you a script yesterday. do you have it?"
2        (0.5)
```

3	kono: bideo no sukuriputo?
	this video LN script
	"this videoscript?"
4	((Students look for the script.))
	((11 lines omitted. Video is shown again.))
12 →	T: hai. jaa chotto sukuriputo mite kudasai.
	alright well then for a moment script look please
	"alright. well now please take a look at your script."

The two requests illustrate a typical environment for teacher's directives. In both instances, the teacher deploys requests to organize classroom activities and directs the students to do certain actions. Both requests start with a sequence of discourse markers (*hai jaa (ne)*) that indicate the start of a new activity. The first request (1) is done incrementally. First the teacher establishes the referent *kinoo sukuriputo o agemashita yo ne*. 'I gave you a script yesterday.' as an independent syntactic unit. The sentence-final interactional particle *yo* conveys the epistemic stance of certainty, while the particle *ne* indexes common ground (Cook, 1992) and affiliation (Yoshimi, 1999). The teacher then continues the turn adding *motte masu* 'do you have it?' (1), a question hearable as a request to look at the script. When the students do not react after a 0.5 second gap, the teacher self-repairs *sukuriputo* 'script' to *kono: bideo no sukuriputo?* 'this videoscript?'. The explicit formulation of the referent gets the desired uptake as the students start looking for their scripts (3). After the video clip is shown again, the teacher once more directs the students to look at the scripts: *hai jaa chotto sukuriputo mite kudasai* 'alright. well now please take a look at your script' (12). The directive builds on the previous sequence as the students now have the script in front of them. With the referent established, the teacher issues the request with the most common, ordinary-polite, and clear grammatical form V-*te kudasai* 'please V'. Table 3.1 summarizes the teacher's use of request forms during the observed three-hour class periods. The verb form in both requests is the (polite) -*masu* style. Research on classroom discourse in Japan shows that teachers tend to shift between plain and -*masu* style to index the type of activity and 'mode of self' (Cook, 1996).

The two requests direct the students to do routine classroom activities, and their standard forms and sequence structure index the ordinariness of such directives in the classroom context. On occasion, the teacher directs the students to do something out of the ordinary. In Excerpt 1b below, she asks the class to fill in a questionnaire for her own research. Although this assignment benefits the teacher and the students had to spend additional time to complete it, she did not use the most polite forms.

Table 3.1 Teacher's use of request forms

Strategies	Frequency (tokens)	Percentage
1. V-te/V-te kudasai (Please V)	29	55.8
2. N doozo (Please N)	5	9.6
3. V mashoo (Let's V)	4	7.7
4. V-te hoshii n desu ga (I would like you to V but)	3	5.9
5. V-te itadakemasu ka (Would you please V?)	2	3.8
6. V(potential) masu ka (Can you V?)	2	3.8
7. Others	7	13.5

The teacher predominantly used direct request forms, V-te and V-te kudasai (e.g. yonde kudasai or 'Please read'). In a classroom setting in which the context is mutually understood and the participant roles clearly divided, often it is not even necessary for the teacher to specifically indicate what he or she wants students to do. Calling the student's name or adding doozo 'please' after the name served as a directive. The teacher did not use the most conventionally polite request forms when addressing the students. It was only in interaction with the classroom guest that the teacher used conventionally polite indirect forms in class.

Excerpt 1b (Teacher speaking to class)

1 T: chotto mina san ni onegai ga aru n desu kedo:.
    a little everyone P favor   S have N CP but
    "I have some favor to ask all of you."
2   anoo kore mae kurasu de yatta n desu kedo nee.
    uhm this before class in did   N CP   but P
    "uhm we did this in class before, you know"
3   anoo watashi no risaachi: no koto na n desu (.) ga.
    uhm   my   LN research LN thing   N CP (.) P
    "uhm it's regarding my research (.)."
4   ee ashita   to   asatte (.) sorekara doyoo nichiyoo
    er tomorrow and day after tomorrow (.) and Saturday Sunday
    "er tomorrow, the day after tomorrow (.), Saturday and Sunday"
5   yon renkyuu na node (.) kore chotto uchi de ne yatte kite
    four day weekend so (.) this a little home at P do come
    "you have four days off so (.) I'd like you to do this at home"
6   hoshii n desu. chotto kubarimasu node. ((distributes handouts))
    want N CP   a little distribute   so
    "and bring it back. I'll distribute them for now."

The teacher starts the sequence with a series of pre-requests.[3] First she announces that she has a favor to ask of the students (1): *chotto mina san ni onegai ga aru n desu kedo:* 'I have some favor to ask all of you.' This is immediately followed by a reference preparation ('we did this in class before' (2), 'it's regarding my research' (3)). In the next pre-request, the teacher offers an account for why she is giving the extra assignment at this time (4–5), leading into the request *kore chotto uchi de ne yatte kite hoshii n desu* 'I'd like you to do this at home and bring it back' (5–6). With the multiple pre-requests and the want statement *V-te hoshii n desu* 'I'd like you to do V' instead of the more common classroom directive, *V-te kudasai* 'please V', the teacher shows her orientation to the imposition embodied in the request. However, the heavy mitigation notwithstanding, the entire sequence runs off in one extended turn, without giving the students an opportunity to respond. The video clip shows that most students were gazing at the teacher and listening to her, co-constructing their participation status as addressed recipients. A final observation to register is that the teacher produced the long turn with very few perturbations. Apart from three micro pauses, she used *anoo* 'uhm' (2 & 3) and *ee* 'er' (4) at the beginning of a new pre-request, and *chotto* 'a little' (1, 5, 6) as a mitigating device. Other features common in making an imposing request, such as apologetic formulaic expressions or a hesitant delivery,[4] are absent. Falsgraf and Majors (1995) note that teachers' directives in the Japanese classrooms they studied were for the most part highly direct and unmitigated. It appears, then, that by not choosing super-polite forms or other interactional features that are common in making an imposing request outside of the classroom, the teacher orients to the asymmetrical institutional roles of teacher and students.

The teacher's request practices match well with independent observations in the literature, and the video records suggest that the students are socialized to the teacher's style of classroom requests. It is also apparent that in many contexts outside of classrooms, this style of requesting would not be sufficiently polite. Adult L2 speakers of Japanese therefore need exposure to ways of requesting that may be more usable in out-of-class environments. The request episodes with the classroom guest afford such opportunities.

Requests from the teacher to the classroom guest

The following request sequences between the teacher and classroom guest Aya differ from the teacher's requests to class in many ways. In Excerpt 2, the teacher makes two requests to Aya in front of the class.

Excerpt 2 (T: Teacher, A: Aya, B: Brian)

1   T: eeh (.5) aya san, anoo (.) suimasen.
        er   (.5) Aya ms uhm (.) sorry
        "er (.5) Aya,   uhm (.) excuse me."

2   oisogashii tokoro mooshiwakenai n desu ke[do.
    busy place very sorry N CP but
    "I'm very sorry to bother you when you are busy but."
3 A: ((bows)) [hai.
                 yes
                "yes."
4 T: raishuu suiyoobi (.) doo desu ka.
   next week Wednesday (.) how CP Q
   "how about (.) next Wednesday"
5→   kurasu ni mata kite itadakemasu?
    class P again come could
    "would you please come to class again?"
6 A: hai (.) daijoobu desu.
   yes (.) alright CP
   "sure (.) alright."
7 T: daijoobu desu ka. AH yokatta.
   alright CP P oh good PAST
   "alright. OH I'm glad."
8→ B: °huh°
9→ T: de ano dekimashitara ne (.) hoka no hito ni mo
   and FL if possible P (.) other LN people P also
   "and uhm if possible [<would you be so kind also ask"
10 chotto < kiite itadake[(.)nai deshoo ka >
   a bit ask could NEG CP Q
   "ask > other people?"
11 A: [°hai°.
          yes
         "°yes.°"
12 A: hai. natsu yasumi chu aan haru yasumi chuu na node
   yes summer break during um spring break during CP because
   "yes. we are in summer vacation um spring break so"
13 doo ka wakaranai n desu [kedo.
   how Q know NEG N CP but
   "I don't know if anyone is available."
14 T: [ah soo desu ka.
          oh so CP P
         "oh I see."
15 A: hai. °soide yokattara.°
   yes that with good if
   "yes. °if that's all right (with you)°"
16→ T: ja, suimasen kedo, yoroshiku onegaishimasu.[6]
   well sorry but well request
   "well, I'm sorry to trouble you but I hope you will help me."
17 A: ha:i. ((bows))
   yes
   "ye:s."

18	T:	doomo sumimasen.
		indeed sorry
		"thank you very much."
19	A:	sonjaa mata.
		well then see you
		"well then, see you."
20	T:	hai doomo.
		yes see you
		"yes see you."

The teacher marks the beginning of the sequence with an attention getter that identifies Aya as the recipient of the talk, followed by the apologetic formulaic expressions *suimasen.* 'excuse me' (1) and *oisogashii tokoro mooshiwakenai n desu kedo* 'I'm very sorry (to bother you) when you are busy but' (2). These formulae are commonly used in Japanese to preface a request in formal situations, to status-higher recipients, or to out-group[6] members. By addressing these expressions to Aya, the teacher orients to her as an outsider in the classroom setting. With Aya's response *hai* 'yes' (3), the pre-sequence is completed as Aya has shown herself to be in a state of recipiency. The teacher's next action could be heard as a pre-request as she asks whether Aya is available on the following Wednesday (4). However, the teacher does not yield the turn for Aya's response but immediately proceeds to her next action, a request that Aya come to class again (5). The request *kurasu ni mata kite itadakemasu* 'would you please come to class again?' is done with the very polite conventional request form *verb -te itadakemasu* (lit. 'may I partake' or 'I humbly receive from you'). Aya accepts the request with an acceptance token *hai* 'yes', followed by an explicit commitment *daijoobu desu* 'that's alright' (6). By repeating the same expression *daijoobu desu* in her response turn with the sentence final particle *ka* attached to show acknowledgement, the teacher confirms that she and Aya have reached a shared understanding.[7] To this the teacher adds a positive assessment *AH yokatta* 'OH I'm glad', which closes the sequence on an affiliative note. However, in her next turn, the teacher makes yet another request (9 & 10). Following a turn-initial delay, she produces the conditional expression *dekimashitara* 'if possible', set off from the following turn segment by the interactional particle *ne* and a micropause. In this way, the speaker alerts the recipient to a possible request as the next action. The following request *hoka no hito ni mo chotto < kiite itadake (.) nai deshoo ka>* 'would you be so kind also to ask other people' includes the negative form *itadakenai* 'wouldn't you please' with *deshoo*, a tentative form of the copula *da* attached, which is conventionally heard as even more polite than the positive form *itadakemasu* 'would you please'. The formulaic segment *<kiite itadake (.) nai deshoo ka>* 'would you be so kind to ask' is said more slowly than the preceding turn segment, conveying a hesitant, apologetic tone. This is a culturally valued style of speaking when making an imposing request. The slower speed of delivery also allows the speaker to monitor how the interlocutor reacts while the turn is in progress (Kashiwazaki, 1993). Aya acknowledges the teacher's request with the overlapping response token *hai* (11), said softly while the teacher's turn is still under way and repeated at normal loudness at the beginning of Aya's response turn. *Hai* is a multifunctional response token that can be heard, in the two environments in which it occurs here, as an acknowledgement and as an acceptance of the teacher's request. In her response turn (12 & 13), Aya brings up an obstacle to recruiting other classroom guests, namely that her school is in spring recess. After the teacher acknowledges this possible difficulty with *ah soo desu ka.* 'Oh I see.' (14), Aya continues with a softly said °*soide yokattara*° 'if that's all right (with you)' (15). In this way, Aya makes a tentative commitment, conditional on the circumstances. In her next turn, the teacher indicates with a turn-initial *ja* 'well' that a conclusion has been reached, followed by the apologetic formula *suimasen kedo* 'I'm sorry to trouble you' and the polite requestive expression *yoroshiku onegaishimasu* 'I hope you will help me'. Aya politely agrees with an elongated *ha:i* and a bow (17), in response to which the teacher thanks her with an apologetic thanking expression, *doomo sumimasen* 'thank you very much.' (18). Through these co-ordinated actions, the co-participants show to each other that they have come to a shared understanding and are ready to close the sequence. The interaction concludes with a leave-taking exchange (19 & 20).

The request event between Aya and the teacher took place in front of the students, whose posture and gaze indicated that they were attentively following the action.[8] As an audience, the students' participation status was that of 'intended overhearers' (Goffman, 1981) who did not actively take part in the interaction. However, on one occasion, a student uttered an audible sound while the interaction between teacher and guest was in progress. After the teacher confirmed her understanding that Aya promised to come to class again and made a positive assessment *AH yokatta* 'OH I'm glad' (7), Brian aligns himself with that assessment by softly uttering 'huh' (8). In this way Brian shows that he attentively observes the interaction from the sideline and that he understands the upshot of the sequence so far. Through their embodied action and, in this one instance, a student's vocal conduct, the students display their focused recipiency to the event unfolding in front of them.

In the next request episode (Excerpt 3), the discourse roles are reversed: Aya asks the teacher a favor in front of the class.

Excerpt 3 (T: Teacher, A: Aya)

```
1     A: ah   sensee  ima =
         uhm  teacher now
         "uhm teacher now ="
```

2   T: hai.
       yes
       "yes."
3 → A: = ojikan   arimasu ka.
         time (polite) have   Q
         " = do you have time?"
4   T: ah hai nan deshoo?
       oh yes what CP
       "oh, yes, what would it be?"
5 → A: anoo   chotto   okikishitai koto ga aru n desu ga:.
        uhm for a moment wish-to-ask thing S have N CP   P
        "uhm there is something I would like to ask you."
6   T: ee::
       yes
       "ye:s."
7   A: anoo watashi kore kara (.) eetto (.) gogatsu ni °desu ne° =
       uhm   I   from now (.) FL   (.) May   in CP   P
       " =uhm from now (.) uhm (.) in May ="
8   T: hai
       yes
       "yes."
9   A: = yuueechi no samaa sesshon toroo to omotte[ru n desu kedo,
           UH   LK summer session take QT thinking N CP   but
       " =I'm thinking of taking summer session at UH,"
10 T: [aa soo na n desu ka.
                                                 oh so   N CP   P
                                                 "oh I see."
11 A: sono apurikeeshon no shikata   ni tsui[te: =
       that application LK how-to-do P about
       "regarding how to apply for it ="
12 T: [ee:
                                               yes
                                               "ye:s"
13 → A: = oshiete itadakerebaa to omoimashite.
          teach   could if   QT think
         " =I was wondering if you could tell me."
14 T: ah, wakarimashi[ta.
       oh understood
       "oh, I got it."
15 A: [ii desu ka.
                       all right CP Q
                       "is it all right (with you)?"
16 T: ee ii desu yoo. jaa kurasu no ato   ni demo
       yes fine CP FP then class LK after P for example
       "yes, that's fine. so perhaps after class"
17   Chotto hanashi mashoo [ka. =
       for a moment talk shall Q
       "Shall we talk for a moment?"

18   A: [°ha:i.° sore jaa =
                                 yes   well then
                                "°ye:s.° Well then = "
19   T: hai.
        yes.
        "yes."
20   A: = mata kurasu no ato ni.
        again class   LK after P
        "see you again after class."
21   T: hai hai. (.) doo[mo.
        yes yes (.) see   you
        "yes yes (.) see you.
22 → A: [shitsuree shimasu.
                             excuse me
                            "excuse me."
23   T: doomo.
        see you
        "see you."

The interaction gets off the ground in several steps before Aya makes her request. After summoning the teacher's attention (1/2) following a summons-answer sequence, Aya continues with two pre-requests. First she asks whether the teacher is available to talk: *ojikan arimasu ka* 'do you have time' (3). The teacher responds in the affirmative and gives Aya the green light to proceed (4). Aya then announces that she has something to ask of the teacher (5). However, following a common practice in request design (Schegloff, 1980; Taleghani-Nikazm, 2006), Aya's next action is not a request but an account, describing that Aya is thinking of enrolling in the summer session at the University of Hawai'i (9). Through the account, Aya establishes relevant background to her upcoming request so that the request comes across as something reasonable to ask. As the account further delays the request, she also treats the request as a disaffiliative or face-threatening action. After the teacher acknowledges receipt of the news about Aya's summer plans (10), Aya moves into the request by first specifying the topic, how to apply to the university (11), and then asking the teacher to tell her about it (13). The teacher responds with a claim to understanding *ah, wakarimashita* 'oh, I got it' but does not actually accept the request (14). Aya pursues an acceptance (Davidson, 1984) with the question *ii desu ka* 'is it alright' (15) and now successfully generates the agreement she is after. The teacher first answers affirmatively, using the same expression *ii desu* and thereby emphasizing iconically that she and Aya have reached a shared understanding. She then offers the next step towards delivering on her promise by suggesting that she and Aya talk after class (16 & 17). Aya accepts the teacher's suggestion and initiates a pre-closing with *sore jaa* 'well then' (18), from which point onwards the co-participants close the activity.

We noted in our analysis of Excerpt 2 that the teacher used conventionally indirect polite request forms when she made a request of Aya. In Excerpt 3, Aya also produced a conventionally indirect request, but she made the request even more polite by incorporating the conditional structure *oshiete itadakerebaa to omoimashite* 'I was wondering if you could tell me'. Aya also enhanced the politeness level of her utterance by incorporating the polite prefix *o*, which can be attached to a noun, as shown in the word *ojikan* 'time' (3), and by using the humble polite form *okikishitai* 'wish to ask' (5) instead of *kikitai* 'would like to ask'. In Excerpt 2, when she was in the position of either accepting or declining the teacher's request, Aya used a casual closing expression, *sonjaa mata* 'well then, see you' (19). In contrast, her closing formula in Excerpt 3 (22) is the very formal *shitsuree shimasu* 'excuse me' (lit. 'I am going to be rude'). Aya's use of formal-polite expressions in Excerpt 3 suggests that she orients to her role as a requester to a higher status person.

As far as the participation framework is concerned, the students remained in their participation status as an engaged audience with no claims to active participation throughout the request event. Their gaze stayed fixed on the teacher and Aya, their postures were directed towards the scene in front of them, and their body movements were minimal. Through their nonverbal displays, the students showed themselves in a state of keen interest and attention.

Request from the classroom guest to a student

After observing the two L1 speakers of Japanese making requests to each other, it was the students' turn to participate in a request event with the classroom guest. Aya randomly selected one of the students and asked him if he could check a paper she had to write in English. As before, the two participants performed the request episode in front of the class (see Excerpt 4). However, this time around the borders between the two performing participants and the student audience proved more permeable. As we will see, the 'crossplay' between the participants, 'the communication between ratified participants and bystanders across the boundaries of the dominant encounter' (Goffman, 1981: 134), is occasioned by the JFL student's difficulties in participating in the activity on the strength of his own resources.

Excerpt 4 (A: Aya, S: Steve, D: Dina, M: Mary, SS: students)

((Steve is sitting at a corner, Dina is at the other end, and Mary is sitting next to Steve. Aya is standing in the classroom facing her back towards the camera, and then she positions herself towards Steve. The rest of the students are watching her.))

1 A:.h (1) sutiibu san.
       (1) Steve Mr
   ".h (1) Steve."
2 S: hai.
       yes
   "yes."
3   (2.5)
4 A: um (1) etto ima eego no peepaa kaiteru n desu kedo:
       (1) FL now English LK paper writing N CP   but
   "uhm (1) uhm I'm writing an English paper now"
5 S: um eego no peepaa [desu ka.
       FL English LK paper CP   Q
   "uhm is it an English paper?"
6 A: [un eego.
                    yeah English
                   "yeah, English."
7 S: eego no [peepaa desu ka.
       English LK paper CP   Q
   "is it an English paper?"
8 A: [un (.) eego   de peepaa kaiteru n desu kedo,
            yeah (.) English P paper   writing N CP but,
   "yeah (.) I'm writing a paper in English but"
9 chotto (.5) guramaa ni jishin ga nai node, (.5)
   a little (.5) grammar P confidence S not so   (.5)
   "I'm a little (.5) unsure about my grammar so, (.5)"
10 chotto chekkushite moraitai kedo (.) ii? jikan aru?
   a little check would-like-to-receive but (.) ok time have
   "I'd like you to check it (.) is it ok? you have time?"
11 S: chekku shimasu ka.
      check   do   Q
   "do I check?"
12 A: un. chekku shite hoshii n da kedo.
      yeah check   would like   N CP but
   "yeah. I'd like you to check it."
13 S: aa SO desu ka. (.) ano:
      oh so CP P   (.) FL
   "oh, I see. (.) uhm:."
14   (2)
15 A: jikan arimasu ka.
      time have   Q
   "do you have time?"
16   (2)
17 → D: (   )°time°? ((D says this while further leaning towards S))
18   (.5)
19 → S: HAI.
      yes
   "YES."

Talking with a Classroom Guest 59

```
20      SS: hahahaha hahahaha haha ha ((J jumps a bit. The entire class
            bursts into laughter.))
            "hahahaha hahahaha haha ha"
21          (5)
22      M: °(   )° ((M whispers something to S and S looks at her.))
23      A: aa dono ji- (.5) itsu  ga ii    desu?
            FL which   (.5) when S good CP
            "uhm what ti- (.5) when is a good time for you?"
24      S: °itsu  ga° (.) ano: (1.5) rai- (.) raishu:  suiyoobi (.) desu ka.
            when S  (.)    FL  (1.5) nex- (.) next week Wednesday (.) CP   Q
            "when (.) uhm (1.5) is it (.) nex- (.) next week Wednesday?"
25      A: hai. (.) jaa raishuu  no suiyoobi  ni:
            yes  (.) then next week LK Wednesday P
            "yes. (.) then next Wednesday
26          ichioo peepaa mottekuru n de,
            in any case paper bring      N so,
            "I'll bring my paper anyway so"
27          mite kudasai, ranchi taimu ni.
            look please   lunch  time  at
            please take a look at it during lunch time."
28          (1)
29      SS: hahahaha hahahaha haha. ((The class bursts into laughter))
            "hahahaha   hahahaha  haha."
30          ((S looks at Mary. S shakes his head.))
31      A: ranchi taimu (.) isogashii desu ka.
            lunch   time  (.) busy       CP   Q
            "are you busy (.) during lunch time?"
32      S: ah ie  um (1) °um (1) ano: (.5) ie°
            oh no FL (1)  FL (1) FL    (.5) no
            "oh, no uhm (1) °uhm (1) uhm: (.5) no°."
33          (1.5)
34 →    M: hima.
            free
            "free."
35 →    S: HIMA desu.
            free   CP
            "I'm FREE."
36      SS: hahahaha. ((The class bursts into laughter))
            "hahahaha."
37      A: ja:, issho ni gohan tabe nagara (.) mite kudasai,
            then together meal  eat  while   (.) look please
            "then, while eating lunch together (.) please take a look at
38          peepaa eego    no.
            paper  English LK
            "my English paper."
```

39	S:	hai ((nods)) *yes* "yes."
40	A:	jaa, sono (.) mata raishuu ni (.5) aimashoo? *then that (.) again next week P (.5) meet let's* "well then, that (.) let's (.5) meet again next week."
41	S:	.h haha. ((S bends forward and laughs, shaking his head.)) ".h haha."
42	SS:	*hahahaha.* ((The class laughs.)) "hahahaha."
43		((J jumps a bit, looks away from S, and then looks towards S again, while laughing.))
44	A:	°sugoi° ( ) tte n da (2) [doo shiyoo. *great QT N CP (2) how do* "°great° It's that ( ) (2) what shall I do?"
45 →	M:	[°( )°((M whispers something to S.))
46 →	S:	OH (.) hai. *oh (.) yes* "OH (.) yes."
47	SS:	*hahahaha.* ((Everybody bursts into laughter again.)) "hahahaha."

Following a summons-answer sequence (1 & 2), Aya starts with a pre-sequence that prepares the topical context for the request she is about to make (4). Steve's other-initiation of repair (5) leads into a multiple-turn repair sequence in which Steve tries to confirm his understanding that the paper Aya is writing is in English. Aya confirms his understanding and repeats the topically relevant portion of her original pre-request (8), followed by an account expressing uncertainty about her ability to write in English (9). Connecting the pre-requests to the upcoming request with the connector *node* 'so', she does a request in three parts, first by expressing her desire *chotto chekkushite moraitai kedo* (.) 'I'd like you to check it.', followed by two short questions, *ii?* 'is it ok?' and *jikan aru?* 'you have time?' (10). The request gets another other-initiation of repair as Steve displays his candidate understanding *chekku shimasu ka* 'do I check?' (11). Aya's repair ratifies his understanding (12) while also doing an embedded correction of Steve's semantically incorrect form *chekku shimasu ka* with *chekku shite hoshii n da kedo*,[9] upon which Steve makes a claim to understanding by saying *aa SO desu ka.* (.) 'oh I see' (13). The hesitation token *ano* projects more to come, but when after a two-second gap Steve has not resumed his turn, Aya repeats her question 'do you have time?' (15). While her original question was in plain style (*jikan aru?*, 10), Aya now uses the (polite) *-masu* style (*jikan arimasu ka?*). With this style shift, Aya appears to accommodate Steve's limited Japanese proficiency because students learn the *-masu* style first and are more used to hearing it.

After the two-second gap following Aya's question, Dina, a student sitting at the opposite corner from Steve, leans towards Steve and whispers something. The first part of her utterance is not audible but her softly spoken 'time' suggests that she was supplying the English equivalent of Aya's utterance in Line 15, that is, 'do you have time'. With the assistance from his classmate, Steve answers Aya's question affirmatively with a loud *HAI* (19), upon which the entire class bursts into laughter (20). Another bystanding student, Mary, says something to Steve and Steve directs his gaze at her, however what Mary says is not audible.

Aya then moves into the next phase of the request sequence, that is, to make an arrangement for checking the paper. After mutual agreement to meet the following Wednesday (23–25), Aya reiterates her request with the direct request form *mite kudasai, ranchi taimu ni.* 'please take a look at it during lunch time' (27). This is followed by a one-second gap in Line 28 and laughter by the class (29). From Lines 31 to 36, we can see a sequence similar to the one observed earlier. Here Aya asks Steve if he will be busy during lunch hour (31). Steve starts his response with *ah, ie* 'oh, no', followed by perturbations and a repetition of *ie* (32). Orienting to Steve's struggle in producing an answer, Mary offers him the word *hima* 'free' as a solution to the word search that Steve appears to be entangled in (34). Steve appropriates the word and produces *HIMA desu.* 'I'm FREE.', with emphatic stress on the critical element (35). Again, his response triggers laughter from the class (36). Bringing the focal interaction back on track again, Aya reiterates her request (37 & 38) with a direct *mite kudasai* 'please take a look', which Steve accepts with *hai* 'yes' and an affirming nod (39). Aya now moves into the pre-closing by suggesting to meet in a week's time, as they agreed upon earlier (40). In response, Steve shakes his head and laughs, showing that he does not understand her utterance. His laughter is joined by the audience (42) and Aya (43). While everybody else is still laughing, Mary whispers something to S (45). Her utterance is not audible, but Steve's next turn *OH (.) hai.* (46) suggests that Mary translated Aya's laughable utterance (40). Whatever the nature of the assistance, it enables Steve to produce a much delayed agreement to Aya's proposal (46), which prompts another round of laughter (47).

If we compare Aya's request to the teacher in Excerpt 3 with her request to Steve, we note several important differences. In Excerpt 4, after getting Steve's attention, Aya's pre-request immediately prepares the referential context for the request. She does not inquire into Steve's availability to talk or announce that she had a favor to ask, as she did in interaction with the teacher in Excerpt 3. Moreover, the two request episodes differ noticeably in speech styles. In Episode 4, Aya shifted between plain and polite style, whereas in Excerpt 3 she used the polite style throughout the interaction, incorporating humble polite forms and other politeness markers such as a polite prefix. These interactional features, including style shifts in different participant configurations, suggest that interactions with a classroom guest make a wide range of interactional sequences and social indexicals available to students. Such interactions also provide opportunities for constructing a more diverse array of social identities, relationships and discourse roles than JFL classrooms usually afford. In pragmatic, sociolinguistic and interactional perspective, the active participation of a classroom guest can transcend some of the institutional constraints on instructed foreign language learning.

Aya's participation in the request episode with a student was also valuable because she provided assistance for Steve, facilitating his understanding and moving the interaction forward. On several occasions, Steve other-initiated repair of Aya's preceding turn, showing problems in hearing or understanding what Aya had said. In each case, Aya's repairs were designed to address Steve's problem as one of understanding rather than hearing. In response to his first repair initiation *um eego no peepaa desu ka* 'uhm is it an English paper' (5), Aya first confirms Steve's understanding by the affirmative token *un* 'yeah' and then repeats the key word *eego* 'English' (6). This repair does not appear to solve Steve's understanding problem, perhaps because it was said in overlap with the final elements in Steve's preceding turn. Upon Steve's repetition of his repair initiation (7), Aya again starts her repair turn with the affirmative token *un*, but this time she expands the repair by repeating her pre-request *eego no peepaa kaiteru n desu kedo* 'I'm writing a paper in English (4)' almost verbatim, changing only the linking nominal *no* to the particle *de* 'in' (8) before she proceeds to her next action. In this way, Aya assists Steve not only in understanding the object *eego no peepaa* but also that she has to write one and thereby prepares a relevant context for the request. When Steve other-initiates repair of Aya's request *chekkushite moraitai kedo* 'I'd like you to check it' (10) by soliciting confirmation of his candidate understanding (11), Aya follows her previous practice by first ratifying Steve's understanding (*un*). Then she repeats the entire request *chekkku shite hoshii n da kedo* 'I'd like you to check it.', with the only modification of replacing *moraitai* (10) with *hoshii* (12). After Steve has the opportunity to hear the same request twice, he displays understanding without delay, showing that the repair has been successful. Aya's repairs consistently do more than ratifying Steve's candidate understandings with an affirmative token. Through repetition of the problematic element or the entire utterance in which it was embedded, Aya's repairs are recipient-designed to facilitate Steve's understanding (Kasper, 2006; Kasper & Ross, 2007).

It bears pointing out that throughout the request episode, Aya did not resort to such features of 'foreigner talk' as speaking more slowly or simplifying the linguistic form of her utterances. This gave Steve as well as the overhearing students an opportunity to observe and understand request and repair sequences as they occur in talk outside of the classroom.

Earlier we registered differences in audience participation between the request episodes involving the two first language speakers of Japanese and the episode between Aya and Steve. Although in all three events the requests were performed in front of and for the benefit of the student audience as intended bystanders, the crossplay observed in the guest–student episode was absent from the guest–teacher interactions. In Request episode 4, some of the bystanding students engaged in crossplay in response to particular interactional moments, namely when their performing classmate had hearable difficulty producing or understanding an utterance. On four such occasions (17, 22, 34, 45), Dina and Mary helped Steve by providing him with English glosses or Japanese words. The helping students' discourse identity (Zimmerman, 1998) was that of a prompter, literally in Mary's supply of *hima* 'free' (34), spoken for Steve to repeat, metaphorically on the occasions where Dina or Mary glossed an utterance by Aya that Steve did not understand and thereby enabled him to produce a sequentially appropriate turn (17, 45). Steve, in turn, became a crossplayer by virtue of being the addressed recipient of the crossplaying bystanders. On one occasion, he actively sought out his classmates' assistance through gaze and gesture (30). At another moment, he oriented to both of his discourse identities as a crossplayer and performer in the request event. After he received some inaudible assistance from Mary (45), his next turn *OH (.) hai.* 'OH (.) yes.' was composed of two parts, separated from each other by a micropause, each doing a different action, in a different language and addressed to its own recipient. The change-of-state token *OH* (Heritage, 1984), produced in English, responded to Mary's intervention and constructed Steve as a recipient of Mary's assistance. *Hai.* was addressed to Aya, agreeing to her suggestion some turns ago and constructing Steve as a co-participant in the request event.

Toohey (2000) found in a study of learning English at a grade school that children were not allowed to help each other in class, except for certain tasks which were explicitly set up to foster mutual assistance among the children. No such policy exists in the JFL classroom examined in this study. As we have seen, the teacher did not intervene in the interaction between Steve and Aya even when Steve was in trouble. By withholding assistance, she gave the bystanding students the opportunity to assist Steve as a matter of student-organized collaborative learning. In the request episode between classroom guest and student, the performing student received assistance both from the classroom guest as his co-participant in the request event and from his bystanding peers.

Discussion and Conclusion

This study set out to answer three sets of research questions. Based on the analysis of request episodes in the preceding sections, we can summarize our answers as follows.

1. What opportunities for learning how to request in Japanese arise when a classroom guest participates in request episodes? In what ways do request episodes with a classroom guest differ from requests made by the teacher to class?

The request episodes between Aya and the teacher and Aya and a student suggest that interactions with a classroom guest make a wide range of interactional sequences, linguistic resources and speech styles available to students. When making requests to each other, the L1 speakers of Japanese prefaced their requests by inquiring into the co-participants availability to talk and announcing the upcoming request. They deployed polite and humble polite speech styles and a hesitant and apologetic demeanor, both of which are culturally valued practices in requests to higher status persons or out-group members. In contrast, Aya's request to the student, Steve, included prefatory reference preparation but no relationally oriented pre-requests, and the speech style was more casual, shifting between plain and polite -*desu/masu*. By observing how the requests in different participant configurations were organized sequentially and how they were implemented through linguistic, paralinguistic and nonverbal resources, the overhearing students were able to see how discursive practices and resources may be associated with dimensions of social context. The L1 speakers of Japanese also modeled the practice of echoing what the co-participant has said in his or her previous turn (Excerpt 2, *daijoobu desu* 'alright' (6); Excerpt 3, *ii desu yo* 'that's alright' (16)), a common interactional method to affirm that mutual agreement has been achieved (Svennevig, 2004).

To some extent, requests issued by the teacher to the class enable such an association as well. The teacher's requests differed markedly when the requestive goal was a routine action, expected as a matter of course in the JFL classroom, or an unusual request for the teacher's benefit. The most salient difference was that the standard requests were unprefaced and unaccounted, showing that the teacher treated them as preferred, i.e. normatively expectable actions in the classroom context. Through the multiple extensive pre-requests that prefaced the exceptional request, including the announcement of the upcoming request and an account, the teacher oriented to the high imposition of the request. By observing that the same type of action addressed to the same recipients is done very differently on different occasions, the students have the opportunity to register what other social dimensions besides participant categories may be relevant for request speakers. But unlike the episodes with the classroom guest, the teacher's requests to class did not invite extended collaboration with the students. The requests displayed a narrow range of speech styles and did not feature the hesitant-apologetic demeanor as seen in the L1 Japanese speakers' interactions. In sum, while teacher talk does comprise requests addressed to students on a regular basis, their range, sequentially, linguistically and stylistically, is narrow compared to that afforded in interactions with a classroom guest.

2. What participation frameworks emerge during request episodes with a classroom guest?

In the examined episodes, the classroom guest performed request events with the teacher or a student in front of the class. While in the requests issued by the teacher to class, the students were the collective addressed recipient, in the request episodes with the classroom guest, the addressed recipient was not the students but the party to which the request was made. The request episodes with Aya unfolded as performances, staged before an audience of classroom members. In these activities, the overall participation framework was modeled on that of a theatrical audience watching a performance as collective intended overhearers. During the request episodes between Aya and the teacher, the boundaries between performers and audience remained intact. On one occasion, during a request made by the teacher to Aya, an overhearing student made an approving remark, but that comment was not addressed to the performers, nor did it get an uptake from them or, for that matter, the remaining audience. But although the student's comment did not affect the participation framework, it came at a critical point in the request event and showed his understanding of the action so far. Except for this incident, the overhearing students displayed through their gaze and posture that they were in a state of active attentive recipientship throughout the performances.

In contrast to the request episodes between the two L1 speakers of Japanese, during the request event between classroom guest and a student, the boundaries between audience and performers were crossed on several occasions. Each time crossplay was initiated in response to the student performer's trouble in understanding what his co-participant in the request event had said, or when he had problems in producing a turn. On such occasions, an overhearing student would take on the discourse role of a prompter, assisting the performer to progress in the interaction. For the most part, the prompters oriented to their participant status as support staff by whispering to the performer. Through this practice they indicated that their intervention did not make claims to ratified participation in the performance. Compared to their theatrical models, the mediating roles of the prompters were more extensive. They supplied Japanese words for the student performer to plug in his turn and in so doing helped him overcome problems in speaking, and they provided English glosses of Japanese utterances made by the co-performer that the performing student had problems understanding. In addition to unsolicited interventions by overhearing students, the performing student also solicited help from specific audience members through gaze and gesture, and he oriented to the assistance received from a prompter through a vocal display produced in English. Crossplay was thus initiated by either a bystanding student or the performing student, but the occasion was invariably the performing student's difficulties at particular moments in the request interaction.

3. What kinds of assistance are made available to the students during request episodes with a classroom guest?

During the request episode with the classroom guest, the performing student received assistance from two sources: his co-performer and the overhearing students. Aya would only help on demand, that is, in response to Steve's other-initiations of repair. On all of these occasions, her repairs were recipient-designed in such a way that they provided more material than a response token to confirm Steve's candidate understandings. Through repetition of the problematic utterances, Aya gave Steve the opportunity to listen yet another time and achieve understanding the second or third time around. In this way, the co-performers reached levels of mutual understanding before moving on to the next step in the request episode.

As we have shown, interacting with the classroom guest in the request episode afforded demonstrable benefits for the performing student. But what was in it for the overhearing students? The participant status of non-performing bystanders would seem to render the concept of assisted performance inapplicable by definition. Unlike the performing student, the overhearers were not under the interactional demands of having to understand the co-performer's turn and connecting it to the interaction thus far in order to produce a relevant response (Ohta, 2001). The demands and benefits of moment-to-moment monitoring, inferencing and projecting what comes next were inescapable for the performing student but less pressing for the audience. As overhearers with no ratified parts as contributors to the interaction, audience members can tune in and out at any time, allowing themselves to direct their attention elsewhere, or nowhere. While this is a possible scenario, it was not what we saw in the examined class session. First, as the video record documents, the entire student audience displayed consistent focused attention to the performances in front of them, suggesting that they were indeed following and interpreting the request event as it unfolded. Secondly, in the request event with the student performer, the crossplaying students demonstrated through their interventions their understanding of the action at those particular moments – in fact the interventions followed from *their* understanding and their recognition of the performing student's *non-* understanding. Finally, yet another source of evidence for the bystanding students' ongoing analysis of the unfolding interaction are the laughter episodes during the request event with the student performer. The onset of the collective laughter coincided with the overhearing students' registering that Steve was in interactional trouble, either not being able to understand what Aya had said or by searching for a word or expression to continue his turn. Upon hearing indications of such difficulties, the overhearing students turned their heads and gaze towards Steve before starting to laugh. Whether the student audience did learn from the performance cannot be said with any certainty. But through their embodied actions and vocal conduct, the overhearing students showed that they did pay close attention to the scene in front of them, and thereby to the affordances for learning how to make requests in Japanese.

Appendix 3.1. Transcription Conventions and Abbreviations

Transcription Conventions

[	overlap
?	rising intonation
.	falling intonation
,	continuing intonation
:	elongated syllable
::	longer elongated syllable
H	audible breathing
.h	in-breath
h	out-breath
text	marked stress
TEXT	spoken loudly
< text >	spoken slowly
°text°	spoken softly
(1.5)	length of significant pause in seconds
(.)	micropause
=	latched talk
-	word cutoff
( )	unsure hearings
((behavior))	paralinguistic behavior

Abbreviations

CP	Copula verb *be* in various forms
FL	Filler

LK	Linking nominal
N	Nominalizer
NEG	Negative morpheme
O	Object marker
P	Particle
Q	Question marker
QT	Quotation marker
S	Subject marker

Notes

1. The IRF is neither universal to all classroom settings globally (Cook, 1999), nor is it immutably fixed in settings where it does predominate (van Lier, 1988).
2. Aya was often chatting with students who were sitting next to her when the instructor arrived at the classroom. Also, after class some students would come over to her desk and say hi before they left the classroom. These conversations were predominantly held in English, whereas the talk during the official class lessons was mainly conducted in Japanese. Through their language choice, the students and Aya framed their talk as institutional interaction or ordinary conversation respectively.
3. Pre-requests (Schegloff, 1980, 1988) project a request as a possible next action. Among other things, they can serve to explore whether a condition for the request is met. As pre-requests delay the upcoming request, they can also be understood to mark the request as a dispreferred action, that is one that is face-threatening or disaffiliative (Lerner, 1996; Taleghani-Nikazm, 2006).
4. Excerpts 2 and 3 below are examples of the conventional hesitant style.
5. The polite formulaic expression *yoroshiku onegai shimasu* is used in many situations in Japanese. Literally, *yoroshiku* means 'appropriately' and *onegai shimasu* 'to ask a favor'. In a request context, the expression is conventionally used as an appeal to the recipient to accommodate the request. Thus, we rendered it as 'I hope you will help me'.
6. For the distinction between in-group and out-group (*uchi-soto*) in Japanese society, see Bachnik and Quinn (1994).
7. Svennevig (2004: 489) observes an equivalent response format in Norwegian: 'A repeat plus a final response particle, "ja" (yes), constitutes a claim of understanding'.
8. During the class period in which Request episodes 2 and 3 were recorded, the video camera was stationed in the same position, focusing on the overhearing students rather than the performing guest and teacher. However Aya's body movements came into view on occasion.
9. From Steve's discourse perspective, the correct form would be *chekku shite hoshii n desu ka* 'I would like you to check'.

References

Bachnik, J.M. and Quinn, C.J. (eds) (1994) *Situated Meaning. Inside and Outside in Japanese Self, Society, and Language*. Princeton, NJ: Princeton University Press.

Bardovi-Harlig, K., Hartford, B., Mahan-Taylor, R., Morgan, M. and Reynolds, D. (1991) Developing pragmatic awareness: Closing the conversation. *ELT Journal* 45, 4–15.

Belz, J.A. and Kinginger, C. (2002) The cross-linguistic development of address form use in telecollaborative language learning: Two case studies. *Canadian Modern Language Review/Revue Canadienne des Langues Vivantes* 59, 189–214.

Chaudron, C. (1988) *Second Language Classrooms*. Cambridge: Cambridge University Press.

Cook, H.M. (1992) Meanings of non-referential indexes: A case study of the Japanese sentence-final particle *ne*. *Text* 12, 507–539.

Cook, H.M. (1996) The use of addressee honorifics in Japanese elementary school classroom. In N. Akatsuka, S. Iwasaki and S. Strauss (eds) *Japanese/Korean Linguistics* (Vol. 5, pp. 67–81). Stanford, CA: Center for the Study of Language and Information.

Cook, H.M. (1999) Language socialization in Japanese elementary schools: Attentive listening and reaction turns. *Journal of Pragmatics* 31, 1443–1465.

Davidson, J. (1984) Subsequent versions of invitations, offers, requests, and proposals dealing with potential or actual rejection. In J.M. Atkinson and J. Heritage (eds) *Structures of Social Action* (pp. 102–128). Cambridge, UK: Cambridge University Press.

Duff, P.A. (1995) An ethnography of communication in immersion classrooms in Hungary. *TESOL Quarterly* 29, 505–537.

Ellis, R. (1994) *The Study of Second Language Acquisition*. Oxford: Oxford University Press.

Falsgraf, C. and Majors, D. (1995) Implicit culture in Japanese immersion classroom discourse. *Journal of the Association of Teachers of Japanese* 29 (2), 1–21.

Goffman, E. (1981) *Forms of Talk*. Oxford: Blackwell.

He, A.W. (2000) The grammatical and interactional organization of teacher's directives: Implications for socialization of Chinese American children. *Linguistics and Education* 11, 119–140.

He, A.W. (2003) Novices and their speech roles in Chinese heritage language classes. In R. Bayley and S.R. Schecter (eds) *Language Socialization in Bilingual and Multilingual Societies* (pp. 128–146). Clevedon, UK: Multilingual Matters.

Heritage, J. (1984) A change-of-state token and aspects of its sequential placement. In J.M. Atkinson and J. Heritage (eds) *Structures of Social Action* (pp. 299–345). Cambridge: Cambridge University Press.

Kanagy, R. (1999) Interactional routines as a mechanism for L2 acquisition and socialization in an immersion context. *Journal of Pragmatics* 31, 1467–1492.

Kashiwazaki, H. (1993) Hanashikake koudou no danwa bunseki: Irai youkyuu hyougen no jissai o chuushin ni [Discourse analysis of requests with phatic communication]. *Nihongo Kyooiku* 79, 53–63.

Kasper, G. (1997) The role of pragmatics in language teacher education. In K. Bardovi-Harlig and B. Hartford (eds) *Beyond Methods* (pp. 113–136). New York: McGraw-Hill.

Kasper, G. (2006) When once is not enough: Politeness in multiple requests. *Multilingua* 25, 323–349.

Kasper, G. and Ross, S. (2007) Multiple questions in oral proficiency interviews. *Journal of Pragmatics* 39, 2045–2070.

Kinginger, C. (2000) Learning the pragmatics of solidarity in the networked foreign language classroom. In J.K. Hall and L.S. Verplaetse (eds) *Second and Foreign Language Learning Through Classroom Interaction* (pp. 23–46). Mahwah, NJ: Erlbaum.

Kinginger, C. and Belz, J.A. (2005) Socio-cultural perspectives on pragmatic development in foreign language learning: Microgenetic case studies from telecollaboration and residence abroad. *Intercultural Pragmatics* 2, 369–421.

Lantolf, J.P. and Thorne, S.L. (2006) *Sociocultural Theory and the Genesis of Second Language Development.* Oxford: Oxford University Press.

Lerner, G.H. (1996) Finding "face" in the preference structures of talk-in-interaction. *Social Psychology Quarterly* 59, 303–321.

Lo, A. (2004). Evidentiality and morality in a Korean heritage language school. *Pragmatics* 14, 235–256.

Long, M.H., Adams, L., McLean, M. and Castaños, F. (1976) Doing things with words: Verbal interaction in lockstep and small group classroom situations. In J. Fanselow and R. Crymes (eds) *On TESOL '76* (pp. 137–153). Washington, DC: Teachers of English to Speakers of Other Languages.

Mehan, H. (1979) *Learning Lessons.* Cambridge, MA: Harvard University Press.

Mori, J. (2002) Task-design, plan and development of talk-in-interaction: An analysis of a small group activity in a Japanese language classroom. *Applied Linguistics* 23, 323–347.

Mori, J. (2004) Negotiating sequential boundaries and learning opportunities: A case from a Japanese language classroom. *The Modern Language Journal* 88, 536–550.

Morita, N. (2000) Discourse socialization through oral classroom activities in a TESOL graduate program. *TESOL Quarterly* 34, 279–310.

Ohta, A.S. (1995) Applying sociocultural theory to an analysis of learner discourse: Learner–learner collaborative interaction in the zone of proximal development. *Issues in Applied Linguistics* 6, 93–121.

Ohta, A.S. (1997) The development of pragmatic competence in learner–learner classroom interaction. *Pragmatics and Language Learning* 8, 223–242. Urbana, IL: University of Illinois at Urbana-Champaign.

Ohta, A.S. (2001) *Second Language Acquisition Processes in the Classroom: Learning Japanese.* Mahwah, NJ: Lawrence Erlbaum Associates.

Ohta, A.S. (2005) Interlanguage pragmatics in the zone of proximal development. *System* 33, 503–517.

Poole, D. (1992). Language socialization in the second language classroom. *Language Learning* 42, 593–616.

Schegloff, E.A. (1980) Preliminaries to preliminaries: "Can I ask you a question?" *Sociological Inquiry* 50, 104–152.

Schegloff, E.A. (1988) Presequences and indirection: Applying speech act theory to ordinary conversation. *Journal of Pragmatics* 12, 55–62.

Sinclair, M. and Coulthard, M. (1975) *Towards an Analysis of Discourse.* Oxford: Oxford University Press.

Svennevig, J. (2004) Other-repetition as display of hearing, understanding and emotional stance. *Discourse Studies* 6, 489–516.

Taleghani-Nikazm, C. (2006) *Request Sequences: The Intersection of Grammar, Interaction and Social Context.* Amsterdam & Philadelphia: John Benjamins.

Tateyama, Y. (2001) Requests in Japanese as a foreign language (JFL) classroom discourse. Paper presented at the American Association for Applied Linguistics Annual Conference, St. Louis, MO, February.

Tharp, R.G. and Gallimore, R. (1988) *Rousing Minds to Life: Teaching, Learning, and Schooling in Social Context.* New York: Cambridge University Press.

Toohey, K. (2000) *Learning English at School: Identity, Social Relations and Classroom Practice.* Clevedon: Multilingual Matters.

van Lier, L. (1988) *The Classroom and the Language Learner.* London: Longman.

van Lier, L. (2000) From input to affordance: Social-interactive learning from an ecological perspective. In J.P. Lantolf (ed.) *Sociocultural Theory and Second Language Learning* (pp. 245–259). Oxford: Oxford University Press.

Vygotsky, L.S. (1978) *Mind in Society: The Development of Higher Psychological Processes*. Cambridge, MA: Harvard University Press.

Willet, J. (1995) Becoming first graders in L2: An ethnographic study of language socialization. *TESOL Quarterly* 29, 473–503.

Yoshimi, D.A. (1999) L1 language socialization as a variable in the use of *ne* by L2 learners of Japanese. *Journal of Pragmatics* 31, 1513–1525.

Zimmerman, D.H. (1998) Identity, context and interaction. In C. Antaki and S. Widdicombe (eds) *Identities in Talk* (pp. 87–106). London: Sage.

Chapter 4
Pragmatic Performance: What are Learners Thinking?

TIM HASSALL

Introduction

The study seeks to reveal the mental processes underlying the performance of sensitive speech acts by adult learners of a second language (L2). As this is still a new research goal, the study is open-ended and exploratory in nature. It asks learners to report whatever they were thinking and then examines those reports to gain insights into what they know about pragmatics and how they acquire pragmatic knowledge and ability. It also aims specifically to clarify the relationship of two cognitive tasks: the task of acquiring knowledge and that of acquiring control over attention to knowledge (cf. Bialystok, 1993). A further aim is to assess the value of verbal report data for investigating learner pragmatic knowledge and acquisition. The subjects of the study are two groups of Australian learners of Indonesian: a low intermediate group of foreign language (FL) learners and an upper intermediate group of foreign/second language (FL/SL) learners.

Background

Thoughts underlying L2 pragmatic performance

The standard way of examining mental processes during performance of a task is to elicit verbal reports. These are either 'think aloud' reports provided concurrently or retrospective reports provided shortly afterwards while memory traces can still be retrieved (Ericsson & Simon, 1993). While many studies have used verbal reports to examine what L2 learners are thinking while they do language tasks (see e.g. Cohen, 1998: 35; Faerch & Kasper, 1987; Kasper & Rose, n.d.), virtually none set out to investigate what learners are thinking while they do pragmatic tasks. By these I mean tasks where interpersonal meaning is paramount – such as face-threatening speech acts. To my knowledge only two published studies in English have attempted to do so.[1]

Robinson's (1992) study evaluated verbal reports for their ability to reveal the pragmatic knowledge of learners. She had learners make written refusals in six situations during a written Discourse Completion Task, and examined their mental processes by eliciting both concurrent and retrospective verbal reports from them. Certain learners did reveal pieces of knowledge they possessed about making refusals. However very little evidence emerged about acquisition of pragmatic knowledge or ability.[2] One reason is that the learners were not asked in their retrospective reports to report their actual thoughts, but rather to provide reasons or explanations for their behaviour (see Ericsson & Simon, 1993; Kasper & Rose, n.d.). Also the learners sometimes had to wait as long as an hour before giving their retrospective reports, so that they had sometimes forgotten their thoughts from during the task itself (see Robinson, 1992: 64).

As for mental processes underlying spoken pragmatic performance, these have been investigated by Widjaja (1997). She used oral roleplay combined with retrospective verbal reports to investigate how female Taiwanese learners of English refused invitations for a date and what factors affected their refusals. As with Robinson's (1992) study above, the learners were asked to comment on their behaviour rather than to reveal what they had been thinking during the task itself. Nevertheless, their verbal reports did on occasion reveal the state of their pragmatic knowledge. Their reports also revealed two instances where their weak control over attention to knowledge, rather than deviant knowledge itself, was evidently the cause of their behaviour (although Wijaya does not comment on those cases). However, no evidence of them acquiring pragmatic knowledge or ability apparently emerged from their reports. To sum up, these earlier studies show that verbal reports by learners can help to reveal their pragmatic knowledge. And the present study will exploit the potential of this data source more effectively still by obtaining reports on what learners were actually thinking during their spoken pragmatic performance.

Learner Pragmatics

Sociopragmatics versus pragmalinguistics

Thomas (1983) usefully distinguishes between two types of pragmatic knowledge: 'sociopragmatic' and 'pragmalinguistic'. The former refers to knowledge about the social context – the weightings of factors such as status or social distance which will affect choice of linguistic form. Pragmalinguistic knowledge is knowledge about the relation between linguistic forms and the pragmatic meanings they carry.

Bialystok's two-dimensional model: Knowledge versus control

Bialystok (1993) argues that acquiring knowledge is of relatively minor importance for adult L2 learners of pragmatics. She acknowledges that they must acquire a certain amount of knowledge, in the form of an increasingly explicit understanding of L2 pragmatic features. However she asserts that the crucial process for them is acquiring control over attention to their knowledge. They generally produce inappropriate utterances not because their knowledge is deviant but because they cannot access it rapidly enough to use it when they need it. This claim of Bialystok (1993) has yet to be verified empirically. Her claim that acquiring knowledge itself is a minor task tends to be challenged by the few data-based studies that assess it (e.g. Barron, 2005; Hassall, 2001). However the importance of her second dimension, control over knowledge, is hard to assess rigorously without introspective data. One study that uses diary data from learners (DuFon, 1999) manages to identify gaps between what learners know about address terms and how they actually use them. This finding, as Kasper and Rose point out, does suggest that 'pragmatic awareness and processing control may be unrelated dimensions' (Kasper & Rose, 2002: 25). In addition, one study that uses diary data from a single learner (Hassall, 2005) identifies certain pragmatic features for which the acquisition of control over attention to knowledge was crucial. The present study will examine the roles of those two dimensions of Bialystok's model and the interactions between them more thoroughly than has been done to date.

Effect of learning environment on L2 pragmatics

Learners who learn the language while living in the target culture tend to regard pragmatics as important, showing for instance greater sensitivity to pragmatic errors than to grammatical errors (Bardovi-Harlig & Dörnyei, 1998; Niezgoda & Röver, 2001). The high importance they place on pragmatics seems to be because they interact daily with natives of the target culture. On the contrary, learners who learn the language in a classroom outside the target culture appear to be less sensitive to appropriateness and to place more importance on grammatical accuracy instead (Bardovi-Harlig & Dörnyei, 1998). It is also true that FL learners who are highly motivated and capable can succeed in extracting pragmatic input even from their relatively poor environment, and so manage to develop a high sensitivity to pragmatics as well (Niezgoda & Röver, 2001). And what is more, as Kasper and Rose (2002) point out, not all FL classrooms are poor sources of pragmatic information. Even so, learning the language in the target culture tends to make learners more sensitive to the importance of pragmatics because the amount and quality of relevant input and the opportunities for relevant practice tend to be greater than in a classroom back home.

Does an FL or an SL environment best help one acquire pragmatic competence? As Kasper and Rose (2002) observe after summing up the literature, it is a myth that living in the target culture is always a good way to learn pragmatics. Some second language learners may in fact have little exposure to pragmatic information and/or few chances to practise using it. Nevertheless, a great many second language environments are far richer in both those respects than at least more traditional FL classrooms. And for the learning of sociopragmatics specifically, the evidence does suggest that living in the target culture is more conducive than studying in an FL classroom (see Kasper & Rose, 2002: 145–146, 268).

Indonesian address terms and terms of self-reference

Indonesian has a great many terms of address (see e.g. Jenson, 1988). An important one for this study is the second person pronoun *Anda*. This term is appropriate only for addressing distant equals, such as strangers of roughly one's own status. *Anda* should therefore not be used to address people of higher status than oneself, for whom respectful terms such as *(Ba)pak* and *(I)bu*, kin terms literally meaning 'father' and 'mother', are more suitable. Nor should *Anda* be used to address familiar people such as friends, for whom an intimate term such as the pronoun *kamu* is more appropriate.

As for terms of self-reference, Indonesian again offers a choice to speakers. One option is the first person pronoun *saya*. It carries a fairly neutral social message. While especially common in formal situations, it is also acceptable when talking to familiars and/or when talking in informal contexts. Another option for self-reference is to use the first person pronoun *aku*. This pronoun, unlike the more neutral *saya*, is marked for informality or familiarity or both (Quinn, 2001: 555).

Method

Subjects

The subjects were 19 students from an undergraduate programme in Indonesian at an Australian university. Subjects were attracted by advertisements on campus and were paid for their participation. One group, who will be referred to as Low learners, consisted of 12 subjects near the beginning of the second-year level of study of the language. They were all of low intermediate (or in one case upper elementary) proficiency. The other group, the High learners, comprised seven subjects who had first completed four to five semesters of study of Indonesian in Australia and then studied for a full year at a university in Indonesia, a sojourn from which they had recently returned. This group had therefore learned Indonesian as both a foreign and a second language. All were of upper intermediate (or in one case low advanced) proficiency. Comparing these two groups allows a cross-sectional study of acquisition of pragmatics. The two groups represent different points along a route of learning common in many countries, by which undergraduate learners first undertake formal classes as FL learners in the home country and then spend one year abroad as SL learners in the target culture.

Procedure

The data were collected using a method of oral roleplay combined with retrospective verbal reports. Verbal report is the standard method of studying the mental processes underlying performance of a task and is often used in L2 research (see e.g. Cohen, 1998; Faerch & Kasper, 1987; Gass & Mackey, 2000). With retrospective verbal reports, subjects retrieve the memory traces of the thoughts they had during the task and directly verbalise them shortly after the task itself is finished (Ericsson & Simon, 1993: 16).

Learners all performed the same four roleplay situations involving a face-threatening speech act: two requests and two complaints (see Appendix 4.1). They also performed three distractor situations on which no verbal reports were obtained, in order to help them focus on the roleplay task itself and so minimise the reactive effect of the verbal reporting on their mental processes (cf. Ericsson & Simon, 1993: xvii; Kasper & Rose, n.d.). All roleplays were performed on the basis of a written cue (see Appendix 4.2). The order of the situations was systematically varied to eliminate bias but the second, fourth and fifth roleplays were always distractors.

All the learners' roleplays were performed with an Indonesian partner. For half of the sessions this partner was a female teaching assistant and for the other half a male postgraduate student. A preliminary training session was conducted for both partners. A trial data-elicitation session on a single pilot subject was also conducted, which proved useful, especially in revealing how long the various stages of the procedure took and in giving the researcher practice in handling the equipment smoothly and unobtrusively. All roleplays were videotaped and audiotaped by the researcher, and the verbal reports were audiotaped.

The procedure for obtaining verbal reports on pragmatic performance was based on recommendations by Kasper and Rose (n.d.), and was as follows.[3]

(1) The learner read the written cue and indicated when ready to begin the roleplay.
(2) The researcher started the video camera and signalled to the participants to begin.
(3) As soon as the learner had produced the request or complaint, the researcher stopped the roleplay and asked: 'What were you thinking when you said that? Say what you were thinking from start to finish.'

(4) The learner verbally reported his or her thoughts.
(5) The video recording of the roleplay was replayed segment by segment one or more times as a stimulus to recall, while the learner again reported his or her thoughts. During this activity the learner was given the remote control and instructed to pause the video whenever s/he wanted to say something; the researcher also stopped the video himself manually at times if the learner did not. The verbal cue used by the researcher during this stage was: 'What were you thinking [then]?'
(6) The researcher instructed the two participants to resume the roleplay.

Sessions lasted between 35 and 50 minutes. After the last session had been conducted the researcher transcribed all the target roleplays (up the point of interruption) and all the learners' verbal reports.

Analysis

The data were classified by examining the transcripts of verbal reports and coding the data into categories and subcategories (displayed in Table 4.4.1 and Table 4.4.2). This taxonomy was developed by making a tentative classification based on a subset of the data and then continuing to test and revise those categories against more and more of the data until they needed no more changes (see Kasper & Rose, n.d.). The taxonomy allows comparisons of the number of thoughts of various types reported by High versus by Low learners. The inter-rater reliability of the coding was tested by having a second rater, an Australian university teacher of Indonesian who was a PhD student of applied linguistics, independently code a sample of the data. She independently coded four entire verbal report protocols (of the 76) using the same coding categories, and the codings by the two raters yielded an inter-rater reliability score of 87.7%.

Purely qualitative observations were also made by noting any pieces of data that were interesting from the point of view of pragmatic acquisition. Some of these were noted during the process of transcribing the data or coding it; others were noted later by examining the transcripts after the coding process was finished.

Findings and Discussion

Amount of attention paid to pragmatics

This was assessed in purely quantitative terms, by calculating what proportion of learners' reported thoughts were about pragmatics. The Low (FL) learners reported thinking about pragmatics a lot less often than they reported thinking about purely linguistic planning of their speech act (see Table 4.1). The type of thoughts they most commonly

Table 4.1 Types of mental processes reported by learners

What reported thoughts were about	Low subjects (n=12)		High subjects (n=7)		All subjects (n=19)	
	n	Mean	n	Mean	n	Mean*
Verbal planning	140	11.7	27	3.9	165	8.7
Pragmatics (i.e. politeness/social appropriateness)	52	4.3	46	6.6	100	5.3
Conversational management	12	1.0	6	0.9	18	0.9
Emotion/affect	6	0.5	2	0.3	8	0.4
Total	210	17.5	81	11.6	291	15.3

*Refers to the mean number of instances per learner of that type of report (e.g. Low learners report 140 instances of verbal planning, which is equivalent to a mean of 11.7 instances per learner)

reported were searching for lexical items to convey their propositional meaning or thinking of strategies to deal with the problem of such gaps in their vocabulary. While they did report thinking about pragmatics fairly often as well, that was much less common – about half as frequent.

This suggests that FL learners, even when performing pragmatically sensitive tasks, pay more attention to expressing their propositional message with adequate clarity than they do to being adequately polite. Other researchers have formed the same impression based purely on performance data (e.g. Edmondson *et al.*, 1984; Koike, 1989). One reason why this might be so is a cognitive reason. Unlike native speakers, L2 learners cannot perform low-level verbal planning tasks automatically and unconsciously. These tasks still demand a good deal of conscious effort from them and so consume most of their language processing capacity. This means they are unable to pay much attention to pragmatics without suffering cognitive overload. Another important reason is learning environment. Traditional FL teaching is not very rich in pragmatic input or practice. FL learners in traditional classroom settings – such as these Low learners – tend to mainly perform language tasks where propositional meanings must be expressed clearly and accurately but interpersonal meanings matter little. This learning environment naturally affects their priorities during language tasks. They come to regard propositional clarity and accuracy as paramount, and so they concentrate on it even when performing tasks where interpersonal meanings are crucial, such as face-threatening speech acts like requests or complaints.

With the group of High (FL/SL) learners, findings were quite different. They reported thinking about pragmatics more often than thinking about linguistic planning or anything else (see Table 4.4.1). So the two groups of learners seem to have different priorities in what they think about while performing these face-threatening speech acts.

One reason the High learners might think mainly about pragmatics is simply that they are a good deal more proficient in Indonesian than the Low group. This allows them to perform many low-level processing tasks automatically. That frees up more processing capacity to be devoted to other tasks instead – such as thinking about politeness.[4] Their learning environment is another reason that they might think mostly about pragmatics while performing these speech acts. This High group has just spent one year living in the target culture, studying alongside Indonesian students and regularly interacting with Indonesians in a range of situations. Their experiences during this year have probably made them more aware of the importance of speaking appropriately – more aware than the Low learners, who have never lived in Indonesia. This confirms the claim of Bardovi-Harlig and Dörnyei (1998) that living in the target language community tends to make learners sensitive to the importance of pragmatics, while learning the language in a traditional language classroom tends to make them attach more importance to linguistic accuracy and propositional clarity instead.

Pragmatic knowledge and acquisition

The learners' reports revealed a wide range of thoughts about pragmatics (see Table 4.2). These reports shed light on both their knowledge and their acquisition of pragmatics.

Sociopragmatics

In one situation verbal reports reveal that both Low and High learners possess accurate knowledge of sociopragmatics. In another situation they reveal that High learners possess more accurate knowledge than Low learners do.

Asking the lecturer for an extension on an essay deadline. Reports by both Low and High learners in this situation reveal they know that the lecturer has markedly higher status than the student and must therefore be addressed respectfully. Four of the Low learners report their social perceptions of this situation, and the reports of all four reveal that knowledge, while five of the seven High learners report their social perceptions, and the reports of all five reveal the same knowledge. A typical example of a Low learner's report in that regard is:

(1) I was keeping in mind that I had to show respect because it was my LECTURER-and so I knew I had to call him *Pak* ['father']-so that was easy.

This sociopragmatic knowledge is specific to the target culture, which is marked by a strong hierarchical norm (see e.g. Draine & Hall, 1990; Mulder, 1989: 45). These Australian learners cannot have simply transferred this knowledge from their L1 culture, as lecturer–student relations in Australia are affected by the strong egalitarian social norm that prevails in that culture (see Wierzbicka, 1991), so that status differences between lecturer and student in such a situation are smaller than in Indonesia and need not be marked so overtly.

This shows us that Low learners have managed to acquire some sociopragmatic knowledge in their formal classroom environment. That success can be attributed to the pragmatic instruction they were given. While they received little pragmatic input and practice in general, they had been taught this particular piece of knowledge, both in their first year course and again at the start of their second year course. They were told that lecturers in Indonesian are addressed by their students by the kin terms *(Ba)pak* 'father' or *(I)bu* 'mother' to show respect, and that this practice reflected a hierarchical norm prevailing in Indonesia, where status relationships were more marked than in Australia. They had also

Pragmatic Performance: What are Learners Thinking? 81

Table 4.2 Reports of thoughts related to pragmatics (politeness/appropriateness)

Type of pragmatic thought reported	Low subjects (n =12)		High subjects (n =7)		All subjects (n =19)	
	n	Mean	n	Mean	n	Mean*
Assess social variables → make a pragmatic choice based on assessment (e.g. assess Status or Social Distance or Size of Offence → select address term or register or level of politeness)	18	1.5	20	2.9	38	2
Select degree of politeness → make a pragmatic choice based on selection (e.g. decide to be 'fairly polite' → select Maaf 'Excuse me' as an Attention-getter)	8	0.7	4	0.6	12	0.6
Search for/select strategy (i.e. primary semantic content to express) (e.g. decide to state fact of own previous occupation of seat as way to complain about other student taking seat in library)	8	0.7	6	0.9	14	0.7
Decide to include a supportive move (e.g. to include an explanation as support for a request)	3	0.25	5	0.7	8	0.4

Table 4.2 (Continued)

Type of pragmatic thought reported	Low subjects (n =12)		High subjects (n =7)		All subjects (n =19)	
	n	Mean	n	Mean	n	Mean*
Search for/select semantic content for a supportive move (e.g. decide to refer to own illness as explanatory content in asking for extension on essay deadline)	3	0.25	8	1.1	11	0.6
Search for/select lexicopragmatic item (e.g. a term of address)	4	0.3	0	—	4	0.3
Evaluate linguistic choice for politeness while or after executing it (e.g. straight after making a complaint, wonder 'did that sound rude?')	8	0.7	3	0.4	10	0.5
Total	52	4.3	46	6.6	98	5.2

*Refers to the mean number of instances per learner (e.g. Low learners report eight instances of searching for/selecting a strategy, which is equivalent to a mean of 0.7 instances per learner) practised this knowledge, being encouraged to address their teachers as *Pak/Bu* during class time in order to get used to it. This instruction was apparently enough for them to develop firm representations of the relevant knowledge. And this supports the claim that giving FL learners explicit metapragmatic information together with opportunities for communicative practice is an effective way of teaching them pragmatics (see Kasper & Rose, 2002: 259–269 for a review of research on approaches to L2 pragmatic instruction).[5]

Complaining to a fellow student who has taken your seat in the library. In this case the High learners display sociopragmatic knowledge that is closer to the target norm than that of Low learners. In Indonesia, the size of the offence – moving aside another's books which were left on the desk and sitting in his or her seat – is smaller than it is in Australia. This reflects a lower value placed on personal space broadly (including a much lower concern for privacy). Having one's seat in the library taken in this way does not evoke such a strong feeling of infringement as in Australia; the feeling that one has marked out one's territory and had it violated. Indonesian students would therefore be more likely than Australians not to complain at all in this situation. And the High learners' reports showed that they perceived the situation according to target norms. Of the four High learners who reported on their social perceptions of the situation, all four revealed that they felt uncomfortable complaining. They perceived the offence as slight – to the point that it probably did not merit a verbal complaint. Their verbal reports were as follows:

(2) I wouldn't say ANYthing (*laughs*)-I'd just find another seat-there's always another seat SOMEwhere (*laughs*)

(3) is it my fault?-or is it his fault?-does it MATTER that-that he's got my chair?-will I sit somewhere else? will I ask him to move?-for me, I don't really care

(4) for me to say ANYthing in this situation I would have had to be quite annoyed otherwise I'd just have picked up my books and found somewhere else to sit-because it's a quiet place-and if I've left my books it's obvious that someone else can take my place ...

(5) yeah-with this one [i.e. this situation] I really had no idea what to say really-um-like with the others I I sort of had something I wanted to SAY but this one ... I just couldn't see how to approach it-like it was kind of EMBARRassing to come up to him and hassle him

All four High learners above seem to feel that the offence does not justify a verbal complaint. However, the reports by Low learners reveal quite different sociopragmatic perceptions. Of the four who reported on their perceptions in this situation, all seem to regard the offence of the other student as sizeable. Their reports were as follows:

(6) I wanted to tell her-I thought it was WRONG because my stuff was there-and the only way I could approach that was by sort of pointing out that there's other people's books there so obviously she should have known not to sit there.

(7) I was going to say *Buku-buku pindah-mengapa* ['The books have moved-why?'] but then I decided to say something about her sitting in my CHAIR-because that's what was important-I mean it was my chair she could SEE that

(8) I was trying to work out how not to be TOO rude but still show her that I was annoyed that she'd taken my place

(9) I just wanted to be a bit of a smart-arse and just ask if it was a special seat because I was annoyed at him-that's all[6]

The High learners evidently have more advanced knowledge than Low learners in this situation. The Low learners have simply transferred social perceptions from their first language and culture, while the High learners have formed perceptions close to those of L2 natives instead. The High learners were greatly aided by their recent year abroad in acquiring this knowledge. Neither group had been taught it in the classroom in Australia, and it might in fact be difficult to teach in such a setting as it is subtle, even nebulous, knowledge. So this finding supports the contention that second language settings are more conducive to learning *socio*pragmatics specifically than foreign language settings are.

Pragmalinguistics: A case study

By focusing on the single area of terms for address and self-reference, we discover a lot about these learners' pragmalinguistic knowledge and acquisition of it.

Inappropriate use but accurate knowledge. Perhaps most significantly, we find instances where learners behave inappropriately but are revealed to possess accurate knowledge. An example is where a Low learner addresses her lecturer twice as *Anda*. As *Anda* is only appropriate for addressing distant equals and not people of higher status, this creates a rude impression. Her request is this:

(10) ... esai ini-harus:-um 1 mengambil   untuk <u>Anda</u>-hari INI? um -
This essay-I must-um (1) give it to <u>you</u>-today um -
apakah saya -um - bisa: (1) um ... mengam/-mengambil-untuk <u>Anda</u> -
can I-um-can I (1) um ... give-give it to <u>you</u> -
(inbreath) *besok*?
(*inbreath*) tomorrow?

Pragmatic Performance: What are Learners Thinking?

After making this request, the learner reports

(11) I was keeping in mind I was talking to a university lecturer-and so call him *BAPAK* not *Anda*

That shows she knew the relevant constraint on *Anda* – don't use it to superiors. And she apparently never notices that she twice called him *Anda*, even when watching her own performance on video. This shows very weak control over attention to knowledge that *Anda* is wrong for superiors and vividly illustrates that pragmatic knowledge and control over attention to it are unrelated dimensions for learners.[7]

Another example where control over accurate knowledge is revealed to be at issue concerns a High learner. He addresses a boarding house mate as *Anda*, in asking him to check an assignment for language errors. This creates an impression of aloofness because *Anda* indexes high social distance, as if he were addressing a stranger. However, after that request he reports:

(12) I was thinking because it was a *kos* [boarding house] mate I could use informal language but-then I called him-*Anda*-and I knew straight away I shouldn't have.

This shows that the High learner knew a second constraint on the use of *Anda* – don't use it to familiars. This is a more esoteric constraint than the earlier one (on using *Anda* to superiors) in the sense that these learners are not taught this second constraint in class. We can therefore expect the Low (FL) group not to know about it. This High learner seemed not to know either but his report reveals otherwise.

In these cases, then, the learners' performance belies the true state of their knowledge. Their reports each time reveal that they had the requisite knowledge and were unable to access it in order to use it.

Inappropriate use of a feature with deviant knowledge. Conversely, the reports can reveal when the 'face-value' explanation for a pragmatic infelicity is the best one instead and the learner did simply have inaccurate knowledge. An example is when a Low learner calls a lecturer by the unusual term *Tuan*. This address term does index high status but is used almost exclusively to foreigners and is never used to a lecturer. She uses it twice, to bizarre effect, when embarking on a request for an extension on an essay deadline:

(13) uh selamat sore Tuan ... boleh saya:-uh berbicara-dengan-um-Tuan
    uh, good afternon 'Tuan' ... may I-uh talk with 'Tuan'
(inbreath) u:m-tentang:-esai   saya?
    (*inbreath*) um-about-my essay?

About this unusual choice of hers, the learner simply reports:

(14) before I started I thought that I should treat the lecturer with respect and so I addressed him as *Tuan*.

This reveals that the learner had firm, but deviant, knowledge about how to address the lecturer. Her sociopragmatic knowledge was accurate but her knowledge of the linguistic means to convey the necessary respect was not.[8]

Appropriate use of a feature but unstable knowledge of it. When learners do use a pragmalinguistic feature appropriately, their verbal reports can still help us. They may for example reveal that this successful performance rests on shaky knowledge. In one such case a Low learner asks a boarding house mate to check her assignment for language errors, and in doing so addresses her by the familiar *kamu*. This is an appropriate address term to use. But the learner reveals afterwards that she did not know whether *kamu* was appropriate or not:

(15) it was a friend so I had to address her as something like that but it was hard to come up with a word that showed I knew this person?-I was going to say *Anda* and then I-I think I said *kamu* but I didn't-I STILL don't know which one is right

In fact, this Low learner had unstable representations of knowledge about *kamu* and *Anda*. And looking at this Sample (15) together with Sample (12) earlier allows us to sketch out a more accurate path of acquisition of knowledge by these learners. Performance alone would suggest that the High learner of (12) did not know that *Anda* was wrong for familiars, while the Low learner of (15) did know. But those reports reveal that the opposite is true. The Low learner did not know this constraint while the High learner did. His knowledge is more target-like due to his year of living abroad, even though his performance on that occasion was less so.

Appropriate use of a feature with weak control over it. When learners use a feature appropriately their reports can, alternatively, reveal that control rather than knowledge is shaky. An example is below where a Low learner successfully addresses her lecturer by the respectful term *Ibu* 'mother':

(16) ... u:m-esai-saya?-ya:ng-   sa:ya (inbreath) perlu-memberi
     um-my- essay-which-I (*inbreath*) need-to give
    kepada:-u:m – Ibu-hari ini? ...
    to-um-'mother'-today? ...

After this performance, the student reports as follows:

(17) (*pausing the video*) YEAH see that was -where I first thought about it I was going to call her ANDA-but you can't really do that if you're talking to a lecturer.

This report confirms what we might suspect from the learner's hesitation just before producing the word *Ibu* 'mother' in Sample (16), namely that she had trouble finding the right address term. It also reveals the more precise detail that she first mentally selected *Anda* and then discarded it.

Non-use of a feature but accurate knowledge of it. Lastly, verbal reports help us understand some cases where learners do not use a given pragmalinguistic feature. This is striking in the case of the familiar first person pronoun *aku*. None of the learners in the study, High or Low, ever refer to themselves by *aku*. They always refer to themselves (acceptably enough) by the mildly formal pronoun *saya*. Do they know about *aku* then? The Low learners almost certainly do not, as they are not exposed to it or taught about it during their formal study in Australia. But the reports by three High learners reveal they do know about *aku*. All three actually wanted to use *aku* in one situation where it would have been appropriate: asking a boarding house mate for help with an assignment. The reason they did not use *aku* is that they could not access their knowledge about it. Here is a striking illustration of this, where a High learner calls herself *saya* instead of *aku* three times:

(18) ... um: saya perlu selesai ini ya ini tugas... tapi saya ndak tahu
      um, I need to finish this, yeah, this assignment ... but I don't know
      kalau ini: bagus atau salah-bisa-apa checking-ini untuk saya?
      if this is fine, or if it's wrong-can you-what check-this for me?

In her report afterwards this learner reveals that she thought *aku*, not *saya*, was a suitable term to use. In fact she even believes she *did* call herself *aku* rather than *saya*.[9]

(19) ... and I used *aku* because it's an informal situation. 1 [*Researcher: so/- were you thinking that you should use* aku?] well-no it's just I felt more relaxed saying *aku* than *saya*.-I find *aku*'s a word that's just so easy to use-it's not conscious.-if I actually THINK then I'd be using the word SAYA

And even on video playback this learner clearly never notices that she used *saya*, not *aku*, in contradiction of her own claim – a display of very weak control over her knowledge of *aku*. Similarly, with two other High learners in the same situation, their verbal reports reveal clearly that they knew *aku* was appropriate and that it was lack of control over attention to that knowledge which stopped them, too, from using it.

The reports of those three learners show that by living in Indonesia for the last year they have acquired pragmalinguistic knowledge about terms of self-reference. Unlike the Low learners they know that one can choose between *saya* and *aku*, and know the social factors that make *aku* appropriate. But *saya* has remained the term they select automatically in all situations, due doubtless to their early classroom learning. Therefore their knowledge can be detected only by introspective data.

Implications for Bialystok's model

A range of basic terms of address and self-reference in Indonesian lack English equivalents and carry subtle yet important social meanings. Therefore Australian learners need a lot of new pragmatic knowledge to use them – perhaps more knowledge than Bialystok's (1993) model suggests. But the more valuable insight from this case study concerns control over attention to knowledge. By examining learners' performance alone we cannot appreciate how hard it is for them to acquire this control, nor how vitally the lack of it affects their performance. Verbal reports such as those above make this possible.[10] They thus reveal the important truth behind Bialystok's claim that acquiring control is the primary task for adult learners of pragmatics, regardless of whether that claim is overstated.

The verbal reports above also illustrate the continuum-like nature of the dimension of control within that model of Bialystok (1993). Our control over pragmatic knowledge may be so weak that what we know bears no relation to what we do (see Sample 11), or nearly strong enough for us to act on our knowledge (see Sample 12), or, while still shaky, finally strong enough for us to hesitantly put our knowledge into action (see Sample 17).

More broadly, the above case study allows us to sketch a possible process of acquisition within Bialystok's (1993) two-dimensional model. The Low group possess basic accurate representations of knowledge about Indonesian terms of self-reference, namely that *saya* is widely appropriate; and have already acquired firm control over that knowledge. They also possess basic accurate representations of knowledge about address terms, such as that *Anda* is wrong to address superiors – but have yet to acquire firm control over them. As for the High learners, by now they have discarded those simple representations and formed richer ones. They know also that *aku* is a second option for self-reference, and that *Anda* is not used to address familiars. However this 'advanced' knowledge that they possess has yet to be adequately controlled. Thus all the learners face a constant task of gaining better control over ever-changing states of knowledge.

Pragmalinguistics: More complex forms

The above dealt with single words like pronouns. Using more complex forms poses new challenges for learners, so that verbal reports yield new insights. Several reports by Low learners are a good illustration. They reveal that the learners wanted to say something different from what they actually did say and by settling for 'second best' changed the pragmatic force of their speech act.

In one such example, a learner employs a very direct strategy to complain to her room neighbour about the loud music coming from her room late at night. She commands her neighbour to stop. But her report reveals that she had not intended to use that strategy at all. Her actual complaint was this:

(20) u:m musik Anda-terlalu BANYAK-berhenti:i
      um your music-is too MUCH – stop.

In (20) above the learner uses an imperative *Berhenti* 'Stop' to her neighbour. But afterwards she reports on this complaint as follows:

(21) I didn't have the vocab to say what I WANTED to ... I wanted to say the music's too loud? can you turn it down?

So the learner had not intended to complain so bluntly, by saying *Berhenti* 'Stop'. Instead she had planned to use a more indirect strategy, a conventionalised question about the addressee's ability to perform the action ('*Can* you...?'). That is the archetypal strategy for making requests in her first language of Australian English (cf. Blum-Kulka & House, 1989). But dealing with the lexical challenges of conveying the concepts 'loud' and then 'turn down' apparently took all her language processing capacity. She therefore abandoned the strategy she had chosen, along with the relatively polite interpersonal meaning it conveys, and settled for producing a single word, *Berhenti* 'Stop', that would at least convey the illocutionary and the propositional components of her message.

Reports by other Low learners reveal similarly thwarted pragmatic intentions. One learner is forced to abandon her plan of providing an explanation in support of her request for an essay extension, because the semantic content that she had planned for that explanation proves too hard to put into words. Another is forced to abandon her plans to add an aggravating move ('I want to sleep!') to reinforce her complaint to a room neighbour who is playing loud music, because she can't think of the word for 'sleep'. In these cases too it is only through their verbal reports that we know their pragmatic intentions, and hence know what forms they regarded as appropriate to use, and so can gain a fuller idea of their pragmatic competence. In all these cases the learners are demonstrating 'modality reduction'. This entails discarding certain interpersonal content from one's plan for a speech act and executing the speech act without that content instead. An early paper by Kasper (1979) identified this phenomenon but it has rarely been mentioned since. The cases above suggest that intermediate learners often reduce modality as a strategy to solve perceived linguistic problems, so that what they actually say belies their 'original' pragmatic intentions.

The research procedure: Evaluation

This method of using retrospective verbal reports proved most helpful for understanding the pragmatic performance of learners. However one stage of the present procedure should be discarded. This is the early step of halting the roleplay immediately after the speech act has been uttered to elicit an instant verbal report. That step did succeed in eliciting a great many useful reports of details of mental processes, and also neatly reduced the time lag between a subject having the thoughts and reporting them. However, the verbal instruction at that point to 'say everything you were thinking from start to finish' often amounted to ignoring constraints on short-term memory. When a verbal task lasts longer than 10 seconds, subjects are unable to recall an extended sequence of thoughts that might represent their mental processes from start to finish of that task (Ericsson & Simon, 1993: xvi).[11] So in future studies of this type the roleplays should simply be allowed to play out to their end before verbal reports are elicited through the stimulus of video playback.

Conclusion

This was an exploratory study using retrospective verbal reports. A quantitative comparison shows that a High (FL/SL) group of learners has become more sensitive to the importance of pragmatics than a Low (FL) group due to a year spent in the target culture. A qualitative analysis also sheds light on sociopragmatics. The Low learners were found to have acquired some knowledge of it even in a traditional classroom setting. However the High learners were shown to have subtle knowledge of sociopragmatics that the Low learners did not possess, confirming claims that it is more easily learned within the target community.

Bialystok's (1993) model is explored through a case study of pragmalinguistics. This demonstrates the range of relations that the two dimensions of knowledge and control can have to actual pragmatic performance. While the findings show that acquiring knowledge is a larger task than Bialystok suggests, they also vividly reveal the enormity of the task of gaining control over attention to knowledge – a dimension whose importance Bialystok especially stresses.

Learners are also found to employ a problem-solving strategy of modality reduction, whereby their pragmatic intentions are concealed by what they actually manage to say and are only revealed by introspective data.

Finally, the study demonstrates that verbal reports are valuable for revealing mental processes that underlie pragmatic performance. They reveal knowledge otherwise concealed, and help to illuminate the process of acquiring it and learning to use it.

Acknowledgement

This study was funded by a research grant from The Australian National University.

Appendix 4.1. Roleplay Situations

Requests: (i) asking a lecturer for an extension on an essay deadline (ii) asking a fellow-college resident to check an assignment for language errors

Complaints: (i) your college neighbour in the next room is playing music too loudly (ii) your seat in the library has been taken by another student

Distractors: (i) asking a stranger for a light for your cigarette (request) (ii) your meal in a restaurant is taking too long to be served (complaint) (iii) you have forgotten to bring your classmate's book to campus (apology)

Appendix 4.2. Sample Written Cue for Roleplay Participants

(Situation: asking a lecturer for an extension on an essay deadline)
i) *Subject's cue* (bilingual):
You have not yet finished writing an essay that must be handed in today. Go to see your lecturer in his/her office.

Anda belum selesai menulis sebuah esai yang harus diserahkan hari ini. Temuilah dosen Anda di kantor.

ii) *Partner's cue* (monolingual):
You are a lecturer. A foreign student will come to see you in your office. The student has not finished an essay which is due today.

Notes

1. Cohen and Olshtain (1993) also examine learners' thoughts while performing face-threatening speech acts but confine their study to purely linguistic aspects of speech production.
2. See Robinson (1992: 59) for one such claim only, which pertained to general knowledge states rather than to knowledge in a specific situation.
3. I am grateful to Gabi Kasper for supplying me with that work.
4. The fact that High learners reported fewer thoughts *overall* than Low learners suggests that they are able to do much of their pragmatic planning automatically as well. And in fact they often used appropriate lexical modifiers of speech acts, for instance, without reporting on it afterwards.
5. Findings from several recent studies suggest that implicit instruction can be as effective as explicit instruction: see for example Alcón (2005) and Martínez-Flor and Fukuya (2005).
6. This learner had used a deliberately impolite strategy of asking a sarcastic question *Apakah-kursi ini – istimewa?* 'Is-this seat-special?'
7. This weak control can be partly explained by the formal instruction that these learners have received. They learn *Anda* earlier, and more intensively, than any other term of address.
8. This particular learner, who was an avid self-studier, must have found the term *Tuan* somewhere in a book herself. She was certainly not taught it in class.
9. This shows that even lowly valid segments of verbal report consisting of false 'recalls' can indirectly yield valuable insights into pragmatic ability.
10. This exploration of Bialystok's model is confined to pragmalinguistics. It would be hard to do the same type of case study for sociopragmatics. For one thing, if a learner commits a pragmatic infelicity and afterwards reveals in a verbal report that his or her sociocultural perceptions were accurate, we cannot conclude that he or she must have lacked control over those perceptions. It might just as easily have been pragmalinguistic ability that was lacking.
11. Kasper and Rose (n.d.) are clearly aware of the cognitive constraints on the use of this step, as they cite only very short pragmatic subtasks as examples for its use.

References

Alcón, E. (2005) Does instruction work for performing pragmatics in the EFL context? *System* 33 (3), 417–435.

Bardovi-Harlig, K. and Dörnyei Z. (1998) Do language learners recognize pragmatic violations? Pragmatic versus grammatical awareness in instructed L2 learning. *TESOL Quarterly* 32 (2), 233–262.

Barron, A. (2005) Learning to say 'You' in German: The acquisition of sociolinguistic competence in a study-abroad context. In M. DuFon and E. Churchill (eds) *Language Learners in Study Abroad Contexts* (pp. 59–88). Clevedon: Multilingual Matters.

Bialystok, E. (1993) Symbolic representation and attentional control in pragmatic competence. In G. Kasper and S. Blum-Kulka (eds) *Interlanguage Pragmatics* (pp. 43–57). New York: Oxford University Press.

Blum-Kulka, S. and House, J. (1989) Cross cultural and situational variation in requesting behaviour. In S. Blum-Kulka, J. House and G. Kasper (eds) *Cross-Cultural Pragmatics: Requests and Apologies* (pp. 123–154). Norwood, NJ: Ablex.

Cohen, A. (1998) *Strategies in Learning and Using a Second Language*. London: Longman.
Cohen, A. and Olshtain, E. (1993) The production of speech acts by EFL learners. *TESOL Quarterly* 27 (1), 33–56.
Draine, C. and Hall, B. (1990) *Culture Shock Indonesia* (2nd edn). Singapore: Times Editions.
DuFon, M.A. (1999) The acquisition of linguistic politeness in Indonesian as a second language by sojourners in naturalistic interactions. Unpublished PhD thesis, University of Hawai'i at Manoa.
Edmondson, W., House, J., Kasper, G. and Stemmer, B. (1984) Learning the pragmatics of discourse: A project report. *Applied Linguistics* 5 (2), 113–127.
Ericsson, K.A. and Simon, H. (1993) *Protocol Analysis*. Cambridge, MA: The MIT Press.
Faerch, C. and Kasper, G. (eds) (1987) *Introspection in Second Language Research*. Clevedon: Multilingual Matters.
Gass, S. and Mackey, A. (2000) *Stimulated Recall Methodology in Second Language Research*. Mahwah, NJ: Lawrence Erlbaum.
Hassall, T. (2001) Modifying requests in a second language. *International Review of Applied Linguistics* 39 (4), 259–283.
Hassall, T. (2005) Learning to take leave in social conversations: A diary study. In M. DuFon and E. Churchill (eds) *Language Learners in Study Abroad Contexts* (pp. 31–58). Clevedon: Multilingual Matters.
Jenson, K. (1988) Forms of address in Indonesian. *I.T.L: Review of Applied Linguistics* 81/82, 113–138.
Kasper, G. (1979) Communication strategies: Modality reduction. *Interlanguage Studies Bulletin Utrecht* 4, 266–283.
Kasper, G. and Rose, K.R. (2002) *Pragmatic Development in a Second Language*. Malden, MA: Blackwell.
Kasper, G. and Rose, K.R. (n.d.) Verbal protocols. Unpublished manuscript.
Koike, D.H. (1989) Pragmatic competence and adult L2 acquisition: Speech acts in interlanguage. *The Modern Language Journal* 73 (3), 279–289.
Martínez-Flor, A. and Fukuya, Y.J. (2005) The effects of instruction on learners' production of appropriate and accurate suggestions. *System* 33 (3), 463–480.
Mulder, N. (1989) *Individual and Society in Java: A Cultural Analysis*. Yogyakarta: Gadjah Mada University Press.
Niezgoda, K. and Röver, C. (2001) Pragmatic and grammatical awareness. In K.R. Rose and G. Kasper (eds) *Pragmatics in Language Teaching* (pp. 63–79). Cambridge: Cambridge University Press.
Quinn, G. (2001) *The Learner's Dictionary of Today's Indonesian*. Sydney: Allen & Unwin.
Robinson, M.A. (1992) Introspective methodology in interlanguage pragmatic research. In G. Kasper (ed.) *Pragmatics of Japanese as Native and Target Language* (Technical Report # 3) (pp. 27–82). Honolulu: University of Hawai'i at Manoa, Second Language Teaching and Curriculum Centre.
Thomas, J. (1983) Cross-cultural pragmatic failure. *Applied Linguistics* 4 (2), 91–112.
Widjaja, C. (1997) A study of date refusal: Taiwanese females vs. American females. *University of Hawai'i Working Papers in ESL* 15 (2), 1–43.
Wierzbicka, A. (1991) *Cross-cultural Pragmatics: The Semantics of Human Interaction*. Berlin: Mouton de Gruyter.

Chapter 5
Learning Pragmatics in Content-based Classrooms

TARJA NIKULA

Introduction

This paper is a qualitative study of pragmatics in content-based instruction, i.e. classrooms where the target language is used as the medium of instruction. In European contexts, the term content and language integrated learning (CLIL) has become widely used as an umbrella term for various forms of implementation (e.g. Dalton-Puffer & Nikula, 2006b; Marsh, 2002) and the acronym CLIL will also be used in this paper. While questions of teaching and learning pragmatics have frequently been considered in the context of foreign language classrooms (for overviews, see Kasper & Rose, 2002; Rose & Kasper, 2001), there is less research on pragmatics in content-based instruction (but see Dalton-Puffer, 2005; Nadasdi *et al.*, 2005). Such research is needed, however, especially as decisions to implement foreign language mediated instruction are often motivated by arguments that can be directly related to pragmatics. For example, the learners are expected to acquire the target language in a more naturalistic way than in formal language teaching and to develop better communicative skills through using the language as part of their everyday practices.

Rather than focusing on pragmatics-related learning outcomes, this paper explores classroom discourse in CLIL settings, offering insights into how pragmatic concerns are taken into account at the local level of interaction and into the nature of CLIL classrooms as environments for pragmatic learning. This paper is part of a larger project, 'Discourse-pragmatic perspectives on classroom interaction', funded by the Academy of Finland, in which data from both EFL and CLIL classrooms are investigated in order to gain a better understanding of local practices of language use in these settings.

Pragmatics and Content-Based Classrooms

Earlier research has given ample evidence of pragmatics as an important area of second and foreign language proficiency and as something that cannot easily be turned into clearly defined learning objectives owing to its diffuse and context-sensitive nature (for overview, see e.g. Jeon & Kaya, 2006). Research on pragmatics and classrooms has to date mostly concentrated on language classrooms. The main focus has been on whether or not teaching pragmatics in language classrooms is necessary, and on the relative merits of explicit and implicit teaching of pragmatics (e.g. Bardovi-Harlig, 2001; Koike & Pearson, 2005; Rose, 2005). These studies have shown that pragmatic development can be enhanced by teaching, and that explicit instruction seems to have an advantage over implicit instruction.

As regards classrooms where the target language is the medium of instruction, such as immersion and CLIL classrooms, studies focusing on explicit instruction of pragmatics are rare (but see Lyster, 1994; Rehner & Mougeon, 2003). The main reason for this is probably that these classrooms are seen as environments where learners are expected to acquire pragmatic competence through exposure, with little need for explicit instruction. However, there are studies that have explored immersion students' learning outcomes in terms of sociolinguistic skills (e.g. Nadasdi *et al.*, 2005; Rehner *et al.*, 2003). What these studies have shown is that students' language use does not correspond to that of native speakers as regards sociolinguistic variation: they use vernacular and informal variants more rarely and formal variants markedly more than native speakers; in other words, despite their mastery of the formal aspects of language, there are shortcomings as regards contextually appropriate language use.

Also in the area of CLIL research, studies focusing on pragmatics are still quite few. Learning outcomes of CLIL have more often been assessed from the viewpoint of target language skills and subject matter mastery (e.g. Jäppinen, 2003; Jiménez Catalán *et al.*, 2006; Vollmer, 2006). However, there are some studies on the pragmatics of interaction in CLIL classrooms which have emphasised that students' pragmatic proficiency needs to be related to the varying contextual conditions of classrooms (Dalton-Puffer, 2005; Dalton-Puffer & Nikula, 2006a; Nikula, 2005). For example, in their study of directives, Dalton-Puffer and Nikula (2006a) suggest that the type of register (whether instructional or regulative) and the object of request (whether for goods or services) have an important role in what to consider pragmatically appropriate language use in CLIL settings. Gassner and Maillat (2006) suggest that when investigating pragmatics in CLIL classrooms, attention should also be paid to larger discourse-level features. They comment, for example, on CLIL classrooms being conducive to students' organisational skills as regards participation in ongoing discourse (e.g. collaborative construction of turns). Nikula (2005, 2007), similarly, draws attention to the fact that discourse practices in CLIL settings often offer students more opportunities for active participation than those in EFL classrooms.

Framework for Analysis: Discourse-pragmatic Approach to Learning Pragmatics

This paper differs from many earlier studies on pragmatics in adopting a discourse-pragmatic perspective on classroom interaction (see Nikula, 2005). This has implications for how pragmatics and learning are conceptualised and for the ways of carrying out the analysis; these implications will be discussed in this chapter.

Earlier research on interlanguage pragmatics has mainly relied on SLA theoretical constructs. As a result, there has been more interest in measurable learning outcomes than in interaction and its relationship to learning. Further, the SLA tendency to itemise language into its constituent parts also has its counterpart in interlanguage pragmatics research, notably in its tendency to concentrate on specific speech acts; earlier research on interlanguage pragmatics covers an impressive repertoire of speech acts (see Jeon & Kaya, 2006 for overview). The speech act focus has also had a direct impact on methodology in that both the use and acquisition of L2 pragmatics has most often been studied using elicited data (e.g. discourse completion tests). Elicited data is useful in allowing efficient control of contextual variables. This is important when conducting quantitative research, which has been the prevailing approach in studies on interlanguage pragmatics. Quantitative studies have provided important information about how learners understand and produce speech acts and valuable insights into the processes of learning L2 pragmatics. However, it is also useful to complement these studies with qualitative discourse-based analyses on how learners convey pragmatic meanings in naturally occurring interactions where contextual effects and constraints, rather than being clearly defined, are multifaceted and in constant flux. Huth and Taleghani-Nikazm (2006: 54), when arguing for the use of naturally occurring data in teaching pragmatics, point out that while elicited data may work well in demonstrating learners' explicit knowledge of L2 pragmatics, 'they tend not to reflect learners' ability to apply their socio-pragmatic knowledge in naturally occurring conversations'. Because the way learners apply their pragmatic knowledge in authentic language use is a central concern in this study, it is based on naturally occurring discourse data.

Using discourse data to explore L2 pragmatics means that a speech act approach becomes problematic. For example, unlike in elicited data, there is no guarantee that particular speech acts will occur often enough to warrant analysis. Hence, assessing participants' pragmatic skills cannot be based solely on how appropriately they perform specific speech acts. Instead, pragmatic proficiency needs to be seen in relation to the overall management of interaction. Therefore, this paper advocates an *in situ* perspective on pragmatic skills, according to which pragmatic success is a matter of local accomplishment, best investigated by paying close attention to the ways in which participants give expression to pragmatic meanings as the interaction unfolds.

Using data with several L2 speakers as discourse participants also makes it difficult to conceptualise language learning as an individual process, which has been customary in SLA research. Even though there are SLA studies that focus on classroom interaction, these have either tended to emphasise its role as input for individual learners and an opportunity to practise output, or explored which interactional choices (usually those of the teacher) help learners in the language acquisition process (for overview, see Larsen-Freeman & Long, 1991). However, in recent years socioculturally oriented views of language learning that emphasise learning as a joint, social accomplishment have gained more ground (e.g. Hall & Verplaetse, 2000; Lantolf, 2000). Sociocultural views are applied in this study because of the importance they accord to social interaction and participation. The view of language learning in this paper also draws on the argument by Brouwer and Wagner (2004: 34) according to which 'learning a language is [...] essentially a question of learning to participate in communication with other speakers'. Such views see interaction and learning as inseparable, which is why also pragmatic learning and pragmatic skills need to be looked at in relation to their social contexts.

Data and Methods of Analysis

The data for this paper come from a larger pool of EFL and CLIL classroom recordings collected by the Department of Languages of the University of Jyväskylä. This paper focuses on three 90-minute seventh-grade physics lessons (a group of six students, aged 13) and three 90-minute ninth-grade biology lessons (a group of nine students, aged 15) taught in English. The recordings were made in an ordinary state comprehensive school with students from all social backgrounds. The classrooms were video and audio recorded with the consent of the teachers, the students and their parents. The school is a medium-sized school in a moderately big Finnish town (ca. 70,000 inhabitants) and it offers an extensive CLIL programme in which all subjects except Finnish language and literature are taught in English. Participation in the programme is voluntary, which is reflected in the small group sizes in the data looked at: most students in the school receive their education in Finnish. There are differences in the students' background in that while most of them have been exposed to English in Finnish contexts only (through formal language instruction and everyday encounters via modern technology and media), some have lived abroad with their families and have thus more prior experience of using English. The students' skills in English are relatively good, which makes it interesting to see how they deal with pragmatic aspects of language use when basic language skills are not an issue. All the students, except for one native speaker of English in the biology group, are native speakers of Finnish.

As for the teachers, they are also native speakers of Finnish; both are subject specialists with no qualifications as foreign language teachers. Both teachers have studied English at school but otherwise their background differs in that while the physics teacher has studied in a British university, the biology teacher has mainly gained his skills in English by travelling abroad and by using English in both professional contexts and in his hobbies (information based on teachers' interviews). That the teachers are subject specialists rather than language specialists is reflected in the fact that language very rarely becomes an issue in these classrooms and when it does, it is in matters pertaining to vocabulary rather than to pragmatics. Pragmatics, then, is taught neither explicitly nor implicitly in these classrooms. This is why the viewpoint in this paper is on learning rather than teaching, with the aim of exploring whether CLIL classrooms as interactional contexts provide students with opportunities to learn pragmatics implicitly.

In outlining the discourse-pragmatic approach above, emphasis was placed on understanding how learners convey pragmatic meanings as interaction unfolds. Hence, the aim is, as Kasper and Rose (2001: 2) put it, to investigate 'how people accomplish their goals and attend to interpersonal relationships while using language'. The problem with this aim is the all-pervasiveness of pragmatics, which makes it necessary to find a workable analytic solution between the two extremes of focusing on certain prespecified elements of language use only and trying to take into account all matters relevant to pragmatic meaning making. In this paper two important aspects of language use have been selected as starting points for analysis. The first starts from more formal aspects of language and the other from more contextual-functional features. Firstly, although it can be argued that all language choices carry pragmatic meanings of some sort, it is fruitful to pay attention to linguistic elements that have *primarily* pragmatic functions. Discourse markers and pragmatic particles are the most obvious examples of these (e.g. Fraser, 1996) but it is also, in the light of earlier findings on L2 pragmatics, useful to pay attention to degrees of directness in students' performance. This brings into focus various indirectness strategies ranging from the use of modal verbs to mitigating adverbs and parenthetical expressions. Secondly, analytic attention will be directed to those instances of interaction in particular where face concerns are likely to emerge. These include, for example, participants negotiating disagreements, resolving misunderstandings and making initiatives. By using this two-layered approach, which combines formal and functional viewpoints, it is possible to focus on specific features of classroom talk without losing sight of the complexity of interactional phenomena, and in this way reveal something about CLIL classrooms as environments for pragmatic learning.

Analysis

Given that the theme of this paper is pragmatic learning, the analysis will focus on students' language use. This does not mean ignoring the teachers' contributions, as understanding interaction obviously requires that attention be paid to all participants and their actions. However, the focus is always on students' performance and what classroom interaction suggests about the way they accomplish pragmatic meaning-making.

Rather than being a homogeneous entity, classroom language is always variable, the variation depending, for example, on the types of activities, e.g. whether teacher fronted or group work activities, as well as on their purpose, e.g. whether to introduce learners to a new topic or to review homework (see e.g. Walsh, 2006). Depending on such contextual constraints, interpersonal concerns are at times in the background. For example, Dalton-Puffer (2005: 1282) argues that information delivery by teachers may be considered a speech function completely sanctioned in the institution 'school', with face issues not important. However, there are situations when face concerns surface; these often arise because of the inherent power asymmetry between teacher and students and the different rights and obligations that go with these institutional roles. These roles, in addition to being defined by the institutional context, also need to be realised at the level of language use to take effect. This is why pragmatic proficiency in classrooms largely relates to the ability to use language in ways that both reflect and (re)create the roles as teachers and students. If participants perform actions that challenge or violate the expected role constellation, face concerns are likely to arise (Brown & Levinson, 1987), which is why it is useful to explore students' language use in these situations in particular.

Negotiating misunderstandings and disagreements

Misunderstandings and disagreements are treated together here because they both require repair sequences: both often result in negotiations where some kind of resolution is sought. It will be of special interest in this section whether students' ways of handling repair sequences reflect any pragmatic concerns.

Extract 1 from a physics lesson is from a situation where students are writing the results of an experiment on the blackboard, after having been engaged in moving a big spring on the floor. Their task was to count the number of waves formed in the spring after one powerful hand movement, and now they are presenting their results. Liisa and Anne had been working as a pair and now there is disagreement between them about how to count the waves. (In all the extracts, the names are pseudonyms. The transcription conventions used in the extracts are presented in Appendix 5.1.)

Extract 1

1	Liisa	when we have the waves like this (.) I go-
		you just counted that there's one (.) two (.) three=
	Anne	=no **I** don' count it like that (.)
	Liisa	what countin' look like
5	Anne	I counted (lot like °this°)
	Julia	< look Liisa >
	Liisa	well then how did Julia get three then↑
	Julia	here's=
	Anne	=I dunno=
10	Julia	=one (.) here's two (.) an here's a half
	Anne	I counted like this one two three
	Liisa	[> there weren't that] many there weren't that many <
	Anne	[(x) (still now)]
	T	yeah that's the way =
15	Liisa	=> cause you counted six < (1.0)
		you said there were six [cause there ain't that many]
	Anne	[but how come you (got it)] okay (.) seven an eight
	Liisa	> no because that was the (xx) < how to **count** them
20	Anne	no but I didn't coun' it like tha'
	Liisa	I just said an example (1.0) it's hard to °count them right°
	Anne	I know I **can**'t count them =
	Julia	=hei haluutsä pyyhkii tä ((to Liisa))
		'hey do you wanna erase this'

The extract suggests that disagreements with fellow students on how to perform a task can be expressed directly without face redress: the girls produce direct disagreements (Lines 3, 12, 16, 19, 20), three of them beginning forcefully with the word 'no'. However, Liisa's utterance in Line 7 suggests that she attempts to modulate her differing opinion by expressing it in a question form, together with pragmatic markers *well then* at the beginning and *then* at the end. Also her rising intonation adds to a sense of uncertainty. Towards the end of the extract Liisa (Line 21), after having defended her viewpoint until then, seems to seek resolution to the disagreement by saying that she was just giving an example, and admitting to the difficulty of the task. Anne readily agrees with this, which brings the negotiation to its conclusion, as is also suggested by the fact that it is at this point that Julia, who has been writing another pair's results until now, enters the conversation and changes the topic, her language switch into Finnish further emphasising a transition from how to count waves to other matters.

As regards students expressing direct disagreements with the teacher, there are hardly any such instances in the data, which serves as a clear indication of the teacher's powerful role. Usually direct disagreements with the teacher occur in situations involving classroom management or decision making rather than matters of subject content, as is shown in the following extract, where Leena disagrees with the teacher's position that they are going to have a quiz that very day. This exchange takes place at the beginning of a lesson, during what Walsh (2006: 68) calls the managerial mode of classrooms; that Leena uses Finnish rather than English to challenge the teacher is probably an indication that the lesson proper has not begun yet as the students rarely use Finnish during instructional phases.

Extract 2

T	that's what I told you last time=
Leena	=eiku sää sanoit perjantaina
	'no you said on Friday'

Extract 3 is an example of a situation where Mikko expresses his reservations about what the teacher says about babies' hearing abilities when in the womb. In Lines 1–3, after repeating a question asked by a student, the teacher says that babies can hear when in the womb. Anna's question in Line 4 seems to indicate she has some doubts about this, as does Mikko when he offers his opinion in Lines 6 and 8. The way he begins his utterance with a cluster of elements that reduce its pragmatic impact (*yeah but just like*) suggests he does not want to assert his viewpoint too forcefully. That he is pragmatically quite skilful also shows in the way he begins his second disagreement in Line 12 with the *yeah but* construction, thus choosing to disagree with partial agreement. In addition, his view of the sounds as mere gurgles in the stomach is heavily hedged with downtoning *just like* preceding the expression, and vagueness marker *and stuff* and appealing *right* following it. Combined with the rising intonation, the overall impression is that he is seeking confirmation from the teacher and is prepared to adjust his view.

Extract 3

1	T	can the baby hear when it's in the womb.
	Leena	yeah

	T	I think it can. (1.4)
	Anna	what is [there to hear]
5	T	[voices]
	Mikko	yeah but just like muffled like grunts [(of xx) stomach]
	Leena	[it it it starts talking]
	Mikko	[I bet that's all (he) [(xx)]
	Leena	[if you go to] (xx[x])
10	T	[yeah] it's has it has
	T	ears of course and they are ready and yeah (.) it can hear.
	Mikko	yeah so but it's just like gurgles of stomach and stuff right↑
	T	yeah but some (.) in in some cases they say that it's it's good

In Extract 4, from another biology lesson, Leena finds herself in a situation where the teacher does not understand her question and she has to negotiate the misunderstanding without embarrassing either herself or the teacher, i.e. there is great potential for face threat. In Lines 1–2, the teacher is finishing his explanation of why it may be dangerous for babies to be delivered feet first. As Lines 16–17 eventually show, Leena wants to know why babies do not keep on breathing through the umbilical cord on those occasions but she has difficulties formulating the question (Lines 5–6), as suggested both by the rising intonation and *or something like that*. The teacher replies in Line 8 but does not succeed in providing the information Leena is looking for, which leads her to attempt a reformulation in Line 9, signalling with *yeah but* her dissatisfaction with the teacher's reply. The teacher still has difficulties understanding, which makes Leena's third round of reformulation in Line 14 even more of a threat both to her own and to the teacher's face, which she seems to acknowledge both by recourse to the particle 'but', this time as *no but*, and also by the particle *like*. At this point Markus joins the conversation in Line 16 and reformulates Leena's question, also using the particle 'but' in *but just like* to add a sense of tentativeness to his reformulation.

Extract 4

1	T	if the brains are without without oxygen. (.) um (.) too long so that that will cause a damage which cannot be cured. (1.5)
	Leena	but they get oxygen when they're in the the the womb↑ (1.0)
	T	pardon
5	Leena	they get oxygen when they're in the womb↑ or something like that or how can they [breathe] if they're in (1.4)
	Helena	[(blood)]
	T	they don't breathe.
	Leena	yeah but why do they start breathing when they're (.) like

Learning Pragmatics in Content-based Classrooms 103

```
10                 nine months (.) when [they come (x English)]
       T                                 [when they come out]
       Leena       [yeah]
       T           [because] they have to.
       Leena       no but (.) why can't (.) they come like legs first. (1.0)
15                 because (2.0) [(xx)]
       Markus                    [but just] (.) like why can't they breathe if their
                   head's still in there and the feet are just out.
```

The extract shows that in authentic situations, unlike in many discourse completion tasks, second/foreign language users may be confronted with situations that require an ability to persist in pursuing problematic talk, trying out new strategies when those already tried fail. Leena shows great persistence in trying to reach her communicative goal and also shows concern for interpersonal aspects while doing so. However, it also seems evident that she does not have available a very wide range of linguistic means to convey pragmatic meanings as she mainly resorts to the particle 'but' as a pragmatic device, either on its own or in combinations *yeah but*, *no but* and *but just*. When native speakers' language use in disagreements and other face-threatening situations has been explored, pragmatic particles such as *well*, *you know* and *I mean* have often been found to be important carriers of interpersonal meanings (e.g. Müller, 2005). The complete absence of these pragmatic particles in the extract above and their rarity also in other meaning negotiations suggests that they form an aspect of pragmatics that foreign language learners probably need to be made aware of and notice before they will be able to make full use of them.

The extracts above have shown that the interpersonal level of meaning making is present as students deploy a range of means to reduce the pragmatic impact of their messages even though their overall pragmatic repertoire may remain limited. In all the above instances, meaning negotiations were started when students reacted to other speakers' contributions by either disagreeing with them or attempting to repair the other party's misunderstanding. In the following, attention will be turned to student initiations, usually in the form of questions. Students' questions, rather than being reactive, begin interactional sequences and involve potential face threats because interaction in classrooms is usually controlled by the teachers.

Student initiations

Sunderland (2001) argues that research on the IRF structure in classrooms has highlighted the role of teachers as the ones who both begin and close off the sequences, and less attention has been paid to initiations by students (but see Ohta & Nakaone, 2004). In the following, the focus will be on students' questions to teachers which, given the asymmetrical power between the teacher and the students, offer a good opportunity to explore whether the students attempt to take this institutional role constellation into account in language use.

The rights and obligations associated with the roles as teachers and students have a great impact on classroom language use. This also shows in how questions are performed. Dalton-Puffer and Nikula (2006a), for example, argue that on the whole, asking content-related questions directly seems to be accepted linguistic behaviour by both teachers and students in CLIL classrooms. However, while direct questions often occur in the present data, there are also occasions when students modify or flag their questions. In the following, the contextual factors at play in this variation are explored as they may offer important insights into students' pragmatic awareness.

It seems that the students' institutional role as learners, which provides them with the obligation to be attentive and learn, also gives them the right to seek further information from the teacher and ask for clarification on content topics in a direct manner: there seems to be little if any need for face redress on such occasions, as illustrated by Extracts 5 and 6 from a biology lesson and a physics lesson, respectively:

Extract 5

```
1   T       and during this time the pregnant mother should be very careful (1.0)
            about um (.) what what she eats or or drinks.
    Leena   what are you allowed to eat or drink
5   T       pardon
    Leena   what are you allowed to eat or drink °during that° that stage.
    T       anything which is healthy. I I mean that um (1.5) for example
```

Extract 6

```
1   T       so we have a hundred newtons (1.0) um at the distance of
            one metre↑ (1.0) so it gets us um (.) one hundred (.) newton
            metres um (1.2) clockwise (2.0)
    Eeva    why is it clockwise
5   T       because it's on this on the right side.
    Eeva    o:h.
```

In both examples, the teachers are in the process of explaining new content area knowledge when they are interrupted by students asking for more specific information (Extract 5, Line 3; Extract 6, Line 4).

Students' directness seems to imply that they are in no doubt about the relevance of their questions and therefore redress neither their own face nor that of the teacher. This is in interesting contrast to questions that are less clearly related to the immediate interactional surroundings and that are often performed in more hesitant ways. In Extract 7, the teacher has begun instructing the class about a task with springs when Liisa interrupts him by asking a question about frequency, a term that has been discussed earlier on during the lesson. Unlike with the earlier extracts above, there are signs of interactional work in that she both paves the ground for her question with *hey can I ask something* (Lines 2–3), and postmodifies it by explaining her reasons for asking (*yeah but I mean like cause moment is the force that goes this way*, Lines 10 and 12), thereby signalling her awareness of her question as something not directly related to what the teacher was saying.

Extract 7

```
1     T        but first of all we need to get these (1.0) [slinkies]
      Liisa                                                 [hey can I-]
               can I [ask] something
      T              [wave]
5     T        yeah
      Liisa    is it frequens-s frequency like force but it's like aa [(x)xx]=
      T                                                               [no]
      T        =it has nothing to do with force it's just (.)
               it's called ef because it starts with ef but=
10    Liisa    =yeah but I mean like=
      Julia    =so it was [like this]
      Liisa               [cause moment] is the (force that goes) this way
               is- is frequency the force that goes like ((obscure noises))
      T        aa (.) no frequency is not a force it's just (1.0) frequency is (1.5)
15             ((explanation continues))
```

Similar pragmatic sensitivity is shown in Extract 8 from a biology lesson. The day's topic concerns dominant and recessive genes and the teacher has asked students to consider themselves in terms of the colour of their eyes, ability to roll their tongues and whether they have straight or curly hair. The type of hair has been discussed before this extract and the discussion has now moved on to a new topic, the ability to roll a tongue. However, Mikko still has on his mind something about hair and, probably because he realises that his question is off the current topic, he flags it with *can I ask about the hair*, in Line 4, and as in the above extract, he also presents reasons for his question, this time before the question itself (Line 6 *cause I was like mine my my hair used to be like really really blond and now it's dark*).

Extract 8

```
1   Leena   can't roll my [tongue]
    T                      [let's] let's look what what kind of people
                    you are
    Mikko   can I ask about the] hair↑
5   T       yeah
    Mikko   why cause I was like mine my my hair used to be like really
                    really blond and now it's dark [why is that↑ ]
    Leena                                          [everyone used] to have really
                    really blond [hair
10  Mikko                        [why is that]
    T                             [it it it] (.) it may change (1.0) and of cours:e
                    it has always this genetic background (1.0) um you have
                    you have that kind of genes (.)
```

The extracts above suggest that questions by students are not as rare as Sunderland (2001: 2) describes them in language classrooms. The CLIL students ask plenty of questions, often ones directed to the teacher. Moreover, they do so in context-sensitive ways, which seems to point towards some level of pragmatic awareness about different situations requiring different types of interpersonal work. It is not possible to say on the basis of this data alone whether such awareness is the result of their regular participation in CLIL classes. However, as practically all interaction in CLIL classrooms is conducted in English, they at the very least provide students with opportunities to practise different kinds of questions in English, whereas in language classrooms students have often been found to participate in classroom activities in L2 but to ask questions in their L1 (e.g. Canagarajah, 1995: 181).

On the overall style of CLIL classroom talk

The extracts above have indicated that when moments of potential face threat occur, students' language use points towards some degree of pragmatic awareness. In this section, the focus is shifted to more general characteristics of talk in these classrooms, with special attention to conversational and informal style because this has an impact on the overall pragmatic atmosphere of these settings.

It has already become evident from the data extracts above that interaction in present CLIL classrooms is largely dialogic, with students as active participants. In this respect, the classrooms seem to differ significantly from foreign language classrooms, which have often been criticised for offering students limited opportunities to act as fully fledged conversational participants. It has been argued that this is especially the case if interaction is structured around the IRF sequence, which easily restricts students' language use so that they only end up producing brief replies (e.g. van Lier, 2001). Furthermore, Nikula's (2005) findings suggest that conversations in EFL classrooms tend to be very materials-centred, i.e. the participants often talk about characters and events depicted in the textbooks, which results in a rather detached style where personal opinions are rarely expressed and students' own understandings seldom developed. In contrast, students' contributions in the present data are usually more complex than one word replies. They also often adopt a personal perspective on matters, which makes the overall tone of talk more involved and conversational than in many language classrooms. That is, CLIL classrooms seem to offer students opportunities to practise pragmatics of conversational participation.

To illustrate the students' active conversational role, it is useful to take a look at situations where they are involved in interactions not only with the teacher, as in most of the above extracts, but also with each other. The students in these classrooms quite often become engaged in lively multiparty conversations which are significant pragmatically in often helping to create a sense of community. It is thus important to bear in mind that pragmatic proficiency is not only about avoiding face threats but also about knowing how to participate in interaction in ways that build rapport. In Extract 9, from a biology lesson, the students and the teacher are involved in a lengthy discussion about when the class was supposed to have a quiz. The personal dimension is clearly visible in that the students speak from their own perspectives, state their personal opinions and take stands (see Tannen, 1984). That the talk has mainly social functions is revealed by the jocular tone and bursts of laughter; frequent overlaps and latched turns also point towards an involved atmosphere. Students are quick to react to each other's and the teacher's comments here, which points towards alertness and an ability to function in one's L2 during unpredictable real-time conditions.

Extract 9

1	T	so it's nine against one
	Mikko	no I'm with you
	Aron	[what]
	T	[((laughs))]
5	Anna	I'm [on nobody's side]
	Maria	[let's make a compromise]
	Markus	yeah a quiz=
	Helena	=I'm [(x)]
	Aron	[< no >]
10	Anna	[((laughs))]
	Mikko	[yes he said wednesday] > I've prepared for today I'm not < > gonna read twice. <

	Anna	[I'm not sitting (xx)]
	T	[yeah yeah but the only only thing] which count here is me
15		because I'm the dictator.
	Mikko	yeah
	Leena	<no>
	Anna	I don't remember what you said so I'm not going to
		go on anybody's side

Extract 10 shows that multiparty conversations are not only a matter of organisational talk but also occur when subject content is being handled. This example comes from a physics lesson after the group has completed a calculation. In Line 3, Sonja exclaims that she finally understands the exercise. The teacher seems to be starting to close off the topic in Lines 4–5 when Anne, Eeva and Laura announce that they still find it hard to understand the calculation (Lines 6–8), echoing each other's words while doing so. As in Extract 9, the students adopt a personal rather than a detached perspective to the task at hand. Moreover, it is noteworthy how there seems to be joint meaning construction going on in the way Eeva and Laura co-operate in explaining what they find hard to understand in the calculation (Lines 9–14), smoothly building on each other's turns and continuing where the other leaves off.

Extract 10

1	T	easy to guess that it must be (.) a hundred newtons as well.
		(2.5) but it all has to do with the moments (2.8)
	Sonja	oh now I get e (1.0) now I get how you do e (2.9) that was easy.
	T	so that's (.) yeah that's what- that's all of the question here (.)
5		summarised (.) I think
	Anne	no I don't get it [still]
	Eeva	[I still] don't really I
	Laura	I [don't]
	Eeva	[(you) get] the hundred newtons there.=
10	Laura	=why is it in the [like middle. Like if you put] in the middle
	Sonja	[cause (x) if you (xx)]
	Laura	hundred newtons
	Eeva	yeah why is in the middle there cause it's the centre but why
		is it a hundred.
15	T	well the centre of mass is here ((explanation continues))

Due to its conversational tone, language use in the present CLIL classrooms is also rather informal in style, a feature that has been visible in most of the above extracts. This is in interesting contrast to those studies in immersion contexts that have pointed towards learners' language use being overly formal and their having difficulties with more informal and vernacular styles, probably due to having acquired the language in the formal context of classrooms with the emphasis on academic style (e.g. Rehner *et al.*, 2003). The reasons for the informal style in the present data may partly lie in the students being non-native speakers of English with less varied style repertoires than native speakers of English. Another reason may be that teaching in CLIL classrooms is not very tightly tied to teaching materials for the simple reason that as yet, there are few CLIL materials in English available in Finnish schools. As a result, teaching is often carried out through classroom talk rather than active engagement with written materials. Thus, rather than being regrettable, the lack of CLIL teaching materials may have its advantages from the viewpoint of students' spoken pragmatic skills.

Discussion

This paper has explored the nature of CLIL classrooms as environments for pragmatic learning and pragmatic meaning making. The findings suggest that pragmatic matters are relevant in these classrooms and that interpersonal concerns come into play, for example when students negotiate disagreements and misunderstandings and make initiations. However, the linguistic repertoire with which they convey pragmatic meanings is not as versatile as that of native speakers. For example, the scarcity of discourse markers and pragmatic particles is a noticeable feature of their talk. Nevertheless, they clearly attempt to monitor degrees of directness in situations with potential face threat. The image of students' pragmatic skills is thus more positive than has been suggested by studies which have tested students' skills in foreign language classrooms. While this may be due in part to the relative fluency of CLIL students when using English, the effect of the context is also worth considering, for it may well be that when authentic situations so demand, one tries harder to convey pragmatic meanings than when practising pragmatics in language classrooms. That is, there is a difference between pragmatic meaning making as something that is considered in the abstract, and as something that has a direct bearing on how one is perceived as a social actor.

It is clear that focusing on cross-sectional classroom data does not make it possible to explore how CLIL exposure supports learners' pragmatic development; doing this would require longitudinal data. Developing pragmatic skills in CLIL classrooms is also problematic in another sense: how to define the target for this development in a context where, as usual in European CLIL classrooms, the language used is not the native language of any of the participants who, moreover, share the same L1. Dalton-Puffer (2005: 1291) is right in arguing that CLIL classrooms in fact resemble lingua franca situations in this respect. Hence, the question of norms becomes more problematic in a CLIL scenario than in immersion and EFL classrooms where language learners are usually expected to approximate native speaker norms to be pragmatically successful. As a legacy of SLA-based thinking, such assumptions seem to treat language proficiency as a psychological-cognitive, context-independent entity. However, if language learning is seen in more social and contextual terms as 'learning to participate in communication with other speakers' (Brouwer & Wagner, 2004: 34), and if pragmatics adds to this the ability to attend to interpersonal relationships while doing so, it also seems possible to treat pragmatic success as a local accomplishment rather than as something that needs to be related to a situation-external, context-independent native speaker norm. This is in line with Bardovi-Harlig's (2005: 75) point that in interlanguage pragmatics, there ought to be more focus on interactional success rather than on convergence with native speaker norms. In this respect, the CLIL data looked at shows that even if the participants may not use exactly the same pragmatic strategies that native speakers would use in similar situations, their language use is not devoid of interpersonal concerns. They also seem to succeed in accomplishing their interactional goals without causing offence. Looked at from a pragmatic perspective, then, the strength of CLIL classrooms – especially for learners who already possess relatively good skills in English – lies in the opportunity they provide for students to participate in a range of activities which bring about various social demands that they have to try and take into account while using their L2. To what extent their ways of attuning to pragmatics of interaction would be similar in out-of-school practices with English is obviously hard to assess on the basis of their classroom conduct only. Because generalising from classroom contexts is difficult, more research is needed in the future on how learners use their language resources across different situations, with different social constellations. However, I hope this study has managed to indicate that approaching pragmatic success as interactional accomplishment rather than as a repository of skills may in important ways complement the image we have of language learners' pragmatic abilities.

Acknowledgement

Financial support from the Academy of Finland is gratefully acknowledged.

Appendix 5.1. Transcription Conventions

overlapping [speech] [text]	overlapping speech
(.)	a short pause that is not timed, less than a second
(2.5)	a pause, timed in seconds
text = = text	latching utterances
boldface	prominent speech
exte:nsion	noticeable extension of the sound or syllable
cut off wo-	cut off word or truncated speech
°high circles°	spoken more silently than surrounding utterances
•dark circles•	laughing voice
.	falling intonation
↑	rising intonation
< text >	spoken more slowly than surrounding utterances
> text <	spoken more rapidly than surrounding utterances
((text))	transcriber's comments
(text)	transcriber's interpretation of unclear word(s)
(x)	unclear speech, probably a word
(xx)	unclear speech, probably a phrase
(xxx)	longer stretch of unclear speech

References

Bardovi-Harlig, K. (2001) Evaluating the empirical evidence: Grounds for instruction in pragmatics? In K.R. Rose and G. Kasper (eds) *Pragmatics in Language Teaching* (pp. 13–32). Cambridge, MA: Cambridge University Press.

Bardovi-Harlig, K. (2005) Contextualizing interlanguage pragmatics. In A.E. Tyler, M. Takada, Y. Kim and D. Marinova (eds) *Language in Use. Cognitive and Discourse Perspectives on Language and Language Learning* (pp. 65–84). Washington: Georgetown University Press.

Brouwer, C.E. and Wagner, J. (2004) Developmental issues in second language conversation. *Journal of Applied Linguistics* 1 (1), 29–47.

Brown, P. and Levinson, S. (1987) *Politeness. Some Universals in Language Usage.* Cambridge: Cambridge University Press.

Canagarajah, S.A. (1995) Functions of codeswitching in ESL classrooms: Socialising bilingualism in Jaffna. *Journal of Multilingual and Multicultural Development* 6 (3), 173–195.

Dalton-Puffer, C. (2005) Negotiating interpersonal meanings in naturalistic classroom discourse: Directives in content-and-language-integrated classrooms. *Journal of Pragmatics* 37, 1275–1293.

Dalton-Puffer, C. and Nikula, T. (2006a) Pragmatics of content-based instruction: Teacher and student directives in Finnish and Austrian classrooms. *Applied Linguistics* 27 (2), 241–267.

Dalton-Puffer, C. and Nikula, T. (eds) (2006b) *Current Research on CLIL*. Special issue of *VIEWZ – Vienna English Working Papers* 15 (3).
Fraser, B. (1996) Pragmatic markers. *Pragmatics* 6 (2), 167–190.
Gassner, D. and Maillat, D. (2006) Spoken competence in CLIL: A pragmatic take on recent Swiss data. *VIEWZ – Vienna English Working Papers* 15 (3), 15–22.
Hall, J.K. and Verplaetse, L.S. (eds) (2000) *Second and Foreign Language Learning through Classroom Interaction*. Mahwah, NJ: Lawrence Erlbaum.
Huth, T. and Taleghani-Nikazm, C. (2006) How can insights from conversation analysis be directly applied to teaching L2 pragmatics? *Language Teaching Research* 10 (1), 53–79.
Jäppinen, A.-K. (2003) *Ajattelu ja sisältöjen oppiminen vieraskielisessä opetuksessa* [*Thinking and Content Learning in Bilingual Education*]. Jyväskylä: The Centre for Applied Language Studies.
Jeon, E.H. and Kaya, T. (2006) Effects of L2 instruction on interlanguage pragmatic development. In J.M. Norris and L. Ortega (eds) *Synthesizing Research on Language Learning and Teaching* (pp. 165–211). Amsterdam: John Benjamins.
Jiménez Catalán, R.M., Ruiz De Zarobe, Y. and Cenoz, J. (2006) Vocabulary profiles of English foreign language learners in English as a subject and as a vehicular language. *VIEWZ – Vienna English Working Papers* 15 (3), 23–27.
Kasper, G. and Rose, K.R. (2001) Pragmatics in language teaching. In K.R. Rose and G. Kasper (eds) *Pragmatics in Language Teaching* (pp. 1–9). Cambridge: Cambridge University Press.
Kasper, G. and Rose, K.R. (2002) *Pragmatic Development in a Second Language*. Oxford: Blackwell.
Koike, D.A. and Pearson, L. (2005) The effect of instruction and feedback in the development of pragmatic competence. *System* 33 (3), 481–501.
Lantolf, J.P. (ed.) (2000) *Sociocultural Theory and Second Language Learning*. Oxford: Oxford University Press.
Larsen-Freeman, D. and Long, M. (1991) *An Introduction to Second Language Acquisition Research*. London: Longman.
Lyster, R. (1994) The effect of functional-analytic teaching on aspects of French immersion students' sociolinguistic competence. *Applied Linguistics* 15, 263–287.
Marsh, D. (2002) *CLIL/EMILE – the European Dimension. Actions, Trends and Foresight Potential*. European Commission Report, Public Services Contract DG EAC 36 01 Lot 3.
Müller, S. (2005) *Discourse Markers in Native and Non-Native English Discourse*. Amsterdam: John Benjamins.
Nadasdi, T., Mougeon, R. and Rehner, K. (2005) Learning to speak everyday (Canadian) French. *The Canadian Modern Language Review* 61 (4), 543–563.
Nikula, T. (2005) English as an object and tool of study in classrooms: Interactional effects and pragmatic implications. *Linguistics and Education* 16 (1), 27–58.
Nikula, T. (2007) The IRF pattern and space for interaction: Observations on EFL and CLIL classrooms. In C. Dalton-Puffer and U. Smit (eds) *Empirical Perspectives on CLIL Classroom Discourse* (pp. 179–204). Frankfurt: Peter Lang.
Ohta, A.S. and Nakaone, T. (2004) When students ask questions: Teacher and peer answers in the foreign language classroom. *IRAL* 42, 217–237.

Rehner, K. and Mougeon, R. (2003) The effect of educational input on the development of sociolinguistic competence by French immersion students: The case of expressions of consequence in spoken French. *Journal of Educational Thought* 37, 259–281.

Rehner, K, Mougeon, R. and Nadasdi, T. (2003) The learning of sociolinguistic variation by advanced FSL learners. The case of *nous* versus *on* in immersion French. *Studies in Second Language Acquisition* 25, 127–156.

Rose, K. (2005) On the effects of instruction in second language pragmatics. *System* 33 (3), 385–399.

Rose, K.R. and Kasper, G. (eds) (2001) *Pragmatics in Language Teaching*. Cambridge, MA: Cambridge University Press.

Sunderland, J. (2001) Student initiation, teacher response, student follow-up: Towards an appreciation of student-initiated IRFs in the language classroom. Centre for Research in Language Education (CRILE) Working papers 55, University of Lancaster.

Tannen, D. (1984) *Conversational Style: Analyzing Talk Among Friends*. Norwood, NJ: Ablex.

van Lier, L. (2001) Constraints and resources in classroom talk: Issues of equality and symmetry. In C. Candlin and N. Mercer (eds) *English Language Teaching in its Social Context* (pp. 90–107). London: Routledge in association with Macquarie University and The Open University.

Vollmer, H. (2006) Subject-specific competence and language use of bilingual learners: The case of geography in grade 10 of secondary schools in Germany. A paper in the seminar 'English as the Medium of Instruction in European Schools', ESSE Conference, London, August 30, 2006.

Walsh, S. (2006) *Investigating Classroom Discourse*. London: Routledge.

Chapter 6
Computer-mediated Learning of L2 Pragmatics

MARTA GONZÁLEZ-LLORET

Introduction

Correct sociopragmatic use of addressivity in Spanish, although essential for successful communication, may be difficult to acquire in the traditional language classroom. This longitudinal study investigates how synchronous computer-mediated communication (SCMC) may aid second/foreign language learners in their development of addressivity through interaction with expert speakers of the target language. A microanalytical analysis of the data shows that participants engaged in collaborative interactions and extended language use, including multiple repair sequences initiated by the expert speaker, which resulted in the improvement of the student sociopragmatic knowledge and pragmalinguistic competence.

Addressivity

According to Braun (1988), addressivity can be accomplished mainly through the use of three forms: (1) *Forms of address*. These are pronouns referring to the collocutor(s). (2) *Verb forms of address.* Reference to the collocutor is expressed by means of inflectional suffixes. (3) *Nouns of address.* Substantives and adjectives which designate collocutors or refer to them in some other way (e.g. kinship terms and titles). Of all these forms, pronouns of address have been the most investigated as indexing addressivity, probably because pronouns are independent forms, and are not influenced by other factors such as tense and aspect, which imprint greater variation and difficulty.

Pronouns of address, although once described quite straightforwardly by Brown and Gilman (1970) as being a dichotomy between a simple or intimate pronoun of address (T) used to express familiarity/solidarity and intimacy, and a polite, distant or secondary pronoun (V) used to express formality/distance/hierarchy, have proved to be much more complicated (Braun, 1988; Morford, 1997; Mühlhäusler & Harré, 1990). Morford (1997) proposes that the complexity of the pronoun system is due to two different but related orders of indexicality. The first order involves social relationships (solidarity, intimacy, hierarchy), while the second one refers to aspects of the speakers' identity (social class, political orientation).

The Special Difficulty of the Spanish Addressivity System

Spanish, as well as French and German, has a dual system of pronouns of address which is complicated for students as the different forms are used to index formality, deference, hierarchy, respect (*usted, su*) or informality, solidarity and intimacy (*tú, tu*). However, unlike French and German, Spanish is a pro-drop language in which subject pronouns are almost always implicit in the verb form and therefore less salient to language learners. In addition, the addressivity system in Spanish is highly complex; not only does it reflect solidarity and power (Brown & Gilman, 1970), but because it also includes geographical and dialectal variations, and is deeply rooted in the social and historical context of each of the 20 countries and numerous communities where Spanish is used. The use of terms of address is anything but simple or transparent to foreigners entering the community, and it is nothing like the normative forms that can be found in written materials (D'Ambrosio, 2004). The addressivity system is an extremely variable and complex system, not only related to personal characteristics, such as age and gender, that also seem to vary from country to country, but largely embedded in the sociocultural and economic context of the speakers.

As the native speaker participants in this study were in Spain, special attention was paid to the addressivity system in Spain. Studies of address focusing on Spain are scarce, but they agree that Spanish speakers in Spain tend to prefer the use of *tú* as a form of symmetry rather than considering issues of power; with new generations using almost exclusively the informal forms *tú* and *vosotros* (Blas Arroyo, 1994). In Spain, people tend to consider social factors such as age, gender and class, as well as degree of acquaintance (Rossomondo, 2002), age being the most definite factor, when using *usted*, followed by social class or status, with a tendency to reciprocate regardless of the pronoun (Schwenter, 1993). The question is then: is it possible for L2 students to develop their sociopragmatic and pragmalinguistic competence in a classroom? Is interaction with native speakers helpful? Can this interaction happen in an on-line environment?

Development of Addressivity in the Classroom

Although instruction seems to be a key element in the acquisition of pragmatics (Jeon & Kaya, 2006; Kasper & Schmidt, 1996), the foreign language classroom may offer a limited environment for learning, as the opportunities for human interaction are restricted (Kasper, 2001; Kasper & Rose, 1999; Lyster, 1994), the materials that the students are exposed to are artificial and decontextualized (Bardovi-Harlig *et al.*, 1991), and may not generate the sociolinguistic input that is needed in order for learning to take place. Given these limitations, studies on the teachability of pragmatic competence in the language classroom have been attempting to find those techniques and methods that positively affect pragmatic learning (Alcón, 2002; Bardovi-Harlig & Mahan-Taylor, 2003; House, 1996; Martínez-Flor *et al.*, 2003; Rose & Kasper, 2001, see also Alcon and Martínez-Flor's (2005) special issue of *System* on Pragmatics in Instructed Language Learning).

Although there are hardly any studies on Spanish SLA and addressivity, there are a few studies that have researched the development of pronouns of addressivity in languages other than Spanish, such as for instance Lyster (1993, 1994) in French; DuFon (1999) in Indonesian; and Norris (2001) and Belz and Kinginger (2002, 2003) in German. The data in these studies suggest that students are able to correct their inappropriately overgeneralized use of pragmatic forms with focused instruction (Lyster, 1993, 1994). However, the sociolinguistic use as well as the developmental process of address forms vary greatly among learners (DuFon, 1999; Norris, 2001), partly because of the influence that learners' personal beliefs and motivations may have for the developmental process (Belz & Kinginger, 2002, 2003; DuFon, 1999). In addition, although the choice of appropriate pronoun may seem clear to native speakers, students have problems deciding between formal and informal pronouns, and they tend to use formal address pronouns less often but more sociopragmatically accurately (Norris, 2001).

Belz and Kinginger conducted a series of studies on the development of the informal pronoun (T) through electronic social contact, through telecollaborative projects among students in the USA, Germany and France (Belz & Kinginger, 2002, 2003; Kinginger, 2000). These studies point out that American students exhibited free variation on their use of V and T at the beginning of the interaction (despite explicit instruction from their teachers to use T with their key-pals). Several students corrected their use immediately after receiving explicit feedback from their key-pals (Belz & Kinginger, 2003) while others took longer to develop the accurate use of T and V. Belz and Kinginger point out that feedback which is highly meaningful (*'critical incident* with respect to socialization into appropriate T/V use'; Belz & Kinginger, 2003: 9 italics in original) may be the detonator for change (Belz & Kinginger, 2002). Belz and Kinginger's data also suggest that the gradual, slower change shown by some of the participants was probably due to a lack of domain of the grammatical system once the sociopragmatic system was understood (Belz & Kinginger, 2003).

Following this line of research, this study also explores the potential of SCMC as an environment conductive to the development of sociopragmatic and pragmalinguistic competence, and particularly the development of addressivity.

The potential of SCMC lies in the way it allows students to interact with other speakers of the language and provides opportunities for more experienced speakers to offer assistance or feedback and engage in collaborative dialogue, which is believed to promote language development (Foster & Ohta, 2005; Ohta, 2001; Swain, 2000; Swain & Lapkin, 2001). Furthermore, during interaction in SCMC students are forced to produce language constantly in order to co-construct the interaction, and they have the opportunity to reflect and look back at their language (at least the interaction in which they are engaged) as the entire interaction is still available to them. This feature allows students to compare their language with that of their interlocutors, thus increasing the possibility that students notice any 'holes' on their linguistic knowledge and repair them (Swain & Lapkin, 1995). These opportunities for students to reflect on their language are occasions for second language learning (LaPierre, 1994; Swain, 1998); they are 'micromoments of cognition' (Markee, 2007) in which learning is occurring.

Case Study

Participants

The participants in this study, all part of a larger project, were sixteen second-year Spanish language students at the University of Hawaii interacting with nine Spanish speakers, students at the University Jaume I, in Castelló, Spain. This level was chosen for three reasons: first, at this level students already have enough grammatical competence that they can engage in limited interaction with native speakers of the language; second, in order to be able to establish comparisons with similar existing studies that also targeted this level (Belz & Kinginger, 2002, 2003; Kinginger, 2000); and third, to allow for comparison of intact classes of the same level, in which the project was integrated as part of a semester-long curriculum. Students were paired up according to their schedules to connect with their Spanish key-pals. The participants from Spain were very similar to the American participants in age and gender. They were also university students learning English and approximately the same age. Students worked in groups of two American students and one Spanish student on a project-based task in Spanish for 10 weeks, and at a later time they engaged again in SCMC interaction, this time in English, to help shape the final oral project for the students' English language class in Spain. The students arranged their meeting times with their partners and connected outside of class time at their convenience (a necessary measure given the large time difference between the two locations). This study is a case study of the interactions of one of those

16 students, Vero (a pseudonym), with her chat-pal in Spain, A_m, and her project mate, Jeff.

This student was chosen because her interactions reflect the optimal conditions that may lead to pragmatic development (length of interactions, student engagement and native speaker engagement in the learning process). In addition they were chosen for reasons similar to those presented by Belz and Kinginger (2002): the participants showed great variation in their use of addressivity at the beginning of the project and the Spanish partner provided several instances of explicit feedback.

The online environment

The instructors in both universities agreed to use Yahoo! Messenger as the medium of interaction; it allows for cross-platform use (Apple and PC), it is free, it is easy to download, install and use, and it allows for the storage of the conversations in the students' computers. As with most chat tools, there is a window for writing messages (the lower one in this case), and a window where the messages appear in the order they are received by the server (the top window) with a time stamp of when the message is posted by the server. At the bottom of the window the message '(name) is typing a message' appears when another participant is typing and before that message is sent. This feature was also considered desirable as it may prompt students to wait longer for another participants' message before they self-select as next speaker in the absence of an incoming message.

Another reason for selecting Yahoo! was that it is not an open-to-the-public type of chatroom. No one can enter a conversation unless they are invited into the room. With Yahoo! Messenger it is possible to form groups easily by adding all the members of one group to one account, so all participants can see who is connected and able to participate. If a participant is not connected, the others still can leave messages or email his/her Yahoo! account from within the messenger program. Finally, Yahoo! allows the participants to save their interactions to a folder in their computer, which the students then forwarded via email to their respective teachers. The project lasted 10 weeks. Although a full semester (16 weeks) would have been preferable, this was impossible due to conflicting schedules between university calendars in Spain and the USA. However, it is important to note that although the project lasted 10 weeks, interactions for each group happened at different times and varied greatly in duration (from 30 minutes to 2 hours). The group presented in this paper interacted eight times in the 10 weeks and their exchanges varied in length between 15 e-turns[1] and 222 e-turns.

The task

Students in groups had to complete a project-based task: a full itinerary for a trip with a detailed budget, including flight information, hotels and any activities, excursions, museums and restaurants that they planned to visit. The students were not provided with information on how to divide the work or how to work in their groups. They were only asked to meet once a week for at least one hour to work on their projects, and they were given instructions on the final product of the collaboration: a detailed itinerary in Microsoft Word format, with pictures and references to all the relevant links of cited Internet sites and other resources, and a detailed budget of how their assigned money was spent. This type of task was selected because it was large enough to require several interactions but not so large that it could not be accomplished in the available time frame. In addition, a needs analysis conducted at the beginning of the semester had revealed that the students were interested in creating a project that had 'traveling' as the main topic. Finally, there is some support to the idea that project-based tasks may produce language in which development may be observed. As Donato and Lantolf (1990: 85) state, developmental processes 'can be observed directly in the linguistic interactions that arise among speakers as they participate in problem-solving tasks'.

Data analysis

This study uses a conversational analytical approach to the data. Such an approach allows an investigation of the fine-grain, in-depth characteristics of the interaction that may make it conducive to language learning. It can help uncover how students engage, how they respond to the medium, and how their interaction is constructed and maintained in a highly contextual environment such as SCMC. A microanalytical analysis helps explore those episodes of the interaction that are believed to be conducive to language learning from an emic perspective, considering them from the point of view of the participants. In this spirit, the language used by the Spanish students and their Spaniard chat-pal was kept unmodified, in spite of typographical and spelling errors, to be faithful to the original interaction. Translation was done by the author and reflects the Spanish conversation as closely as possible. When language errors were present in the learner's data, the translation reflected the general meaning of the sentence, without accounting for the errors, unless the participants themselves oriented to them.

In addition to the qualitative analysis of the data, the study also looks at the frequency in use of address pronouns and verbs that are morphologically marked for formality/distance or informality/solidarity, one of the possible measures of language development to determine improvement of the learner's use of these linguistic features during the duration of the project.

Discussion

The analysis of the data revealed several episodes in which issues of addressivity were apparent to the participants engaged in the conversation. During the first interaction, which was rather short, Vero, one of the Spanish learners, uses the formal pronoun 'usted' in E-turn 3 to initiate the main topic of the conversation, the project-based task. A_m, in E-turn 5, initiates a repair sequence (other-repair) and provides Vero with explicit feedback about the sociopragmatic use of *'usted'*, and demands, with a direct negative command (don't call me *'usted'*), that she uses *'tú'* instead. Vero seems to orient to the feedback in Line 8 when she repairs her error by using the verb in the informal *tú* form.

Episode 1. Interaction 1

1. a_m (1:04:00 AM): Hola, ya he llegado	1. Hello, I am here
2. vero (1:04:53 AM): Hola	2. Hello
→ 3. vero (1:06:02 AM): Nuestro proyecto deberá planear un viaje. ¿Dónde **quiere usted** ir?	3. Our project will have to plan a trip. Where do **you[formal] want** to go?
4. a_m (1:06:28 AM): Me es indiferente.	4. I don't care
→ 5. a_m (1:06:43 AM): No me llames de usted.	5. Don't you[informal] use 'usted' with me.
6. vero (1:07:00 AM): Me llamo es XXXX	6. My name is XXXX
7. a_m (1:07:18 AM): Yo AXXXX	7. I AXXX
→ 8. vero (1:07:52 AM): AXXX...Cuanto anos **tienes**?	8. AXXX... How old are you [informal]?
9. a_m (1:08:00 AM): 18, y **tu**?	9. and you[informal]
10. vero (1:08:20 AM): 30	10. 30

Looking at this interaction alone we could perhaps conclude that A_m's initiated repair was effective in correcting Vero's inappropriate sociopragmatic use and pragmalinguistic forms of addressivity. However, their second interaction, also a brief one, disproves this idea. Although Vero starts with the correct form of the verb *estar 'estas'*, she switches back to the formal in E-turn 15 with the use of the pronoun 'le' and continues with several verbs in the formal *'usted'* in E-turns 17 (*'piensa'* – do you[formal] think), 27 (*'sabe'* – you[formal] know) and 30 (*'puede'* – can you[formal]). However in this interaction the student from Spain does not orient to Vero's errors and focuses exclusively on the topic, asking

Vero to explain more about the task at hand (Line 16, 'Explain yourself [informal]').

Episode 2. Interaction 2

→ 1. a_m (11:22:35 AM): Hola
→ 2. vero (11:22:47 AM): como **estas**?
3. a_m (11:23:23 AM): Bien, i Jeff?

1. Hello
2. How are you[informal]?
3. Well, and Jeff?

→ 15. vero (11:33:04 AM): es tambien ... desde que vamos a los Alpes. Quiza **le** podemos encontar en Espana y donde **pararia** en camino a Suiza? Dos ciudades ...

15. is also ... since we go to the Alps. Maybe we can meet **you[formal]** in Spain and where **would you[formal] stop** on the way to Switzerland? Two cities ...

16. a_m (11:34:39 AM): Explic**ate**
→ 17. vero (11:35:27 AM): asi que **piensa** acerca de eso para esta noche. nuestro profesora dijo que tenemos un presupuesto de 6000 dolares cada.
18. a_m (11:36:14 AM): cada persona?

16. Explain yourself[informal]
17. What do **you[formal] think** about this for tonight. Our teacher said we have a budget of 6000 dollars each

18. Each person?

This 'backsliding' or regression on Vero's development illustrates the importance of longitudinal data that looks at development not as the fruit of only one interaction but rather an extended progression.

Interaction 3, a much longer interaction, includes both Vero and Jeff, Spanish students, and A_m, the Spanish speaker. In this interaction, Vero's language presents a clear fluctuation between the use of formal and informal, also found in Belz and Kinginger (2002, 2003), which seems to suggest that although she seemed to exhibit some sociopragmatic understanding of formal and informal address, she lacks control over the pragmalinguistic forms. Jeff also exhibits a lack of control over the pragmalinguistic forms, although he uses more informal than formal verbs. Jeff's variation is especially evident in several sentences where he alternates both forms.

93. jeff (1:48:19 AM): pero **tu** usas acentos cuando: **dijo**, 'no me digais senor, solo tengo 18'

93. but **you[informal] use** accent marks when: **you[formal] said** 'don't call me sir, I am only 18'

101. jeff (1:51:10 AM): **tu** esta bromeando? **usted** no **ha** salido de Espana?

101. you[informal] are joking? You [formal] have never left Spain?

Jeff also seems to lack sociopragmatic understanding of Spanish terms of address, as illustrated by Episode 3 during his first interaction (the third one for Vero and A_m).

Episode 3. Interaction 3

→   78. jeff (1:44:29 AM): que pasa **senor**?   78. what's up **sir**?
→   79. a_m (1:44:35 AM): atonito   79. in shock
80. vero (1:44:43 AM): posible.. pero no   80. posible but
81. jeff (1:45:06 AM): donde vamos?   81. where are we going?
82. jeff (1:45:08 AM): donde   82. where
83. jeff (1:45:10 AM): donde   83. where
→   84. a_m (1:45:17 AM): no me digais señor:), solo tengo 18   84. don't call me sir:), I am only 18 years old
85. vero (1:45:35 AM): muy joven   85. very young
86. a_m (1:46:04 AM): Pues que me hubiesen parido antes!!   86. Then my mother should have had me earlier!!
→   87. jeff (1:46:08 AM): **puedes** beber el alcohol alli si **tienes** 18 anos?   87. can you[informal] drink alcohol there if you[informal] are 18?

→   97. vero (1:49:55 AM): donde **va** esquiar entonces?   97. Where do **you go[formal]** skiing then?
98. a_m (1:50:04 AM): Hata ahora era menor y no me dejavan ir tan lejos, y no podiamos ir toda la familia.   98. Until now I was a minor and I was not allowed to go so far, and we couldn't go with the entire family
99. a_m (1:50:45 AM): fui una vez a esquiar a Andorra.   99. I went to ski one to Andorra
→   100. vero (1:51:05 AM): si solomente **tu** ... de donde **vas** esquiar?   100. If only you[informal] ... where do you go[informal] skiing?
→   101. jeff (1:51:10 AM): **tu esta** bromeando? **usted** no **ha salido** de Espana?   101. You[inform] are[formal] joking? You[formal] have[formal] not left Spain?
102. a_m (1:52:07 AM): no, solo a andorra, que esta ni a 20Km. de la frontera de España.   102. No, only to andorra, that is only 20Km from Spain's border
103. jeff (1:53:20 AM): pero donde debemos ir para este viaje?   103. But where should we go for this trip?
→   104. a_m (1:53:25 AM): no me llameis de usted!!   104. Do not call [form+pl] me usted [form]!!

105. a_m (1:53:52 AM): me da igual.	105. I don't care
→ 106. vero (1:54:14 AM): Querris **ustedes** venir a Suiza?	106. Would **you [form+pl]** want to come to Switzerland?
→ 107. a_m (1:54:19 AM): me enfadare como me volvais a decir usded!!!!!	107. I am going to get angry if you [informal + pl] call me 'usted' [form] again!!!!!
→ 108. a_m (1:54:32 AM): **OK?**	108. Ok?
→ 109. jeff (1:54:47 AM): **ok**	109. Ok

When Jeff uses the form *'señor'* (sir) to refer to A_m (we know he is referring to A_m as the fact that Vero is a woman is known to all participants), he starts a repair sequence with a strong declaration of surprise in E-turn 79 ('in shock') followed by an explicit request not to be called 'sir' and a sociopragmatic explanation of why the term is inappropriate in this context ('I am only 18') as they are all young students, and a symmetrical and informal use is the norm to be followed. Jeff seems to orient to A_m's repair initiation and repairs his utterance by using the appropriate form twice in E-turn 87 (*'puedes'* can you[informal]) displaying sociopragmatic and pragmalinguistic understanding.

During this exchange Vero displays understanding of A_m's sociopragmatic reason for the need of informal address forms with him in E-turn 85 when she states *'muy joven'* (very young). However, she continues varying both forms, even of the same verb (*'va esquiar'* in E-turn 97 and *'vas esquiar'* in E-turn 100 above), to which A_m orients as still a lack of understanding. Jeff also displays pragmalinguistic variation, even using both forms in the same sentence (E-turn 101). Jeff's explicit use of *'usted'* triggers a new repair sequence, initiated in E-turn 104 by A_m again providing explicit feedback as to the use of the formal *'usted'* (Do not call me *'usted'*!! in E-turn 104), emphasized this time with two exclamation marks, which in chat interaction denotes emphasis, much like raising voice and changing intonation in a face-to-face interaction. Vero, the next speaker, does not orient to the repair and uses the formal explicit pronoun *'ustedes'* again, to which A_m responds by upgrading his repair turn to the condition of a threat (I will get mad if you call me *'usted'* again) followed by five exclamation marks to display emphasis. In addition, A_m self-selects as the next speaker seeking confirmation of the repair (E-turn 108) by using the students' L1, seeking guarantee that his repair turn was understood. Jeff confirms understanding in E-turn 107 (ok) and Vero on her next intervention (E-turn 112).

After this episode, the interaction continues for 102 more turns, but only three forms are second person. Vero seems to switch to the use of an inclusive *'nosotros'* and Jeff reduces his sentences considerably and engages mostly in off-topic digressions.

Before the interaction is over, Jeff uses a *'tú'* form again (160. jeff (2:06:54 AM): *2 de la manana . . . y tu?* '2 in the morning...and you[informal]?') and Vero uses a *'tú'* form almost at the end of the interaction (198. vero (2:11:47 AM): *Que vas a comer?* 'What are you[informal] going to eat?), but she still maintains her plural formal pronoun (E-turn 138: y uds?). Both Jeff's and Vero's decrease in the production of formal forms for the rest of interaction may be seen as an effort to comply with the sociopragmatic norms suggested by the Spanish speaker. Vero's use of the plural pronoun *'uds'* cannot be seen solely as a lack of comprehension of sociopragmatic rules. In classroom settings it is common to use both formal *'tú'* (with classmates) and formal *'usted'* (with the teacher, guests,...), but when either the teacher or a student refers to more than one person, the plural form *'ustedes'* is employed regardless of the formality/solidarity of the context. In the USA the form *'vosotros'* is hardly ever used in the classroom. It is not considered necessary or practical as it is only used in Spain. Therefore, at this point, it is difficult to know whether Vero is using *'ustedes'* as the formal or informal plural form, especially as there is no answer to the turn from either A_m or Jeff, who are engaged in a side interaction, ignoring Vero's turns.

Interaction 4, between Vero and A_m only, happened only one week after the previous one. Although Vero had previously agreed to use the informal forms with A_m, she reverts back to formal (E-turns 13 and 15), which triggers a new repair sequence started by A_m. In E-turn 17, A_m once again provides a very explicit correction, which includes what to do and what not to do (Don't call me *'usted'* use *'tu'* with me).

Episode 4 Interaction 4

→ 13. vero (12:47:08 AM): La cancion **su** manda a mi?
13. The song **you[formal]** send to me?

14. a_m (12:47:34 AM): Si, la cancion que mande el otro dia
14. Yes, the song I sent the other day

→ 15. vero (12:48:34 AM): **Estuvo ud.** el retrato que mande?
15. **Were you[formal]** the portrait I sent?

16. vero (12:49:23 AM): me gusto la cancion. oida a algun canciones americans?
16. I liked the song. Heard any american songs?

→ 17. a_m(12:49:41 AM): Si, lo vi.:" > **No me llames de ud. tratame de tu.**
17. Yes, I saw it.:" > Don't call me 'usted'[form], use 'tu' [inform] with me

18. a_m (12:50:04 AM): Yo no tengo fotos digitales, si encuentro ya enviare
18. I don't have any digital photos, if I find any I will send them

19. a_m (12:50:16 AM): Ok
19. ok

20. vero (12:50:20 AM): ok	20. ok
21. a_m (12:50:38 AM): Que nuvero de cancion era?	21. What song number was it?
→ 22. vero (12:51:51 AM): asi que vamos nosotros a vacationes en los alpes? nuvero 4.	22. So we are going vacationing to the Alps? number 4

After the repair initiation, A_m retakes a different strand of conversation, answering Vero's question in E-turn 15. It is important to note here that these apparently chaotic, unpredictable, multitopic conversations are a common feature of SCMC (González-Lloret, in press; Herring, 1999; Schönfeldt & Golato, 2003). Vero orients to this new strand rather than the repair initiation turn and they both agree to send digital pictures when he gets some. In E-turn 21 A_m initiates a new topic, abandoning the repair sequence. After this, Vero switches to the use of *'nosotros'* (we), and there is no other use of second person for more than 40 e-turns. Although this may seem like an avoidance strategy, Vero is actually explaining what their task is and what type of information they need to find out as a group, and therefore the switch to *'nosotros'* seems to be in agreement with the topic at hand.

The last repair sequence in the data happens later on in the same interaction. In E-turn 61, Vero uses the verb *'tener'* in the *usted* form, and repeats it again in isolation in E-turn 64.

Episode 5 Interaction 4

→ 61. vero (1:10:28 AM): **tiene** skiis o madero de nieve?	61. Do you[formal] have skiis of snow board(literally)
62. a_m (1:10:41 AM): 'madera'	62. 'wood'
63. vero (1:10:50 AM): ok	63. ok
→ 64. vero (1:10:54 AM): **tiene**?	64. Do you[formal] have?
→ 65. a_m (1:10:55 AM): no, no tengo. **usted** si?	65. No, I don't have. Do **you [formal]**?
66. vero (1:10:59 AM): no.	66. No
67. vero (1:11:09 AM): necesitamos pagar unos?	67. We need to pay for some?
68. a_m (1:11:13 AM): nos tocara alquilarlos	68. We will have to rent them
69. vero (1:12:03 AM): Alquilamos en las montanas entonces.	69. We rent them at the mountains then.

Quite unexpectedly, rather than initiating a new repair sequence, like previously, A_m switches to the use of formal *'usted'* himself, using it very explicitly in E-turn 65 (no, I don't have and you[formal] do?). This switch could be seen as a change in formality register, as a reaction to another person's persistence in using the formal, which is a common practice to establish distance with the interlocutor. However, this change is maintained for one turn only, as the next turn from A_m addressed directly to Vero (E-turn 74) is back in the informal form (a_m (1:14:05 AM): *Alguna vez has visto los toros*? Have you[informal] ever seen bullfighting?). Vero does not seem to notice A_m's change in sociopragmatic use and answers the question without any sign of surprise, expanding on the topic with another question. A_m does not insist on what could be viewed as an implicit type of repair, and the conversation continues on the same topic until the bullfighting topic is introduced by A_m in E-turn 74.

Quantitative analysis

Although Vero does not seem to notice the last repair sequence in the interaction, the one in Episode 5 above, the rest of her interaction starts to incorporate more informal verbs and pronouns. Vero's later interactions, until the end of their project, show a progressive change of Vero's linguistics forms towards the use of informal pronouns and verb forms with her interlocutor (see Table 6.1 and Figure 6.1). In her last four interactions, Vero changes her pragmalinguistic use of addressivity from chaotic variation to an exclusive use of the informal, the expert norm established by the Spanish speaker.

Figure 6.1 illustrates Vero's pragmalinguistic development. It shows how Vero's variation between formal and informal evolved towards the sole use of sociopragmatically appropriate informal forms of address.

Conclusion

The microanalysis of the data in this study demonstrates that SCMC is an environment in which students collaborate to construct meaning and carry on project-based tasks. The interactions between the Spanish learner and the Spanish speaker included multiple repair sequences, started by the Spanish speaker, with explicit instruction about the sociopragmatic rules of addressivity between two speakers of similar age. In spite of several clear repair sequences incorporating very explicit feedback, which is supposed to be most effective (Nassaji & Swain, 2000), and in which the Spanish student displayed understanding and acceptance of the rules, her pragmalinguistic knowledge did not change immediately. Her developmental process required several weeks and several language exchanges before it became target-like. This is consistent with research by Alcón (2002: 371), who points out that 'relationship between collaborative dialogue and learners' development of pragmatics is not immediate'. This seems to suggest that pragmalinguistic knowledge functions as any

Table 6.1 Distribution of formal and informal forms of address by participant and interaction

	A_m – Spanish speaker	Vero – Spanish student	Jeff – Spanish student
Interaction 1	3 V-tú 1 pron. tú	1 V-tú	1 pron., 'usted'
Interaction 2	1 V+ te 1 DO pron. 'os'	2 V-tú	3 V-usted 1 IO pron.-le
Interaction 3	9 V-vostros 2 pron. vosotros 1 pron. os	4 V-'tú' 1 V-vosotros 1 pron. tú	3 V- 'usted' 1 pron. 'ustedes'	7 V-tú
Interaction 4	10 V-tú 3 V-te 2 V-vosotros 3 pron. os 1 OD pron. 'te'	1 V-usted 1 pron. usted	5 V-'tú' 1 pron. tú 1 posses. tu	7 V-usted 1 pron. usted 1 pron. su	2 posses. 'su' 1 pron. ↦'usted' 1 señor
Interaction 5	2 V-vostros 1 pron. os	2 V-tu	3 V-usted

Table 6.1 (*Continued*)

	A_m – Spanish speaker	Vero – Spanish student	Jeff – Spanish student
Interaction 6	2 V-tú 1 pron. os	8 V-tú 2 posses tu	1 V-usted 1 posses. su
Interaction 7	1 V-tú	3 V-tú 1 pron. ti	0 V-usted 1 OI se
Interaction 8	1 V-tú 2 pron. os	3 V-tu	0 V-usted	3 V-tú 1 V-vosotros	3 V-usted 1 V-ustedes 1 pron. usted

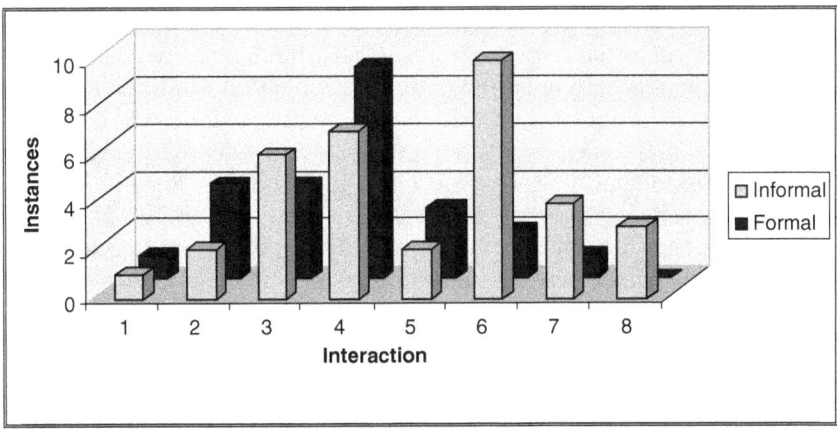

Figure 6.1 Vero's use of formal and informal pronouns and verbs by interaction

other system, where forms may emerge at different times, and they may not emerge equally for all participants (Bardovi-Harlig, 1999; Bardovi-Harlig & Griffin, 2005; Pienemann, 1984). For some students grammatical competence cannot develop 'as quickly as the already present pragmatic concepts require' (Koike, 1989: 287). This is also consistent with results of studies on L1 Spanish pronoun development which suggest that child development of addressivity takes a number of years, progresses in stages and is related to the child's experiences (Anderson, 1998; Gathercole *et al.*, 2002). These results also emphasize the importance of conducting longitudinal studies to be able to observe development (Ortega & Iberri-Shea, 2005). As Kasper and Schmidt (1996: 153) stated, 'longitudinal designs have the greatest potential for uncovering developmental patterns in learners' acquisition of pragmatic competence'.

As for pedagogic implications, this study suggests that SCMC is an excellent environment for the acquisition not only of sociopragmatic knowledge of addressivity, defined here as students' awareness of social rules that direct the use of formal and informal forms of address in a specific context, but also for the development of pragmalinguistic competence given that students can engage for a prolonged period of time in meaningful exchanges and have enough opportunities for language production. SCMC may be a supplement to the traditional classroom by providing students with different contexts and different interlocutors with whom to engage in meaningful communication.

This study opens a door to several opportunities for research. On one side, developmental studies would benefit from research looking at the possible developmental steps for the acquisition of Spanish pronouns and verb morphology by L2 learners. This is an as-yet-unexplored area that would also have pedagogical implications for one-size-fits-all models of language classrooms, which usually do not account for developmental variation. In addition, this one case study would benefit from more research on several other students' development, comparing their developmental patterns for both sociocultural knowledge and pragmalinguistic competence in order to be able to generalize its results. Finally, a deeper look at the role of the native speaker in the interaction and how this affects the students' language development is also an important avenue of study to follow. Do students need a specific type of interlocutor to be able to benefit from SCMC, or would any speaker aid their language development? These and several other questions still need to be answered as part of the exploration of SCMC as a language learning tool, a communication environment which is already becoming deeply embedded in the daily lives of many of our language learners.

Note

1. E-turn refers here to each of the participants' entrances in the exchange. That is, all the text submitted at once by one participant by pressing the enter key, which may vary from one word to several lines of text.

References

Alcón, E. (2002) Relationship between teacher-led versus learners' interaction and the development of pragmatics in the EFL classroom. *International Journal of Educational Research* 37, 359–377.

Alcon, E. and Martínez-Flor, A. (2005) Editors' introduction to pragmatics in instructed language learning. *System* 33 (3), 381–384.

Anderson, R.T. (1998) The development of grammatical case distinctions in the use of personal pronouns by Spanish-speaking preschoolers. *Journal of Speech, Language, and Hearing Research* 41 (2), 394–406.

Bardovi-Harlig, K. (1999) Exploring the interlanguage of interlanguage pragmatics: A research agenda for acquisitional pragmatics. *Language Learning* 49 (4), 677–713.

Bardovi-Harlig, K. and Griffin, R. (2005) L2 pragmatic awareness: Evidence from the ESL classroom. *System* 33 (3), 401–415.

Bardovi-Harlig, K. and Mahan-Taylor, R. (eds) (2003) *Teaching Pragmatics*. United States Department of State. On WWW at http://exchanges.state.gov/education/engteaching/onlineca.htm. Accessed 30.2.2007.

Bardovi-Harlig, K., Hartford, B.A.S., Mahan-Taylor, R., Morgan, M.J. and Reynolds, D.W. (1991) Developing pragmatic awareness: Closing the conversation. *ELT Journal* 45, 4–15.

Belz, J.A. and Kinginger, C. (2002) The cross-linguistic development of address form use in telecollaborative language learning: Two case studies. *The Canadian Modern Language Review* 59 (2), 189–214.

Belz, J.A. and Kinginger, C. (2003) Discourse options and the development of pragmatic competence by classroom learners of German: The case of address forms. *Language Learning* 53 (4), 591.

Blas Arroyo, J.L. (1994) De nuevo sobre el poder y la solidaridad: Apuntes para un análisis integracional de la alternancia TU/USTED. *Nueva resista de filología hispánica* 42 (2), 385–414.
Braun, F. (1988) *Terms of Address: Problems of Patterns and Usage in Various Languages and Cultures*. Berlin: Mouton de Gruyter.
Brown, R. and Gilman, A. (eds) (1970) *The Pronouns of Power and Solidarity*. New York: Free Press.
D'Ambrosio, H.D. (2004) Pragmática, sociolingüística y pedagogía de los pronombres de tratamiento en lengua española. *Estudios de Linguistica Aplicada* 39, 37–52.
Donato, R. and Lantolf, I.J.P. (1990) The dialogic origins of L2 monitoring. *Pragmatics and Language Learning* 1, 83–97.
DuFon, M.A. (1999) The acquisition of linguistic politeness in Indonesian as a second language by sojourners in naturalistic interactions. Unpublished PhD thesis, University of Hawai'i at Manoa.
Foster, P. and Ohta, A.S. (2005) Negotiation for meaning and peer assistance in second language classroom. *Applied Linguistics* 26 (3), 402–430.
Gathercole, V.M., Sebastián, E. and Soto, P. (2002) The emergence of linguistic person in Spanish-speaking children. *Language Learning* 52 (4), 679–722.
González-Lloret, M. (forthcoming) CA for computer-mediated interaction in the Spanish L2 classroom. In G. Kasper and H. Nguyen (eds) *Conversation Analytic Studies of L1 and L2 Interaction, Learning, and Education*. Honolulu, Hawaii: NFLRC and University of Hawaii Press.
Herring, S. (1999) Interactional coherence in CMC. *Journal of Computer-Mediated Communication* 4 (4). On WWW at http://jcmc.indiana.edu/vol4/issue4/herring.html.
House, J. (1996) Developing pragmatic fluency in English as a foreign language: Routines and metapragmatic awareness. *Studies in Second Language Acquisition* 18, 225–252.
Jeon, E.H. and Kaya, T. (2006) Effects of L2 instruction on interlanguage pragmatic development: A meta-analysis. In J. Norris and L. Ortega (eds) *Synthesizing Research on Language Learning and Technology* (pp. 165–211). Philadelphia: John Benjamins.
Kasper, G. (2001) Classroom research on interlanguage pragmatics. In K.R. Rose and G. Kasper (eds) *Pragmatics in Language Teaching* (pp. 33–60). New York: Cambridge University Press.
Kasper, G. and Rose, K.R. (1999) Pragmatics and SLA. *Annual Review of Applied Linguistics* 19, 81–104.
Kasper, G. and Schmidt, R. (1996) Developmental issues in interlanguage pragmatics. *Studies in Second Language Acquisition* 18, 149–169.
Kinginger, C. (ed.) (2000) *Learning the Pragmatics of Solidarity in the Networked Foreign Language Classroom*. Mahwah, NJ: Lawrence Erlbaum Associates.
Koike, D.A. (1989) Pragmatic competence and adult L2 acquisition: Speech acts in interlanguage. *Modern Language Journal* 73, 79–89.
LaPierre, D. (1994) Language output in a cooperative language setting: Determining its effects on second language learning. Unpublished PhD thesis, University of Toronto.
Lyster, R. (1993) The effect of functional-analytic teaching on aspects of sociolinguistic competence: A study in French immersion classrooms at the grade eight level. Unpublished PhD thesis, University of Toronto.

Lyster, R. (1994) The effect of functional-analytic teaching on aspects of French immersion students' sociolinguistic competence. *Applied Linguistics* 15 (3), 263–287.

Markee, N. (2007) Incorporating text and video documents into office hour talk. Paper presented at Pragmatics and Language Learning. Honolulu, HI. March.

Martínez-Flor, A., Usó-Juan, E. and Fernández-Guerra, A. (eds) (2003) *Pragmatic Competence and Foreign Language Teaching*. Castellón: Servei de Publicacions de la Universitat Jaume I.

Morford, J. (1997) Social indexicality in French pronominal address. *Journal of Linguistics Anthropology* 7 (1), 3–37.

Mühlhäusler, P. and Harré, R. (1990) *Pronouns and People: The Linguistic Construction of Social and Personal Identity*. Oxford, UK/Cambridge, MA: Blackwell.

Nassaji, H. and Swain, M. (2000) A Vygotskian perspective on corrective feedback in L2: The effect of random versus negotiated help on the learning of English articles. *Language Awareness* 9, 34–51.

Norris, J. (2001) Use of address terms on the German speaking test. In K.R. Rose and G. Kasper (eds) *Pragmatics in Language Teaching* (pp. 248–282). Cambridge: Cambridge University Press.

Ohta, A.S. (2001) *Second Language Acquisition: Processes in the Classroom*. Mahwah, NJ: Lawrence Erlbaum.

Ortega, L. and Iberri-Shea, G. (2005) Longitudinal research in SLA: Recent trends and future directions. *Annual Review of Applied Linguistics* 25, 26–45.

Pienemann, M. (1984) Psychological constrains on the teachability of languages. *Studies in Second Language Acquisition* 6, 186–214.

Rose, K.R. and Kasper, G. (eds) (2001) *Pragmatics in Language Teaching*. Cambridge: Cambridge University Press.

Rossomondo, A. (2002) Pronominal address forms in Madrid. In J. Lee, K. Geeslin and C. Clements (eds) *Structure, Meaning, and Acquisition in Spanish* (pp. 115–129). Somerville, MA: Cascadilla Press.

Schönfeldt, J. and Golato, A. (2003) Repair in chats: A conversation analytic approach. *Research on Language and Social Interaction* 36 (3), 241–284.

Schwenter, S. (1993) Diferenciación dialectal por medio de pronombres: Una comparación del uso de tú y usted en España y México. *Nueva Revista de Filología Hispánica* XLI, 127–149.

Swain, M. (1998) Focus on form through conscious reflection. In C. Doughty and J. Williams (eds) *Focus on Form in Classroom Second Language Acquisition* (pp. 64–81). Cambridge: Cambridge University Press.

Swain, M. (2000) The output hypothesis and beyond: Mediating acquisition through collaborative dialogue. In J.P. Lantolf (ed.) *Sociocultural Theory and Second Language Learning* (pp. 97–114). New York: Oxford University Press.

Swain, M. and Lapkin, S. (2001) Focus on form through collaborative dialogue: Exploring task effects. In M. Bygate, P. Skehan and M. Swain (eds) *Researching Pedagogic Tasks: Second Language Learning, Teaching and Testing* (pp. 99–118). London: Addison-Wesley Longman.

Part 2
Investigating How Pragmatics Can Be Taught in Foreign Language Contexts

Chapter 7
Using Translation to Improve Pragmatic Competence

JULIANE HOUSE

Introduction

In this chapter I want to make a plea for reintroducing the cross-cultural practice of translation to increase language learners' pragmatic competence. It is high time I believe that the dominance of monolingual practices in language teaching is overcome, and contrastive, transcultural techniques be adopted to enrich the repertoire of pragmatics teaching. The restriction in much of foreign language teaching to monolingual methodologies derives from a mistaken belief that using students' mother tongue endangers their nascent competence in foreign language use, the myth of the negative effect of transfer from the mother tongue and last but not least the influential impact of Anglophone teaching philosophies, and their profit-driven English-only teaching methodologies and textbook industry. Against all this I will argue in this chapter for a reconsideration of translation. The structure of the chapter is as follows: first, because translation is all but forgotten in mainstream foreign language teaching, I will deal with the nature of translation and also present my own translation theory. Secondly, I will give a brief historical outline of how translation has been used in the past in language teaching. Thirdly, I will make a number of suggestions as to how translation might be fruitfully used to improve learners' pragmatic competence.

What is Translation?

The German poet and novelist Heinrich Heine once compared translation with a dance in chains. Others have compared it to a kiss through a handkerchief or the back of a carpet. These metaphors imply that translation is somehow 'not the real thing'. But what exactly is it about translation that makes it so different from 'proper' original text production? Translation is a universal cross-linguistic and cross-cultural social practice at least two millennia old. It comes into being whenever a message produced in one particular language needs to be understood by persons who do not understand that language, and then a translator steps in to remedy this situation. Because the translator is competent in both source and target languages, s/he enables comprehension and communication by providing the intended recipients with a message in a language they understand. Instead of comparing translation to such hopelessly handicapped activities as dancing in chains, hygienic kissing or laying down a carpet bottom-side up, translation can thus also be described by metaphors like 'building bridges', 'carrying a message across' or 'extending horizons' – metaphors which point to the facilitative or enabling function inherent in translation. In this more positive sense, translation can be seen as a service. The deeper reason why translations fulfill this service is the need human beings apparently have to transcend the discourse world set up by their mother tongue(s), their desire not be limited to one particular language. Translations mediate between languages, societies and literatures, and it is through translations that linguistic and cultural barriers can be overcome.

An important characteristic of translation derives directly from this enabling function: translation enables access to something that already exists; it is therefore always secondary communication. Normally, a communicative event happens just once. In translation, however, communicative events are reduplicated for third persons originally prevented from participating in, or appreciating, the original event. This 'reduplication' also lies at the heart of definitions of translation, as we shall see in the next section.

Translation defined

There are many different definitions of translation depending on which factors and conditions are focused on. Here are two classic definitions which focus on the notions of 'text' and 'equivalence' respectively.

A good starting point is Catford's definition. According to him 'translation is an operation performed on languages: a process of substituting a text in one language for a text in another' (Catford, 1965: 1). Catford's focus on 'text' as a critical factor in translating implies that translation does not take place on the level of *langue*, the language system, but on the level of *parole*, i.e. concrete utterances in texts, where the translator must always make a *choice* between several alternative target language linguistic forms that offer themselves as equivalents to the source texts forms; this forced choice is crucial for all acts of translation, not only because all languages differ in form but because the relationship between form and meaning is arbitrary.

The distinction in linguistics between *langue* and *parole*, and the similar one between competence and performance, is important for translation in that it points to crucial differences in both objectives and methods between the fields of contrastive linguistics and translation. While contrastive linguistics tends to focus on the language system, translation is concerned with the realization of that system in acts of communication.

Over and above the notion of 'text', it is the 'bi-directionality' of translation that is of crucial importance, i.e. its simultaneous focus backwards to the 'source language message' and forwards to the (communicative conditions) of the 'target language' (see also Koller, 1995, 2004). This 'double-bind' relation impinges on the meaning of the message and on the way this meaning is to be presented, i.e. its style. Ideas such as these are found in another classic definition of translation by Nida and Taber (1969: 12): 'Translation consists in reproducing in the receptor language the closest natural equivalent of the source-language message, first in terms of meaning and secondly in terms of style'. In this definition the term 'equivalent' is of course the key notion. The 'closest natural equivalent' – here presented as the goal for any translation – needs to be relativized depending on the type of translation produced and which function this translation is to have in the target linguistic and cultural community (see below). Following these basic ideas about the nature of translation, I will now look a bit more closely at translation as a communicative–pragmatic practice.

Translation as communication across cultures

Translating is not only a linguistic procedure, it is also a cultural act, an act of communicating across cultures. Translating always involves both languages and cultures simply because they cannot really be separated; they are inextricably intertwined. Both the social and the historical layer of culture make up what is often called 'the sociocultural context' in which original and translated texts are embedded, and which they also construct in the minds of their readers. This sociocultural context enveloping any text therefore relates not only to the physical environment of text production and reception, but also to its cognitive substrate in the form of expectation norms and values in the minds of authors, translators and recipients as members of a particular linguistic–cultural group.

If language is seen as a social phenomenon, which is naturally bound up with culture, we can say that language both expresses and shapes cultural reality and is embedded in it, and the meanings of linguistic items, from words to collocation, to larger segments of text, can only be understood with reference to its cultural context. Because in translation 'meaning' is of greatest importance, it follows that this meaning cannot be fully understood outside a cultural frame of reference, and it is probably fair to say that in the process of translation not only two languages but also two cultures come into contact. In this sense, translating is a form of intercultural communication in the head of the translator.

But language is not only used in the macrocontext of a particular culture, it is also used with reference to the microcontext of a particular situation. In Halliday's (1994) terms, this context of situation can be divided into three components corresponding to the three metafunctions of language: the ideational (cognitive–referential), the interpersonal and the textual. The context of situation, then, refers to the pragmatic embeddedness of a text. Such a view of the embeddedness of a text in both the situational microcontext and the cultural macrocontext has important consequences for translation: before translation proper, the original needs to be analyzed with reference to both its context of situation and its context of culture. In connection with the above attempts to define translation, the crucial feature of translation as a double-bind phenomenon involving both the (retrospective) ties to the original text and prospective ties to the communicative–cultural conditions on the translation receptors' side were mentioned. Now, the more these communicative–cultural conditions of the receptors differ from those of their counterparts in the original's context, the more important is the 'cultural work' a translator has to do. The concept of translation as a bicultural process in the translator's head presupposes a good knowledge about the two cultures and the way members of the two cultures are wont to assess one another. Understanding the cultural implications of the original text and being familiar with the cultural context into which the new text is to be 'inserted' means knowing at least the following: the situational frame of the text production (conditions, time, place, etc.), the author's intention, attitudes, goals; and the foreign 'cultural world' as depicted in the text and as it is in the real world (in order for the translator to recognize irony and satire). Translation would then involve analyzing the original text in detail, relating it to its source culture context and then to the target cultural context. This idea lies at the heart of my own theory of translation (House, 1977, 1981, 1997). It is based on Hallidayan functional-contextualism but also draws on discourse and corpus linguistics. A basic assumption underlying this theory is that an original and its translation are to be equivalent in meaning, and have an equivalent function. Three aspects of that meaning are particularly important: the semantic, the pragmatic and the textual aspect. Introducing the concept of function presupposes that there are elements in a text which, given appropriate tools, can reveal a text's function. A text's function is to be regarded as the application or use of a text in a particular context of situation. Text and context of situation are not really separate; the context of situation in which the text unfolds is encapsulated in the text through an inextricable connection between the social environment and the functional organization of language. If we want to analyze a text, it must therefore be referred to the particular situation enveloping it, and for this, the broad notion 'context of situation' must be broken down into manageable units.

One way of doing this is using the concepts of Field, Tenor and Mode – three sociolinguistic dimensions of the context of situation jointly characterizing a particular 'Register', or segment of language in use (see Steiner, 2004, who also works with the concept 'register'). Field captures social activity, subject matter or topic including differentiations of degrees of generality or specificity of vocabulary, and the type of verbs used. Tenor refers to the nature of the participants, the author and his or her addressees, the relationship between them in terms of social power and familiarity, the degree of emotional charge, and the author's temporal, social and geographical provenance, intellectual and affective stance, 'personal viewpoint' vis-à-vis the content he is portraying. Important here is the way these sociopsychological phenomena are expressed and reflected in such linguistic systems as modality, tense and aspect or deictic pronouns. Tenor also captures 'social attitude', evident in the text e.g. through different style levels (formal, informal, etc.). Mode refers to both the channel of communication, the spoken or written medium, with many in-between possibilities such as 'written to be read' or 'written to be spoken as if not written', and the degree to which participation is (linguistically) expressed between reader and writer, allowing for various mechanisms creating an (imaginary) dialogue inside a monologic text. Another important part of Mode is the way a text is made 'to hang together' e.g. via repetition, backwards and forwards referring processes inside the text, and the use of forms that take the text 'outside' into the author's and reader's world of experience.

The analysis of the original text and the production of the translation then consist of correlating patterns of linguistic features discovered in the texts with the three contextual register categories Field, Tenor and Mode. Before this analysis can be used to characterize the text's function, another analytic level, 'Genre', incorporated into the analytic scheme – in between, as it were, the Register concepts Field, Tenor and Mode, and the textual function – is to be taken into account. Genre enables one to relate a single textual exemplar to the class of texts with which it shares a common communicative purpose. While register captures the connections between a text and its immediate context, Genre connects the text with the 'macro-context' of the cultural community in which the text is embedded. This translation model is shown in Figure 7.1.

While the analytic process in this scheme yields a particular textual profile characterizing the individual textual function and enabling predictions about the genre shared with other texts, the question remains whether this function *can* in fact be maintained in the translation. This possibility will depend, we might argue, on the type of translation sought for the original. In the framework of the evaluation scheme

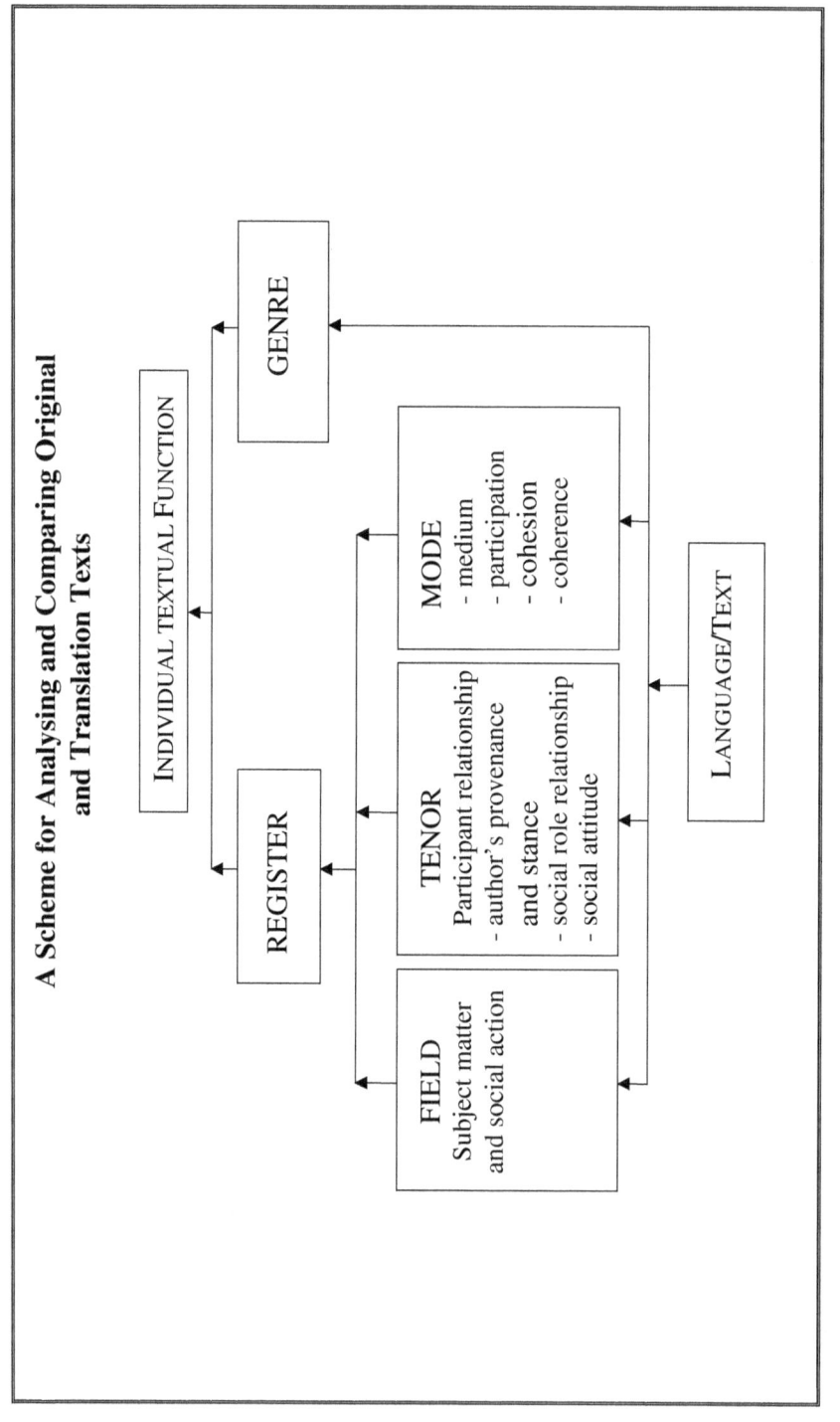

Figure 7.1 A scheme for analyzing and comparing original and translation texts

presented above, these two translation types are called *overt* and *covert* translation. We will look at these in the following section.

Two types of translation: Overt and covert

Translation involves the movement of texts across time and space, and whenever texts move, they also shift frames and discourse worlds. 'Frame' is a psychological concept and is, in a sense, the psychological pendant to the more 'socially conceived' concept of context, delimiting a class of messages or meaningful actions. A frame often operates unconsciously as an explanatory principle, i.e. any message that defines a frame gives receivers instructions in their interpretation of the message included in the frame. Similarly, the notion of a 'discourse world' refers to an overarching structure for interpreting meanings in certain ways.

Applying the concepts of frame and discourse world to the two types of translation, overt and covert translation, we can say that an overtly translated text is embedded in a new speech event, which gives it also a new frame. An *overt* translation resembles a case of 'language mention' (as opposed to 'language use'); the original is left as intact as possible given the need of expression in another language. Relating 'overt translation' to the four-tiered analytical scheme presented above (Function-Genre-Register-Language/Text), an original and its overt translation are to be and can be equivalent at the level of Language/Text, Register and Genre. At the level of the individual textual function, functional equivalence, while still possible, is however of a different nature: it can be described as merely enabling access to the function the original has in its discourse world or frame. But as this access is to be realized in a different language and takes place in the target linguistic and cultural community, a switch in discourse world and frame becomes necessary, i.e. the translation is differently framed, operates in its own frame and discourse world, and can thus reach at best 'second-level functional equivalence'. As this type of equivalence is, however, achieved though equivalence at the levels of Language/Text, Register and Genre, the original's frame and discourse world are co-activated, such that members of the target culture may 'eavesdrop', as it were, i.e. be enabled to appreciate the original textual function, albeit at a distance. In overt translation, the work of the translator is important and visible. As it is the translator's task to give target culture members an unadulterated impression of, and access to, the original text and its cultural impact on source culture members, the translator puts target culture members in a position to observe and/or judge this text 'from outside'. An example of such an overt translation would be a speech given by Winston Churchill at a particular time and a particular location during World War II. Any translation of this speech – a historic event – can never have an equivalent function, it can only give readers an idea of what the original may have meant for its addressees.

By contrast, in *covert* translation, a case of 'language use', the translator can and should attempt to re-create an equivalent speech event. The translation is to act as though it were not a translation. The task of the translator is, in a sense, to cheat and to mislead readers and hide the text's real origin. The translator himself remains invisible, hiding behind the 're-creation' of the original. In a covert translation, the function the original has in its frame and discourse world is to be reproduced as far as possible. A covert translation operates therefore quite 'overtly' in the frame and discourse world provided by the target culture, with no attempt being made to co-activate the discourse world in which the original unfolds. Covert translation is thus at the same time psycholinguistically less complex and more deceptive than overt translation. As true functional equivalence is aimed at, the original may be manipulated at the levels of Language/Text and Register via the use of a 'cultural filter' (see the next subsection). The result may be a very real distance from the original. While the original and its covert translation thus need not be equivalent at the levels of Language/Text and Register, they should be equivalent at the levels of Genre and the Individual Textual Function. Examples of covert translations are translations of advertisements which are to act as though they were originals in order to be as effective and persuasive as their originals. Overt translations are 'more straightforward', as the original can be 'taken over' unfiltered, as it were. Covert translations are pragmatically more complex, they involve the application of a 'cultural filter'.

The concept and function of a 'cultural filter'

A cultural filter is a means of capturing differences in culturally shared conventions of behavior and communication, preferred rhetorical styles and expectation norms in the source and target speech communities. Given the goal of achieving functional equivalence in covert translation, assumptions of cultural difference should be carefully examined before interventions in the original's meaning structure is undertaken by the translator. The unmarked assumption is one of cultural compatibility, unless there is evidence to the contrary. Such evidence can be provided by cross-cultural research which then gives substance to language-pair specific cultural filters. To take an example, in the case of the German and Anglophone linguistic and cultural communities, the cultural filter has been given some substance through empirical contrastive–pragmatic analyses, in which Anglophone and German communicative preferences were established along a set of dimensions such as directness versus indirectness, a focus on content versus an interpersonal focus, and explicitness versus implicitness of expression. In evaluating, for example, the translation of a request in an English original text 'Would you get out of there please' (said by a teacher to a student in a swimming pool) into German as 'Raus hier jetzt!', one would need to take the generally more direct and more content-oriented conventions of requesting in comparable institutional contexts and genres into account in order to assess the appropriateness of the cultural filtering undertaken in this translation.

While contrastive pragmatics and contrastive discourse analyses can make useful contributions to evaluating covert translations, it remains a challenge to assess the adequateness of applications of a cultural filter. Given the dynamic nature of communicative norms and the way research necessarily lags behind, translation critics will have to struggle to remain abreast of new developments if they want to be able to fairly judge the appropriateness of changes through the application of a cultural filter in a translation between two given languages.

Given the distinction between overt and covert translation, cultural transfer would only occur in overt translation, where cultural items are 'transported' from L1 to L2 acting as a sort of 'Verfremdung' in the translated text. In covert translation however, there will never be cultural transfer, only a sort of 'cultural compensation' for L1 cultural phenomena in L2 with the means of L2, and of course the application of a cultural filter whenever necessary and justifiable.

Distinguishing between a translation and a version

Over and above distinguishing between covert and overt translation, another distinction – between a translation and a version – is also important in translation evaluation. A version results from a deliberate turning away from the original; it becomes in a way a new original. Versions are generally produced in two cases: firstly, whenever a special function is overtly added in the process of translating to a translation text in order to reach a particular audience – as is, for example, the case with translated special editions for children or second language learners with deliberate omissions, additions, simplifications or different accentuations of certain aspects of the original, or with popularizations of specialist works designed for the lay public; secondly, a version results, whenever the 'translation' is given a special added purpose. Examples are interlingual versions, translated summaries or abstracts.

When we distinguish different types of translations and versions, we do not mean however that a particular text may be adequately translated in only one particular way. For instance, the assumption that a particular text necessitates either a covert or an overt translation clearly does not hold in any simple way: any text may at a certain time require an overt translation, i.e. even a text such as a tourist brochure – normally a candidate for covert translation – may be viewed as having an 'independent value' of its own that needs to be preserved as much as possible, when for instance its author has become, in the course of time, a distinguished figure, in which case the original text acquires the status of a sacrosanct document.

It seems to me that this theory can be fruitfully applied to using translation to increase pragmatic competence in a foreign language. Before I will expatiate on this, a brief look at how translation has been and still is used in foreign language teaching seems to be necessary.

How Translation Was Used in Foreign Language Teaching in the Past

Translation as the cross-linguistic technique par excellence has a long tradition as an exercise and a test of students' foreign language competence. Translation was and is in the center of the controversy about the role of the L1 in the classroom. A distinction commonly made is the one between translation *from* the foreign language into students' mother tongue and translation *into* the foreign language from the mother tongue. Translation from the foreign language was probably first used in the third century by elementary school teachers of Latin in the Greek communities of the Roman empire (Kelly, 1969: 172). During the early middle ages when Latin was still a 'living language' and the only medium of instruction in the schools, translation is hardly mentioned as a teaching technique. Once the vernaculars were being taught and vernacular translations of the classics gained in popularity, translation gained importance. During the late Middle Ages the technique of 'construing' was combined with translating into the classical languages: The dissection of sentences and words according to their grammatical functions was followed by an establishment of 'vernacular equivalents' with the resulting 'literal' translation being gradually changed into an acceptable vernacular sentence. This procedure became a keystone of classical language instruction – and its influence is felt even today in the habitual (infamous) association of translation and grammar.

At the end of the 18th century the teaching of Latin had turned into a highly formalized ritual full of grammatical rules. This type of instruction was then transferred onto those few modern languages that were beginning to be taught in the schools – although we have only very little information on translation in the teaching of modern languages up to the end of the 18th century, because these languages were usually acquired privately by direct contact with native speaker servants.

Translation *from* the foreign language was the major form of exercise up to the end of the 18th century, and translation *into* the foreign language gained major importance in the textbooks from the early 19th century onwards – the basis of the 'grammar-translation' method was laid. Grammatical rules were to be learnt through their application in the translation of mostly disconnected, artificially constructed sentences – a practice that did gross injustice not only to language as a living, functioning entity but also to translation as a mode of communication. In the latter half of the 19th century this practice provoked opposition by a number of language teaching theorists (among them Gouin and Vietor) who – stimulated by the newly emerging sciences of linguistics and psychology – advocated a more 'natural' approach to language teaching. They emphasized the importance of the spoken mode of the foreign language, and condemned the dominance of translation in foreign language teaching. They initiated the 'direct method movement' whose most extreme proponents made the exclusive use of the foreign language and the abolition of any form of translation one of their trademarks. Later, translation was again tolerated particularly at advanced levels. At the beginning of the 20th century a more balanced view of language teaching was propagated; there was no more *a priori* condemnation of translation: translation *from* the foreign language was used early on to 'make knowledge more exact', and translation *into* the foreign language was used as soon as a thorough knowledge of the foreign language could be assumed (Sweet, 1964: 197).

In the following decades, the main arguments *against* using translation were that translation into the foreign language hinders the practical command of the foreign language, and translation from the foreign language corrupts the command of the native language due to the restraining co-presence of foreign language items in the mind. Arguments *for* using translation in the foreign language classroom were that translation is a means of economically 'semanticising', i.e. efficiently conveying the meaning of foreign language items, and also testing them (Palmer, 1968) – however never as the 'daily bread of language instruction', but as an interesting change in a predominantly monolingual instruction. So despite the influence of the direct method's monolingual dogma, translation was never completely banned. In higher education, translation has in many countries remained important up to the present time: in the foreign language departments of universities, translation of (mostly) literary passages *into* the foreign language has always been widely (if often stealthily) used as a teaching technique and for examination purposes.

This does not mean that there was not continued criticism of the use of translation in foreign language learning and teaching, – particularly of the indiscriminate use of 'the prose' – mainly for its failure to promote natural and creative use of the foreign language. Such criticism gained ground with the advent of the Audiolingual Method which was based on the assumption that language is primarily oral and that communication is the primary purpose of all language learning. Oral skills were therefore most important, the native language was used as little as possible, and translation was rarely used – although never completely banned from the foreign language classroom. It was for instance used in translation drills and for explaining the meaning of foreign language dialogues. However, audiolingual teaching theorists also stigmatized translation as a harmful exercise because the 'intrusion' of the mother tongue would maximize interference and thus endanger the success of the process of learning a foreign language. The opposition to translation as a teaching technique also gained ground because translation was blamed for failing to produce the right kind of bilingualism: 'compound' instead of 'coordinate bilingualism'. For successful language learning achieved through coordinate bilingualism and an ability to 'think in the foreign language', translation was thought to be harmful. It distracts the learner from establishing a relationship between a sentence and the situation in which the sentence is uttered by forcing the learner to relate sentences in the foreign language to sentences in the native language (and vice versa), the result being an undesirable 'merged code'. Such claims along with the conceptual artifact 'compound-coordinate bilingualism' turned out to be unsubstantiated.

In the newer cognitive, communicative and pragmatic teaching trends, pleas have been made for using translation as a basis for exercises in contrastive analysis with advanced learners in order to develop an awareness of contrasts between native and foreign language items and structures (see Stern, 1983, who takes a rare, balanced attitude towards L1 use and contrastive techniques, and see Edmondson & House, 2006). However, alongside all these pro-translation voices there has always been and indeed still is a strong 'camp' of opponents to translation. They think translation is a thoroughly unnatural activity and a highly specialized art, which is either not at all or negatively related to the desired development of the four basic skills: listening, speaking, reading and writing. For beginning learners, translation if often taboo: it is a fifth skill, and as such is of no help in beginners' struggle for basic language proficiency. Particularly in translation from the foreign language it is only passive knowledge which is demanded from students, and this, it is often believed, will negatively influence any further active use of it.

Today the controversy about translation in the language classroom is far from settled, the two most important reasons being firstly that the nature of translation is still little understood by those who plead for or against its use. Any sensible discussion about the extent to which translation can be used in language teaching and the way in which it might be fruitfully used should be done on the basis of a thorough theoretical understanding of the nature of translation, the different types of translation, the limits of translatability, the means of assessing the quality of translation and so on. Secondly, translation is still far too often used to aim at linguistic competence alone, i.e. it is used to illustrate and explain grammatical rules and to drill certain constructions 'made up' for this purpose; to help teachers make students 'understand properly' often contextless linguistic items; to provide teachers with a handy means of large-scale testing of a variety of (mostly unspecified types of) knowledge and skills. In evaluating translations, it is mainly linguistic correctness that is measured. Such uses fail to exploit the real pedagogic usefulness of this complex cross-linguistic activity. It is the strong pragmatic component in translation that makes it so potentially useful in the teaching of foreign languages. In translation exercises one should therefore not only draw learners' attention to the formal properties of source and target sentences alone, but emphasize the importance of situational, contextual meanings. In the following section I will make several suggestions on how translation can be used in this way.

Using Translation to Increase L2 Pragmatic Competence

If translation is used in a way that its pragmatic potential is fully exploited, it would be carried out as an exercise in establishing functional, pragmatic equivalence by relating linguistic forms to their communicative functions as utterances in a context of situation and culture as described above. Translation would thus play an eminently useful role in developing learners' communicative competence. The use of translation in the foreign language classroom would be extended to embrace a whole range of *translation activities* involving, for instance, the explicit comparison of cultural phenomena in the source and target language communities; the creative production of both source and target language texts; the changing of the register dimensions Field, Tenor and Mode in the original, the translation or both; and guided context-sensitive evaluation of translations and versions.

In such a concept of translation activities, both receptive and productive aspects of communicative competence might be improved. All translation activities should however only be conducted with advanced students whose communicative competence is already so developed that they have an overview of the equivalence relations between the two languages and cultures in question. If in translation activities priority is given to the communicative use of language, language ceases to be an isolated subject but appears to be interlocked with other subjects, used to promote pragmatic and intercultural competence (see also Kramsch, 2006, who has recently pleaded for translation as a recommended activity). Translation activities would involve an amalgamation of foreign language and cultural study as well as other subjects so as to facilitate the use of a wide range of fields for the texts chosen. This would help develop a broad communicative competence in the foreign language.

Any activity involving translation can only be sensibly conducted at the level of text; only at this level can both linguistic and extralinguistic context be given full consideration, and only through using texts can the nature of equivalence relations in translation, and the overriding importance of establishing a textual profile for the original text before translating, be fully recognized.

Along with abandoning a preference for translating isolated sentences and lexicogrammatical analysis, another traditional educational belief should also be questioned: the customary differentiation between translation into, and translation from, the foreign language. These two directional 'translation types' are often said to differ in terms of difficulty: translation into a foreign language is considered to be more difficult because it presupposes an excellent knowledge of the foreign language, whereas translation from the foreign language is often thought to require less expertise in the foreign language. In the concept of translation activities I am suggesting here, the kind of 'treatment' of both the original and the translation texts invariably demands an advanced competence level for both translation directions. However, foreign source texts will obviously need more preparatory work with students i.e. a more detailed analysis and explanation of the linguistic–contextual peculiarities of the texts than native language source texts.

Given these general ideas about alternative pragmatic uses of translation in foreign language teaching, here now are some concrete suggestions of how to use translation in such a way as to improve learners' pragmatic competence in the L2.

Translation as a communicative event

Outside pedagogic contexts, translations are communicative actions that fulfill 'real' pragmatic functions such as enabling persons to understand otherwise incomprehensible texts. In translation activities that claim to be useful for developing communicative competence, translations would also need to fulfill such real pragmatic functions, and not mere didactic functions such as informing the teacher as 'translation commissioner' that a learner is able to produce a didactically equivalent text – equivalent according to norms set by the teacher. To convert a translation into a communicatively 'real' act, it needs to be embedded in a (simulated) communicative situation which has a certain plausibility for language learners. Here is a simple example in which students are asked to pretend to relay information to a monolingual speaker, and in which the translation tasks are fully contextualized: 'A neighbor who does not speak German has just received a letter from a German girl written in German. The neighbor has noticed in the letter that frequent reference is being made to the name of her son who is working for an English firm in Hamburg. The neighbor is anxious to understand what is written in the letter because she is afraid it might be bad news. Now she has asked you – a student of German – to give her both a quick summary of the content in English and to later write a "proper" translation for future reference.' In other words, the student is asked to produce an oral version (a résumé) of the source text and a written overt translation. Along this line, a whole range of situations can be constructed in which a 'real' communicative need is being simulated. The translations produced will then be analyzed, evaluated and discussed in groups.

Translation activities might also comprise producing original source texts, making use of learners' creative imagination and building on simulated communicative needs. Learners start from the function of a text and construct the text in accordance with this function and some other data characterizing the register dimensions Field, Tenor and Mode that contribute to this function, as well as from an outline of the content supplied to them. Here are a few simple examples. The teacher gives students the following assignment: 'Write a letter to a girl in another German city. The address of this person was given to you by a teacher. She is of your age and, like you, attends high school. In your letter you will try to win this person over as your new pen-friend, i.e. it is your task to make your letter as entertaining as possible. You will have to demonstrate your interest in your potential friend's personal life.' Following this first step, these native language letters will first be analyzed and then translated into the foreign language: 'Translate this letter covertly into Arabic, i.e. write the "same" letter to a potential pen friend in Muscat making all the necessary changes as to places you might want to see and as to your potential friend's way of life.'

If the dimensions of Field, Tenor or Mode are varied in assignments such as these, learners can be trained in a wide range of communicative situations. They may for instance be asked to write to the managing director of an advertising firm in the native country and request information about the size of the firm, its work routines, etc. This letter will then be analyzed and covertly translated into the foreign language. A maximal contextualization of such assignments can obviously be achieved if the letters are actually sent off.

Another translation activity based on the creation of a native language text is the writing of advertisements for different products, the collection of a corpus of such advertisements, the discussion of the assumptions underlying advertisements and their linguistic peculiarities, as well as their eventual covert translations and evaluations. Covert translations of advertisements imply that allowances are made for differences in the two language communities' geography, climate, history, economy, educational and cultural preferences, stereotypes and 'national characters'.

A more complicated variation of pragmatic translation activities consists of an analysis and translation of a given mother tongue source text followed by a deliberate change in the function of the source text (as it had been revealed in the analysis) followed by a new translation. Thus, a specialist scientific text may be converted into a scientific text directed at a lay audience – a case of intralingual overt version production followed by an interlingual activity. Various other changes along the register dimensions might be conducted in the production of source texts using the imagination of the students and on the basis of these, the original texts will be rewritten. Following this production of a new source text (a version of the original one) in the students' mother tongue, the students are asked to translate this new source text. Changes along the entire textual profile will be discussed in groups.

Other translation exercises include explicit comparisons between overt and covert translation procedures on the basis of the theoretical distinction previously made. Students may here be sensitized to the cultural transposition which may be necessitated in covert translation. Students can for instance be asked to write a letter to a friend in Spain in which they describe an amusing incident which centers on an English text that needs to be translated as part of the letter they are to write. Here are two examples: 'A student forges a letter allegedly coming from his parents. In the body of the letter he clearly, but unintentionally, reveals that it was written by her- or himself, e.g. through the choice of an inappropriate form of address or an incorrect pronominal reference to her- or himself', or 'A notice appears on a board in school with some ambiguity, as for instance in the following case: "The recreation room is to be closed for redecoration next week. Board games should be returned to Mr. Jones and balls to Mr. Smith."' In translating these texts, students will have to translate overtly, but as the function of the overall translation of the letter to the pen-friend is to amuse, the letter writer must seek to explain in the frame-letter how and why the original documents in their particular cultural contexts were funny.

In general, covert translation procedures should be preferred over overt ones in the context of developing communicative competence through translation activities. Thus source texts will have to be found or created that are 'living texts' encapsulating plausible 'linguistic social events' which address two presumably corresponding contemporary groups of addressees. Covert translation activities tend to be of greater interest for learners than literary texts that stem from faraway epochs and are often far too difficult to translate. Here we might also argue against the widespread belief in foreign language teaching circles that so-called 'authentic texts' be preferred to didactically 'manipulated' ones. If we believe in the usefulness of translation activities that embed translation exercises in communicative situations, then didactic manipulation connected with a 'willing suspension of disbelief' is necessary and indeed unavoidable. Through such didactic manipulation 'didactic authenticity' can be achieved, and this can be given preference in translation activities.

To sum up these suggestions for alternative uses of translation in foreign language teaching, an extension of 'translation proper' is advisable such that 'translation activities' now include the production of original texts, of oral and written versions, a deliberate change of register dimensions. If translation is used in this new sense, the 'fifth skill' can be usefully combined with the development of the four basic language skills and also used to promote other types of knowledge.

Translation and interaction

Using a pragmatic-discourse perspective on translation, one might also expose learners to an oral native language dialogue, which is analyzed and converted into a written text in the L2. Here is an example: learners listen to a dialogue in their mother tongue and analyze it on the basis of a set of discourse analytic categories. They then listen to and analyze comparable foreign language dialogues and discuss differences and similarities of interactional norms in the two languages on the basis of these analyses. The learners then create roleplays in their mother tongue based on the dialogues, enact them and translate them covertly into the target language. Finally, they produce written reports (versions) on the roleplays in the target language. In such translation activities, translation can be used in preparation of spontaneous interlingual and intercultural communication.

Another interactive translation activity uses the method of interactive thinking aloud. Pairs of learners jointly translate texts and verbalize their thoughts on their decision and solution processes during the translation process. Such joint translation activity is more motivating than thinking aloud in isolation while translating. Interactive translation tasks are preferable to the traditional boring sentence-by-sentence discussion of learners' translations by the teacher. Instead, learners themselves might be asked to evaluate their own and others' translations. Following their evaluation attempts, they will be asked to justify their decisions in a plenary discussion.

Conclusion

In the past, translation has too often been misused as a tool to improve language learners' linguistic knowledge of the foreign language system.

Its role in language teaching approaches has varied widely across the centuries – from heavy misuse in the grammar-translation method to a ban in direct and audiolingual methods. At the same time, however, translation has rather paradoxically continued to be used – at least in Germany – in higher education contexts as an easy option for grammatical and vocabulary practice and testing. Such uses of translation miss, however, as I have tried to argue, the point of this complex linguistic–pragmatic cross-linguistic activity. I have therefore suggested several alternative, pragmatic uses of translation to exploit the potential usefulness of translation for promoting learners' pragmatic competence and improving learners' ability to recognize and reflect on pragmatic contrasts between native and foreign languages and cultures.

References

Catford, J.C. (1965) *A Linguistic Theory of Translation*. London: Oxford University Press.
Edmondson, W.J. and House, J. (2006) *Einführung in die Sprachlehrforschung* (3rd edn). Tübingen: Francke.
Halliday, M.A.K. (1994) *An Introduction to Functional Grammar* (2nd edn). London: Arnold.
House, J. (1977) *A Model for Translation Quality Assessment*. Tübingen: Narr.
House, J. (1981) *A Model for Translation Quality Assessment* (2nd edn). Tübingen: Narr.
House, J. (1997) *Translation Quality Assessment. A Model Revisited*. Tübingen: Narr.
Kelly, L.G. (1969) *25 Centuries of Language Teaching*. Rowley, MA: Newbury House.
Koller, W. (1995) The concept of equivalence and the object of translation studies. *Target* 7, 191–222.
Koller, W. (2004) *Einführung in die Übersetzungswissenschaft* (7th edn). Tübingen: Quelle and Meyer.
Kramsch, C. (2006) Teaching local languages in global settings. The European challenge. *Fremdsprachen Lehren und Lernen* 35, 201–210.
Nida, E. and Taber, C. (1969) *The Theory and Practice of Translation*. Leiden: Brill.
Palmer, H.E. (1968) *The Scientific Study and Teaching of Languages*. London: Oxford University Press.
Steiner, E. (2004) *Translated Texts: Properties, Variants, Evaluations*. Frankfurt/Main: Lang.
Stern, H.H. (1983) *Fundamental Concepts of Language Teaching*. London: Oxford University Press.
Sweet, H. (1964) *The Practical Study of Languages* (1st edn 1899). London: Oxford University Press.

Chapter 8
Effects on Pragmatic Development Through Awareness-raising Instruction: Refusals by Japanese EFL Learners

SACHIKO KONDO

Introduction

The importance of pragmatic competence in communication has been widely acknowledged in various models of language ability (Bachman, 1990; Canale, 1983; Canale & Swain, 1980). The controversy concerns whether 'pragmatics' can be taught in the language classroom. As pragmatic competence has a close relationship with the sociocultural values and beliefs of the country or the community where the target language is spoken, English as a Second Language (ESL) learners or those learners who live in the target community certainly have an advantage in acquiring this knowledge (Kondo, 1997). They have a better chance of exposure to adequate and abundant input than English as a Foreign Language (EFL) learners. Does this mean that second/foreign (L2) pragmatics cannot be taught in the EFL classroom? Kasper (1997) and Rose and Kasper (2001) extensively discuss results of previous studies on pragmatic instruction and conclude that 'pragmatics' can indeed be taught. Tateyama *et al.* (1997) and Wildner-Bassett (1994) demonstrate that pragmatic routines are teachable even to beginning foreign language learners.

Teaching target norms, which learners are then forced to use, does not seem to be an appropriate way to teach pragmatics, as learners' pragmatic choices are connected with their cultural identities. In her list of the goals that instruction in pragmatics should aim for, Kasper (1997) points out, quoting Siegal (1996), that 'Second language learners do not merely model native speakers with a desire to emulate, but rather actively create both a new interlanguage and an accompanying identity in the learning process'. Kasper further comments that 'Successful communication is a matter of optimal rather than total convergence.' In order to achieve optimal convergence for each learner, it is important to give them the opportunity in the classroom to reflect on their own linguistic choices, compare those choices with pragmatic features of the target language and then to try out the various other options available to them.

One approach that may help learners create their own interlanguage is awareness raising. Rose (1994) introduces active video-viewing activities and suggests that this approach, which promotes pragmatic consciousness-raising, has the distinct advantage of providing learners with a foundation in some of the central aspects of the role of pragmatics, and that it can be used by teachers of both native speakers and non-native speakers. Bardovi-Harlig (1996), endeavoring to bridge the gap between pragmatic research and pedagogy, stresses the importance of helping learners increase their pragmatic awareness, rather than perpetuating the model of a teacher-centered classroom where the teachers 'tell' and the learners 'receive' information.

The present study investigates how Japanese EFL learners' pragmatic behavior changes and how their awareness of pragmatic aspects of their own and the target language is raised through instruction. The instructional methods employed in this investigation were specifically designed, utilizing research-based teaching material, to develop learners' pragmatic abilities and to raise their consciousness of those abilities.

The Present Study

Research goal

Historically, only very limited materials for teaching pragmatics to Japanese EFL learners have been available. The present study aims to examine instructional effects after teaching with methods and materials that were specifically developed for teaching pragmatics to Japanese EFL learners. The material is intended to raise learners' pragmatic awareness and engage them in creating their own interlanguage identity. The instructional design also provides ample opportunity for learners to practice and experiment in different contexts. In the present study, the following goals will be pursued:

(1) to explore whether learners' use of refusal strategies change after explicit instruction; and
(2) to explore what kinds of pragmatic aspects the learners become aware of through explicit instruction.

Participants

The main participants in this study were 38 Japanese learners of English (JE). All were second-year students majoring in English at a Japanese women's junior college. Their approximate English proficiency, tested before the study began, was intermediate–low. None of these JE students had lived abroad for more than two months. Another group of participants were 46 Americans (AE), all of whom were college students in California or Arizona.

Instruction

Thirty-eight Japanese students in two separate classes (18 in each class) received instruction on speech acts once a week for 12 weeks. Each lesson was 90 minutes long. The contents of the 12 lessons were: (1) compliments & response to compliments, (2) thanking, (3) interaction (compliments & response to compliments and thanking), (4) requests, (5) refusals, (6) interaction (requests and refusals), (7) complaints, (8) apologies, (9) interaction (complaints and apologies), (10) proposals, (11) disagreements and (12) interaction (proposals and disagreements).

Teaching material

A textbook developed by Sophia University Applied Linguistics Research Group (Yoshida *et al.*, 2000) was used for instruction. The author of the present paper is one of the authors of the textbook. This book, called *Heart to Heart: Overcoming Barriers in Cross-Cultural Communication* (H to H), was developed based on the results of pragmatic research and specifically aims to teach cross-cultural pragmatics to Japanese EFL learners. Each lesson is organized progressively in five phases: Feeling, Doing, Thinking, Understanding and Using. These phases are designed to help students recognize that 'speaking is doing', to think about their own language use, and to discover common and different aspects of conducting speech acts between Japanese and Americans. In addition, various class activities, such as listening comprehension and roleplays, are provided to improve their linguistic skills (see Kondo, 2003 for more information on the teaching methods).

Goals of instruction

(1) Raising awareness that misunderstandings can be caused by differences in performing speech acts between Japanese and Americans.
(2) Raising learners' awareness of what they know already and encouraging them to use their universal or transferable L1 pragmatic knowledge in appropriate L2 contexts.
(3) Teaching the appropriate linguistic forms that are likely to be encountered in performing speech acts.

Procedure of speech act chapters

(1) Feeling (warm-up) phase
   (a) Listening to two different dialogs and answering questions
(2) Doing phase
   (a) Discourse Completion Task and roleplay

(3) Thinking phase
   (a) Looking at classification of different types of a particular speech act
   (b) Listening to dialogs and writing down key expressions of each type
   (c) Analyzing their own speech act performance according to types
(4) Understanding phase (cross-cultural communication notes)
   (a) Looking at the graphs and making comparisons of speech act performances by Japanese, Americans, and Japanese learners of English
   (b) Discussion in class
(5) Using phase
   (a) Listening and roleplay practice of model dialogs
   (b) Discourse completion and roleplay tasks for new situations

Description of the activities in speech act chapters

1. Feeling (warm-up) phase

The listening comprehension task in this phase is designed to help students to get the feeling of the speech act dealt with in the chapter. The learners hear two different dialogs in a sample hypothetical speech situation and are asked to answer questions about what is happening and how the learner feels about the two dialogs. One of the dialogs represents a typical American way of conducting the speech act concerned, and the other one represents how JE typically respond. In this activity, students are shown and made to understand that the speech act can be realized in different ways. They are then asked to reflect on their particular preference about the way it is conducted.

2. Doing phase

The learners are presented with another hypothetical speech situation (called Situation 1) in which they are asked to respond in a way similar to a Discourse Completion Task, and to roleplay the situation with their classmates. The aim of this phase is for each learner to assess what she can do with her present knowledge prior to any instruction dealing with cultural differences or linguistic expressions.

3. Thinking phase

In this phase students are asked to reflect on and analyze their own speech act performance. H to H presents the learners with various ways of performing the act under consideration. These classifications are simplified versions of 'Speech Act Sets' (Olshtain & Cohen, 1983), which are often used in the research of 'Interlanguage Pragmatics' (Cohen, 1996; Kasper & Blum-Kulka, 1993; Kasper & Rose, 1999). With these, the learners can examine the strategies they used in Situation 1 in the 'Do the

Act' section. An exercise is provided here to help students categorize which expression they used falls into which type of speech act strategy before they analyze their own performance.

For example, in 'refusal' the textbook says, 'Most refusals include expressions stating the reason why you are refusing. The following types of expressions can be used together with expressions stating the reason for refusing.' Then the following five types of strategies and expressions for each strategy (Table 8.1) are introduced (Yoshida *et al.*, 2000: 32). These classifications are simplified versions of 'semantic formulas' and 'adjuncts' (Beebe *et al.*, 1990),[1] which are often used in the research of refusals.

4. Understanding phase (cross-cultural communication notes)

In this phase the students are encouraged to discover the characteristic differences that exist between Japanese and American English when various speech acts are performed. The data presented here come from the following three groups of college students who filled out Discourse Completion Tasks for Situation 1 (see Figure 8.2 on p. 167):

(1) 50 Americans speaking English (A)
(2) 50 Japanese learners of English speaking English (JE)
(3) 50 Japanese speaking Japanese (J)

Students are asked to compare these three groups and discuss similarities and differences in their way of conducting speech acts. The important point in this phase is that the task is designed so that students

Table 8.1 Refusal Types in Yoshida *et al.* 2000. p. 32

Type A: Positive Opinion	That sounds wonderful, but ...
	I'd like/love to, but ...
	I wish I could, but ...
Type B: Thanking	Thank you for the invitation.
	Thanks, but ...
Type C: Apology	I'm sorry, but ...
Type D: Alternative	Maybe some other time.
	Perhaps next time.
Type E: Direct Refusal	I can't go.
	I can't make it.
+ Reason	I already have other plans.
	I have to ...

are involved in active thinking, instead of passively reading descriptions on cultural differences. The students are also asked to analyze the data in graph form, which has the merit of helping them avoid extreme stereotyping, as the graphs show certain tendencies rather than 'one or zero' phenomena. After discussions in small groups, I ask group leaders to share what they talked about with the rest of the class. They raise various issues, such as 'Pragmatic Transfer'[2] (Kasper, 1992; Kasper & Blum-Kulka, 1993), lack of pragmatic or linguistic knowledge, etc. The details of these discussions will be presented in the second part of the 'Results and Discussion' section of this paper.

5. Using phase

Having completed the four previous phases, the students by this time have received sufficient exposure to the vocabulary and expressions that can be used in performing the speech act. They would also be able to use them more or less in accordance with the tendencies seen among native speakers. The aim of the using phase is to provide students with a chance to practice what they have learned up to this point.

First, the students listen to some model dialogs and then participate in roleplaying. Then new situations are provided so that the students can practice writing and roleplaying their own responses. I encourage students to go around the classroom and interact with many partners so that they have sufficient practice. I also ask a few pairs to perform in front of the class so that other students and I can provide helpful comments on their performance. The students end their practice not by just memorizing and repeating what can be called 'an ideal model dialog', but by creating a dialog reflecting both their own identity and the knowledge they acquired in class.

Interaction chapters

H to H is organized around Speech Act chapters and Interaction chapters. Interaction chapters follow every second speech act chapter, and are intended to provide students with a chance to review what they have learned in the two previous speech act chapters and to participate in activities with a much higher interactional and creative component.

Data acquisition

Pre-test and Post-test for Japanese Learners of English (JE)

Pre-test and post-test were administered before and after the 12-week treatment, respectively. The test instrument used was the Oral Discourse Completion Task (ODCT), which requires students to read a written description of a situation and to say aloud what they would say in that situation into a tape recorder. The ODCT consists of eight items, one from each speech act previously instructed. The same situations were used for both pre- and post-test. Situations were given both in English and Japanese to avoid misunderstandings. Students were asked not to write anything down and not to consult a dictionary before they spoke.

Assessment Task for Americans (AE)
Americans (AE) were administered the Written Discourse Completion Task. They were asked to write what they would say in actual conversation rather than what they thought they should say. They completed the same situations as were given to JE subjects.

Discussion data
The classroom discussions conducted in Japanese in the Understanding Phase were audio-taped. First, a tape recorder was placed in one of the discussion groups. Then, all the presentations by each group representative on the content of their group discussions were audio-taped. The same procedure was followed in both classes.

Data analysis

Pre-test, post-test and AE data
Responses to the ODCTs by JE were transcribed for analysis. Out of 38 students who were in the class, 35 students took both the pre and post-test. Responses to the Discourse Completion Task by 45 Americans were analyzed. In the present study, only the following 'refusal' item was analyzed.

Situation 1: A friend of yours, Jennifer, asks you to go on a ski trip with her and her friends next weekend, but you don't feel like going because you don't like some of the people who are going.

The classification used by Kondo (2000, 2001), which is a modified version of the classification developed by Beebe *et al.* (1990),[3] was used for the data analysis (Table 8.2). The number of subjects who used each strategy was counted.

Discussion data
Recordings of learners' discussions were transcribed for analysis and were translated into English for presentation here.

Results and Discussion

Choices of refusal strategies by Americans, learners before instruction and learners after instruction

Figure 8.1 shows the percentage of subjects who used each strategy. Exact numbers and percentages are shown in Appendix 8.1.

Table 8.2 Classification of refusals (semantic formula)

Direct refusals (e.g. 'No', 'I can't', 'I don't think I can')	[Direct]
Statement of regret (e.g. 'I'm sorry')	[Regret]
Statement of positive opinion (e.g. 'I'd love to', 'I wish I could')	[Positive]
Excuse, reason, explanation (e.g. 'I have to study for the test')	[Account]
Gratitude (e.g. 'Thank you')	[Gratitude]
Statement of future acceptance (e.g. 'Perhaps some other time')	[Future]
Indefinite reply (e.g. 'I'm not sure', 'I don't know')	[Indefinite]
Statement of alternative (e.g., 'How about the movies')	[Alternative]
Statement of empathy (e.g. 'No offence to you')	[Empathy]
Good wish to hearer (e.g. 'Have a nice trip', 'Hope you have fun')	[Good]

The words in [ ] will be used to indicate each category in short

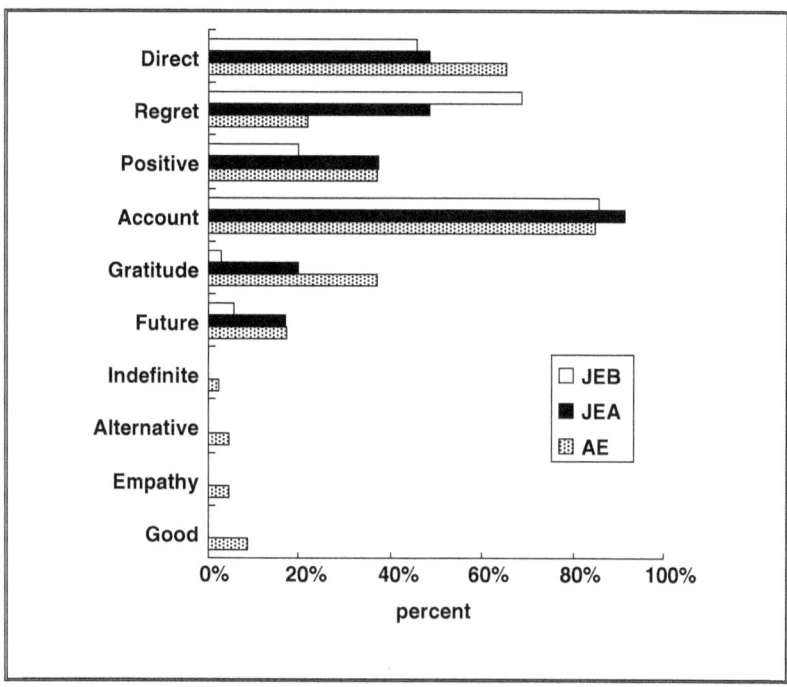

Figure 8.1 Use of strategies by JEB, JEA and AE

Comparison between Japanese EFL learners before instruction and Americans

The comparison between Americans (AE) and Japanese learners before instruction (JEB) shows that there are differences in their choices of strategies, which is consistent with the findings of Kondo (2000), who analyzed how facework[4] in refusal situations is accomplished by Japanese EFL learners and Americans. Japanese learners before treatment preferred using 'Regret', expressions such as 'I'm sorry', more than Americans (JEB 69%, AE 22%). This is probably caused by cultural norms and the tendency of Japanese to prefer to humble themselves to appeal to the empathy of the hearer in order to restore rapport with others (Kondo, 1997; Kumagai, 1993). On the other hand, Americans used 'Positive Opinion', 'Gratitude' and 'Future Acceptance' more often than JEB. This indicates that Americans prefer to use such positive politeness strategies (Brown & Levinson, 1987)[5] more than Japanese when doing facework in refusal situations. The most frequently used strategy was 'Account' for both Americans and JEB. The percentage of those who used this strategy did not differ much between the two groups (JEB 86%, AE 85%).

The followings are examples of responses given by an American and a Japanese learner before instruction respectively.

(1) American Subject 12

Oh, I wish I could, Jennifer, but I have so much catching up to do on my
    [Positive Opinion]   [Account]
studies... thanks for inviting me, though. Hope you guys have a good time.
        [Gratitude]   [Good Wish]

(2) JEB Subject 26

    Sorry, I can't go to ski trip. Because I have a promise the day.
    [Regret] [Direct]   [Account]

American Subject 12 used four types of strategies: a statement of positive opinion, an account, an expression of gratitude and a good wish to hearer. Facework is accomplished by a set of various positive politeness strategies, showing interest in the interlocutor and in what he or she has offered. On the other hand, JEB 26 prefaces her refusal by the expression of regret, 'Sorry', which is a negative politeness strategy. This is followed by direct refusal and an account. Overall, JEB used fewer strategies, resulting in a shorter utterance length than the Americans.

Comparison of choice of strategies between learners before instruction and learners after instruction

The comparison between JEB and JEA shows that there were instructional effects on their pragmatic behavior. 'Regret' was used less frequently by JEA (49%) than by JEB (69%), which demonstrates a change toward the pattern of AE (22%). Three strategies which were underused by JEB, 'Positive Opinion', 'Gratitude' and 'Future Acceptance', were used more frequently after instruction, which also is a move toward the AE use. 'Positive Opinion', expressions such as 'I'd love to' and 'I wish I could', were used by 20% of JEB. However, after pragmatic instruction, 37% of JEA used this strategy, making the percentage exactly the same as its use by AE subjects (37%). 'Gratitude', expressions such as 'thank you', was used by only 3% of JEB, which increased to 20% after instruction, whereas 37% AE used this strategy. 'Future Acceptance', such as 'Maybe some other time', was used by 6% of the JEB, and after instruction the percentage increased to 17%, again exactly the same percentage as Americans (17%).

Strategies which were used by a small number of Americans and by none of the JEB, 'Conditions for Acceptance', 'Indefinite Reply', 'Alternative', 'Empathy' and 'Good Wish', were not taught in the program. Unsurprisingly, none of the Japanese learners after instruction (JEA) used these strategies. This indicates that, unless pragmatic strategies are explicitly taught, they are not likely to be used by learners.

The frequent use of 'Regret' by JEB (69%) shows a strong preference for this strategy by Japanese learners. Although the percentage decreased to 49% after instruction, which certainly was a change toward Americans' way of use (22%), it still shows relatively strong preference by Japanese learners compared to Americans. This indicates that sometimes learners express their identities as Japanese by use of certain strategies they strongly prefer.

Content of accounts

Looking into the content of 'Account', there were interesting changes in learners' use of this strategy. Findings in previous studies such as Beebe *et al.* (1990) and Kondo (2000) suggest that Japanese learners' accounts are less specific than American ones. Beebe *et al.* (1990: 66) report that 'Japanese excuses seem to be less specific than American excuses, and this appears to transfer into the English of Japanese speakers'.

In the present study, specific and unspecific accounts were categorized according to the following definitions:

> Specific: identifying a specific event or state that prevents them from accepting invitations (e.g., 'Next weekend I am going to Monterey Park with my friend.' 'I need to study for the Physics test.')

Unspecific: giving vague reasons for refusals, not specifying place, time, or parties involved (e.g., 'I am busy.' 'I have an appointment.' 'I've already made plans.' 'I have a lot of stuff to do.')

It should be noted here that it is not at all easy to classify every account into these two categories; in reality specificity of accounts fall along a continuum. For example, both 'I have already other plans' and 'My family has already made plans' will be categorized as 'unspecific', however the former is more unspecific than the latter because the latter specifies that 'family' is involved in the event. This issue will be further discussed later in the analysis.

Table 8.3 shows the number of participants who used each category of accounts. The percentage of participants out of the total number of participants who used the 'Account' strategy in each group is shown in parentheses in the table.

The comparison between AE and JEB shows that, as was found in previous studies, fewer Japanese learners use specific accounts than Americans (43.3% versus 51.3%). An interesting finding was that JEA used more unspecific and less specific accounts than before instruction. Further analysis into the content and actual wordings of accounts showed characteristic differences between JEB and JEA. Among unspecific accounts that JEB used, the most frequently used content was 'I have a promise' and 'I don't feel like going'. Four subjects used the former and another four subjects used the latter expression, out of seventeen who gave unspecific accounts (see Example 2 in the previous section). 'I have a promise' is probably a direct translation of '*Yakusoku ga aru node* (Promise exists so ...)', which is an expression that stops in the middle of an utterance leaving the rest vague in order to soften a refusal and make it more polite. The expression, which does not specify the party involved, and which avoids the direct refusal, is commonly used in Japanese refusals, and 'I have a promise' is likely to be a transfer from this Japanese expression. As for the expression, 'I don't feel like going', learners obviously copied and used it from descriptions of the situation in the ODCT (See the description of Situation 1 on p. 159 for exact wordings).

Table 8.3 Number of participants who used specific or unspecific accounts

	AE, N =46	*JEB*, N =35	*JEA*, N =35
Specific	20 (51.3%)	13 (43.3%)	11 (34.4%)
Unspecific	19 (48.7%)	17 (56.7%)	21 (65.6%)
Total	39	30	32

Table 8.4 Examples of accounts used in the textbook

1.	I already have other plans.
2.	My family has already made plans.
3.	I've got to work this weekend.
4.	I can't afford to go on a ski trip right now. I used all my money for my new car.
5.	I've been invited to a party on Saturday.
6.	I need to do homework for my biology class.

Source: Yoshida *et al.* (2000: 32, 33 and 35)

An analysis of accounts offered by JEA found obvious influences of the textbook on their account choices. Table 8.4 shows the examples that appeared in the textbook: 1 and 2 are classified as unspecific, and 3–6 are classified as specific according to the definition used in the present study.

It is interesting to note that although the textbook examples included two unspecific versus four specific responses, 65.6% of the learners who used account strategy chose unspecific accounts. The most frequently used accounts by JEA were 'I already have other plans' by six subjects, followed by 'I'm busy' by four and 'My family has already made plans' by three. This indicates that learners' choice of account expressions was strongly influenced by the examples in the textbook, but they did prefer to model their own responses on the unspecific examples. Only one JEA subject used 'I have a promise', compared to four before instruction, and no JEA used 'I don't feel like going'. Three JEA said they had to do homework, without specifying for which subject, and these have been categorized as unspecific accounts in the present analysis. It is interesting to note that although the textbook example, 'I need to do homework for my biology class', was specific, learners modified it to create a more unspecific version which did not specify the name of the subject being studied. It probably is the case that Japanese learners feel that expressions like 'I need to do homework' or 'I have to study for a test' are specific enough. These expressions are obviously more specific than 'I have a promise' or 'I don't feel like going' in the continuum of specificity, although they are all categorized within unspecific accounts in the present research. I can conclude from the analysis of the content of accounts that, although the textbook may have been influential, learners' preferences for unspecific accounts still remain to some extent even after instruction.

Individual comparisons of before instruction and after instruction

Looking at individual learners' actual wordings in the present data can give us some insight into their pragmatic development. Here are some examples:

(3) Subject 1
JEB: I'm sorry. I have to go grandfather's house with my family.
JEA: Next weekend? Oh, I'm sorry, Jennifer. But my family already made plan. I'm sorry, I can't come. Maybe some other time. Thank you for the invitation.

Subject 1 used only two strategies, 'Regret' and 'Account', before instruction. After instruction, however, she used five kinds of strategy, 'Regret', 'Account', 'Direct', 'Future Acceptance' and 'Gratitude'. It is interesting to note that she not only increased the number of strategies she used, but also used a discourse marker, 'Oh', to intensify her regret and an address term, 'Jennifer', to enhance positive politeness (Brown & Levinson, 1987) by showing intimacy to her interlocutor. Another interesting point is that she used the 'Regret' strategy twice, which seems to be another case of transfer from Japanese and a move away from the American style of doing refusals. Kondo (1997), in a study of apology, shows that multiple uses of the expression 'I'm sorry' can be predominantly analyzed as transfers from Japanese. While her use of account before instruction is specific, her use after instruction is unspecific, adopting one of the examples in the textbook.

(4) Subject 7
JEB: I'm sorry, I can't go on a ski trip. I'm very busy. I must do something.
JEA: I would like to go, but I need to do my homework. Thank you for the invitation.

Before instruction, Subject 7, in addition to 'Account', used 'Regret' and 'Direct' strategies. However, after instruction, instead of these two strategies, she used 'Positive Opinion' and 'Gratitude'. Before instruction, she mentioned the actual object of the invitation, 'a ski trip', which usually is not mentioned in American refusals. On the other hand, she reduced the directness of her refusal by not mentioning the object. What is more, her 'Account' after instruction, 'I need to do my homework', is more specific than before instruction, 'I'm very busy. I must do something.' Still, she did not specify for which subject she needs to do homework.

(5) Subject 30
JEB: I'm afraid I can't. I have to study for test next Monday.
JEA: That sounds good, but I have a previous appointment with my family. Thank you for inviting me though.

While Subject 30 used 'Direct' and 'Account' strategies before instruction, she has come to use 'Positive Opinion', 'Gratitude' and 'Account' after instruction. Linguistic expressions such as 'That sounds good' and 'Thank you for ... though' are ones that she learned in the program, and she has successfully acquired those expressions. Both of her accounts before and after instruction are categorized as 'unspecific' in the analysis because she specified neither the subject to study nor the kind of appointment she has with her family.

(6) Subject 33
JEB: I'm sorry. I have a promise.
JEA: That's sounds wonderful. Thanks, but I already have other plans.

With her 'Account', Subject 33 used 'Regret' before but used 'Positive Opinion' and 'Gratitude' after instruction. Although both of her accounts are unspecific, she changed the wordings from 'I have a promise', which is probably a direct translation of Japanese *'Yakusoku ga aru node'*, to 'I already have other plans', which is an expression from the textbook.

Individual comparisons of learners' choice of strategies reveal that learners increased the number of strategies they used and the lengths of their utterances are longer after instruction. The combination of 'Regret' and 'Account' was the most favored before instruction. On the other hand, learners after instruction combined more strategies to conduct refusals, especially positive politeness strategies such as 'Positive Opinion', 'Account', 'Gratitude' and 'Future Acceptance'.

Awareness raised through class discussions

Learners' discussions after they had analyzed their own speech act performance and the data (see Figure 8.2) presented in the textbook reveal that learners have come to be aware of several pragmatic aspects related to cross-cultural understanding through instruction.

In each class, students were divided into four groups for discussions, each group consisting of four to five students. After group discussions, a spokesperson from each group was requested to provide a summary of that group's discussion to the rest of the class.

During the early stage of their discussions, learners evaluate a graph in the textbook, which shows the speech act strategies used by the three subject groups: Americans speaking English (A), Japanese learners of English speaking English (JE) and Japanese speaking Japanese (J). Almost all the discussion groups noted that Americans use the strategies of 'Positive Opinion', 'Thanking' and 'Alternative' more frequently than Japanese speaking English and Japanese speaking Japanese. They mentioned that, on the other hand, Japanese use an 'Apology'[6] strategy

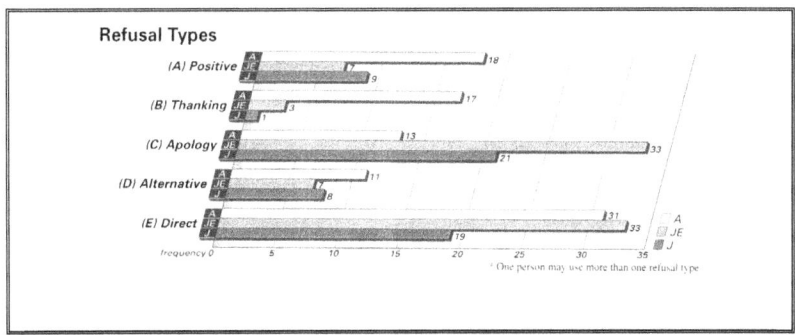

Figure 8.2 Refusal Types and Frequency in Yoshida *et al.* 2000. p. 34

much more often than Americans do (see Table 8.1 for types of strategies).

The following excerpt from the discussion of one group, especially Lines 1 and 2, which occurred at the very beginning of their discussion, illustrates the point. (Excerpts from 1 to 9 were translated from Japanese by the author of the paper. The letters in bold are the pragmatic aspects comprising the points of analysis.)

Excerpt 1

1 S1: Americans use strategies such as [Thanking] and [Positive Opinion] often. On the
      Strategy
2   other hand Japanese like to apologize.
3 S2: We apologize. That's right.
4 S3: And Americans make various comments. Americans use various strategies first to
      Length of Utterance   **Strategy**
5   make a listener feel comfortable, and then refuse. They make long comments first.
      Politeness   **Length of Utterance**
6   On the other hand, Japanese apologize first. This makes the listener feel
                                        Politeness
7   disappointed.
8 S4: That's right.

In this part, the students talk about one pragmatic aspect, that is, the 'length of utterance'. Grice (1975), in his pragmatic theory of 'Cooperative Principle', lists four maxims of conversation that participants in any conversation should adhere to; these maxims are quality, quantity, relevance and manner. Inappropriate utterance length can be a violation of a maxim of 'quantity' or/and 'manner'.[7] Blum-Kulka and Olshtain (1986), studying the relationship between utterance length and pragmatic failure, suggest that cultures differ in the way they judge adherence to the

Gricean maxims, and therefore they are subject to cultural variation. In Line 4 [S3] says 'Americans make various comments' and again in Line 5 'they make long comments first'. By her use of terms like 'comfortable' (Line 5) and 'disappointed' (Line 7), [S3] exhibits her awareness that the length of utterance has something to do with attending to the 'face' (Brown & Levinson, 1987) of an interlocutor. They realize that the longer utterance and the use of various speech act strategies are politeness strategies for Americans and that the short responses that Japanese learners give might sound impolite to the Americans.

Another pragmatic aspect raised by the learners in their discussions was 'Pragmatic Transfer', an influence from the learners' native language and culture on their interlanguage pragmatic knowledge and performance (Kasper & Blum-Kulka, 1993). The following excerpt illustrates this point.

Excerpt 2

1 S1: Japanese learners don't say "thank you." They just say, "I'm sorry."
   Strategy
2 S2: Even in Japanese we don't say "*arigato* (thank you)."
   Pragmatic Transfer
3 S1: No, we don't say that.
4 S4: We don't say "*arigato* (thank you)."
5 S3: I wonder if Americans who speak Japanese say "*arigato*" in refusal situations.
   Pragmatic Transfer
6 S1: I wonder if it is so.
7 S3: This book doesn't tell us about that.
8 S1: I think it would be interesting to see the same kind of data taken from American
9   learners of Japanese. We can request Prof. Kondo to have research on Americans
10   who speak Japanese.

[S1] observes in Line 1 that Japanese learners of English do not say 'thank you'. [S2] then points out in Line 2 that Japanese speaking Japanese do not say '*arigato* (thank you)' either, suggesting the possibility of pragmatic transfer from the native language. They expand their discussion further and talk about the reverse possibility that Americans might transfer their native language behavior in refusal in speaking Japanese (Lines 5–10).

The discussion on 'thanking' strategy continues and it provokes awareness of still other pragmatic aspects. The following comes directly after their discussion in Excerpt 2.

Excerpt 3

1 S4: We don't say "*arigato*" much even in Japanese, so we can't say it in English.
   Pragmatic Transfer
2   We just say "*Gomen, gomen.* (I'm sorry, I'm sorry.)"

3 S3: That's all we say.
4 S2: It sounds blunt.
   Politeness
5 S3: But it would sound strange if we say *"arigato"* in Japanese refusal.
   Appropriateness
6 S1: If we hear *"arigato"*, we feel that the person is accepting, not refusing.
   Misunderstanding
7 S3: So these expressions are different among cultures.
   Culture

In discussion (Excerpt 3) the students bring up the fact that Japanese do not say 'thank you' in refusals, either in English or Japanese. Then [S4] in Line 1 uses a discourse marker 'so' to mark a causal relation between Japanese behavior when speaking in their native language and English, and confirms that it is a case of 'Pragmatic Transfer' from Japanese. [S3] (Line 5) adds that saying *'arigato'* in a Japanese refusal is not appropriate and [S1] (Line 6) follows that such inappropriate use can cause misunderstandings. [S3] (Line 7) concludes this discussion by saying that these pragmatic features are culture-specific.

It was repeatedly mentioned by the students in class that Japanese speakers often use an 'apology' strategy in both Japanese and English. The following excerpt presents an illustration of a student's belief about why Japanese prefer this strategy.

Excerpt 4
1 S3: Japanese learners like to use [Apology] strategy most. They are obedient.
   Strategy
2 S1: Are they obedient?

[S3] (Line 1) says *'sunaodane* (They are obedient.)' to explain why Japanese learners prefer apology. She probably feels that in Japanese culture it is valued to be obedient, and that is the reason why the Japanese often say 'I'm sorry'. The previous studies on apologies (Kondo, 1997; Kumagai, 1993; Kumatoridani, 1993) support this view, suggesting that the Japanese preference for the expression 'I'm sorry' is meant to maintain harmony with an interlocutor by humbling themselves. Japanese prefer this humble approach rather than taking a rational explanatory approach to restore the relationship with an interlocutor. [S1] questions this analysis by saying 'Are they obedient?', but unfortunately the discussion on this point ends here and the students do not expand it further.

The next excerpt indicates that some of the subjects have attributed short responses by Japanese learners to their lack of knowledge about English refusal strategies.

Excerpt 5
1 S1: Japanese learners know few refusal expressions. They know only "I'm sorry."
  Lack of Knowledge
2 S4: That's right. And it sounds somehow cold.
  Politeness
3 S2: Japanese learners use [Direct] strategy. They say, "I can't" directly, because "I'm
4   sorry" is the only expression they know.
  Lack of Knowledge

Both [S1] (Line 1) and [S2] (Line 4) agree that one of the reasons why Japanese learners do not use various refusal strategies is their lack of knowledge about American English refusals. Again, the possibility of threatening others' face by being impolite is brought up here by [S4].

After group discussions, a representative from each group was asked to present a summary of their group discussion. One of the points brought up in this section was the semantic content of speech act strategies. The following is an example:

Excerpt 6
In Japanese we often say, "*Gomen ne, kyowa yoji ga arunnda keredo....* (Sorry, I have something to do today, so...)" We often do not complete a sentence and avoid expressions of [Direct Refusal]. We tend not to give concrete reasons for refusal.
  Content

First of all, this group expressed their awareness that Japanese refusals differ from Americans' in that Japanese uses a strategy of not completing a sentence, thus avoiding direct refusal expressions. Besides, they point out that the reasons Japanese give as accounts of their refusals are not concrete. This analysis is consistent with the findings of the present study (see Content of Accounts section of "Results and Discussion" in this paper on pp. 162–165) and previous studies on refusals of Japanese learners. Both Beebe *et al.* (1990) and Kondo (2000) point out that Japanese give formulaic non-specific reasons in refusals and that this tendency is transferred when they are speaking English.

The following comments by one of the group representatives provide a different perspective:

Excerpt 7
Sometimes Japanese use vague expressions in consideration of the hearer's feelings.
  Politeness
Japanese learners of English (JE) cannot give concrete explanations of the reasons for
  Content
their refusals, because their English ability is limited.
  Limitation of Linguistic Ability

The group representative mentions that the Japanese use vague expressions as a politeness strategy, which suggests that a transfer from Japanese language is at play. In addition to this analysis, she provides another reason for their non-specific explanations or excuses in refusal, saying that they might be caused by the limitation of their linguistic ability. By 'English ability', she probably means the limitation of ability in formal aspects of language, such as vocabulary and grammar. Although it is controversial whether pragmatics precedes grammar or grammar precedes pragmatics (Bardovi-Harlig, 1999; Kasper & Rose, 2002), some learners are aware that the limitation of their linguistic ability may lead to inappropriate speech act performance.

Another group representative talks about the illocutionary force of certain expressions. An illocutionary force is a 'conventional communicative force' achieved in saying something (Austin, 1962).[8]

Excerpt 8
I think both Americans and Japanese want to express their thanks for the invitations, but they have different ways of expressing it. Americans say 'thank you' or
    Illocutionary Force
"I'd love to." On the other hand, Japanese say "I'm sorry". Basically their feelings are the same.

The group representative explains that the illocutionary force that Japanese learners are trying to convey by 'I'm sorry' is probably the same as what Americans are trying to do by using 'thank you' and 'I'd love to'. The point is that the speakers' underlying intent is the same, but they have different conventional realizations. This is an interesting analysis in light of the relatively rich studies focusing on multifunctionality of the Japanese expression *sumimasen* (Coulmas, 1981; Kimura, 1994; Tateyama, 2001; Tateyama *et al.*, 1997). *Sumimasen* is usually translated as 'I'm sorry' in English. However, the expression has functions of both apologizing and thanking. Such complications between certain expressions and the illocutionary force they have make communication difficult when we speak in a second language.

In Excerpt 9, learners express difficulties in understanding the illocutionary force of some expressions.

Excerpt 9
The real intention of saying Japanese "*Mata sasotte ne.* (Please ask me again)" and
Illocutionary Force
English "Maybe some other time" is difficult to understand. These expressions are easy to be misunderstood. It is difficult to understand nuances of these expressions,
    Misunderstanding
especially in foreign languages.

When we use expressions such as '*Mata sasotte ne*. (Please ask me again)' in Japanese and 'Maybe some other time' in English, it is difficult to grasp whether speakers literally mean what they say, because these are formulaic expressions that have highly social functions. Learners here realize that it is difficult to understand illocutionary force even in a native language, let alone in a second language.

Investigating Japanese learners' knowledge about American English refusals through retrospective interviews, Robinson (1991) reveals various types of metapragmatic awareness expressed by learners, such as their pragmatic difficulty as to whether they could apply Japanese pragmatic knowledge to American situations, their linguistic difficulty, and their knowledge about American English refusals. Robinson concludes, quoting Faerch and Kasper (1987), that 'One major task for SL (Second Language) research is to reconstruct learners' IL (Interlanguage) development, i.e. to determine their changing states of competence...'. The instructional approach of the present paper, which utilizes research results to generate classroom discussions, has contributed to some extent to both changing and reconstructing learners' interlanguage.

Conclusion

Teaching pragmatics is a highly complex and challenging task, as pragmatic behavior varies to a large extent depending on social and cultural contexts. However, the present study provides some evidence that pragmatics actually can be taught, and through instruction learners become aware of pragmatic similarities and differences between their native language and the target language.

First of all, the present study has explored how learners' choices of refusal strategies change after explicit instruction. The comparisons between JEB and JEA show that after instruction their choice of refusal strategies changed and became more similar to the American pattern. However, there was evidence that even after instruction, Japanese learners retained some culturally specific characteristics of their pragmatic behavior, which they strongly prefer, as was shown in their use of statements of regret, such as 'I'm sorry'. Moreover, there was evidence that learners were influenced in their choice of content of account by illustrative examples in the textbook. The results indicate that learners have created their own interlanguage, which is influenced both by instruction and by their Japanese identity.

Secondly, the paper has attempted to explore which pragmatic aspects the learners become aware of through explicit instruction. The content of the class discussions after analyzing their own speech act performance, and research data taken from different cultural groups and learners, revealed that the present instructional procedure raised awareness concerning various pragmatic aspects involved in the speech act of refusals. They noticed that both Japanese and Americans attend to the 'face' of an interlocutor and use 'politeness' strategies in refusals, but in different ways. They realized that there can be pragmatic transfer from native languages in the choice of strategies (semantic formulas) and in the semantic content of speech act strategies, and their lack of knowledge about refusals in the target language and their limitation of the linguistic ability can lead to misunderstandings. They even noted that different expressions may be used to express the same feelings, and the difficulty of understanding the illocutionary force of utterances in the L2. The findings show that learners are able to make metapragmatic analyses and can become linguists and discoverers themselves by being actively involved in analyzing, thinking and reflecting on their own speech performance.

Although this paper has some limitations, such as a relatively small number of subjects involved in the instruction and the lack of a control group, I hope that the findings have shed some light on the kinds of pragmatic knowledge learners can acquire through instructions in an EFL setting.

In conclusion, on the one hand, teaching pragmatics, especially in EFL context, is a challenging undertaking, as appropriate use of language is intricately connected with cultural values, situations, interlocutors and other variables. Merely teaching formulaic phrases by rote or forcing learners to conform to 'target norm' is not likely to enhance pragmatic ability. On the other hand, it seems that an awareness-raising approach using research data can sensitize learners to cultural differences and variables involved in language use. It can also contribute to learners' creation of their own interlanguage, providing them a variety of pragmatic options to choose from. Hopefully, learners will be able to apply the pragmatic awareness acquired in class to other settings they may encounter as they use different languages with people from different cultural backgrounds.

Notes

1. Beebe *et al.* (1990) break down refusal responses into semantic formulas (those expressions which can be used to perform a refusal) and adjuncts (expressions which accompany a refusal).
2. Kasper and Blum-Kulka (1993) defines 'pragmatic transfer' as an influence from learners' native language and culture on their interlanguage pragmatic knowledge and performance.
3. As the present study involves only refusals to invitations, not all Beebe *et al.*'s categories occurred. On the other hand, 'Good Wish to Hearer', which was not in Beebe *et al.*'s categories, was added because it occurred in the 'Ski Trip' situation of the present data.
4. Brown and Levinson (1987) define 'face' as the public self-image that every member wants to claim for himself. Certain kinds of acts intrinsically threaten

face, and they are called face-threatening acts (FTAs). Refusal is a FTA which threatens especially the hearer's face, and politeness strategies need to be used to minimize FTAs.
5. Brown and Levinson (1987) categorize two kinds of politeness strategies in doing the Face Threatening Act (FTA) on record with redressive action: positive politeness (roughly, the expression of solidarity) and negative politeness (roughly, the expression of restraint).
6. In the textbook, the category called 'Apology' is used instead of 'Regret' to make it easier for learners to understand.
7. Grice (1975) lists 'Be brief (avoid prolixity)' as one of the submaxims of manner.
8. Austin (1962) subcategorizes speech acts into the following three component acts.

   (a) Locutionary act: the production of sounds and words with meanings.
   (b) Illocutionary act: the issuing of an utterance with conventional communicative force achieved 'in saying something'.
   (c) Perlocutionary act: the actual effect achieved 'by saying something'.

   The intention of the speaker behind the utterance is called 'illocutionary force'. For example, when X says to Y 'are you hungry?', X may intend the question as a request for Y to make X a sandwich.

References

Austin, J. (1962) *How to Do Things with Words*. Oxford: Oxford University Press.
Bachman, L. (1990) *Fundamental Considerations in Language Testing*. Oxford: Oxford University Press.
Bardovi-Harlig, K. (1996) Pragmatics and language teaching: Bringing pragmatics and pedagogy together. In L.F. Bouton (ed.) *Pragmatics and Language Learning* (Vol. 7) (pp. 21–39). Urbana, IL: University of Illinois at Urbana-Champaign.
Bardovi-Harlig, K. (1999) Exploring the interlanguage of interlanguage pragmatics: A research agenda for acquisitional pragmatics. *Language Learning* 49, 677–713.
Beebe, L.M., Takahashi, T. and Uliss-Weltz, R. (1990) Pragmatic transfer in ESL refusals. In S.D. Krashen, R. Scarcella and E. Andersen (eds) *On the Development of Communicative Competence in a Second Language* (pp. 55–73). Cambridge, MA: Newbury House.
Blum-Kulka, S. and Olshtain, E. (1986) Too many words: Length of utterance and pragmatic failure. *Studies in Second Language Acquisition* 8, 165–180.
Brown, P. and Levinson, S.C. (1987) *Politeness: Some Universals in Language Usage*. Cambridge: Cambridge University Press.
Canale, M. (1983) From communicative competence to language pedagogy. In J. Richards and R. Schmidt (eds) *Language and Communication* (pp. 2–27). London: Longman.
Canale, M. and Swain, M. (1980) Theoretical bases of communicative approaches to second language teaching and testing. *Applied Linguistics* 1, 1–47.
Cohen, A.D. (1996) Speech acts. In S.L. McKay and N.H. Hornberger (eds) *Sociolinguistics and Language Teaching* (pp. 383–420). Cambridge: Cambridge University Press.
Coulmas, F. (1981) 'Poison to your soul': Thanks and apologies contrastively viewed. In F. Coulmas (ed.) *Conversational Routine: Explorations in Standardized*

Communication Situations and Prepatterned Speech (pp. 69–91). The Hague: Mouton.

Faerch, C. and Kasper, G. (1987) From product to process: Introspective methods in second language research. In C. Faerch and G. Kasper (eds) *Introspection in Second Language Research*. Clevedon: Multilingual Matters.

Grice, P. (1975) Logic and conversation. In P. Cole and J.L. Morgan (eds) *Syntax and Semantics* (Vol. 3). New York: Academic Press.

Kasper, G. (1992) Pragmatic transfer. *University of Hawaii Working Papers in ESL* Fall, 3–33.

Kasper, G. (1997) Can pragmatic competence be taught? (NetWork #6). On WWW at http://www.lll.hawaii.edu/nflrc/NetWorks/NW6. Accessed 1.10.03.

Kasper, G. and Blum-Kulka, S. (eds) (1993) *Interlanguage Pragmatics*. Oxford: Oxford University Press.

Kasper, G. and Rose, K.R. (1999) Pragmatics and SLA. *Annual Review of Applied Linguistics* 19, 81–104.

Kasper, G. and Rose, K.R. (2002) *Pragmatic Development in a Second Language*. Malden: Blackwell.

Kimura, K. (1994) The multiple functions of sumimasen. *Issues in Applied Linguistics* 5 (2), 279–302.

Kondo, S. (1997) The development of pragmatic competence by Japanese learners of English: Longitudinal study on interlanguage apologies. *Sophia Linguistica* 41, 265–284.

Kondo, S. (2000) Interlanguage refusals: Facework by Japanese EFL learners and Americans. *Publications of Akenohoshi Women's Junior College* 18, 47–62.

Kondo, S. (2001) Instructional effects on pragmatic development: Refusal by Japanese EFL learners. *Publications of Akenohoshi Women's Junior College* 19, 33–51.

Kondo, S. (2003) Teaching refusals in an EFL setting. In K. Bardovi-Harlig, B.S. Hartford and R. Mahan-Taylor (eds) *Teaching Pragmatics*. Washington, DC: US Department of English Language Programs. On WWW at http://exchanges.state.gov/education/engteaching/pragmatics/kondo.htm.

Kumagai, T. (1993) Remedial interactions as face-management: The case of Japanese and Americans. *In honor of Tokuichiro Matsuda: Papers contributed on the occasion of his sixtieth birthday.* Tokyo: Kenkyusha.[d1]

Kumatoridani, T. (1993) Hatsuwa kooi taishoo kenkyuu no tame no toogoteki apurouchi: Nichi-eigo no wabi o rei ni [An integrative approach to contrastive speech-act analysis: A case of apologies in Japanese and English]. *Nihongo Kyooiku* 79, 26–40.

Olshtain, E. and Cohen, A. (1983) Apology: A speech act set. In N. Wolfson and E. Judd (eds) *Sociolinguistics and Second Language Acquisition* (pp. 18–35). New York: Newbury House.

Robinson, M. (1991) Introspective methodology in interlanguage pragmatics research. In G. Kasper (ed.) *Pragmatics of Japanese as Native and Target Language* (Technical Report # 3) (pp. 27–82). Honolulu: University of Hawai'i at Manoa, Second Language Teaching & Curriculum Center.

Rose, K.R. (1994) Pragmatic consciousness-raising in an EFL context. In L.F. Bouton and Y. Kachru (eds) *Pragmatics and Language Learning* (Vol. 5) (pp. 52–63). Urbana, IL: University of Illinois at Urbana-Champaign.

Rose, K.R. and Kasper, G. (eds) (2001) *Pragmatics in Language Teaching*. Cambridge: Cambridge University Press.

Siegal, M. (1996) The role of learner subjectivity in second language sociolinguistic competency: Western women learning Japanese. *Applied Linguistics* 17, 356–382.

Tateyama, Y. (2001) Explicit and implicit teaching of pragmatic routines: Japanese sumimasen. In K.R. Rose and G. Kasper (eds) *Pragmatics in Language Teaching* (pp. 200–222). Cambridge: Cambridge University Press.

Tateyama, Y., Kasper, G., Mui, L., Tay, H. and Thananart, O. (1997) Explicit and implicit teaching of pragmatics routines. *Pragmatics and Language Learning* (Vol. 8) (pp. 163–177). Urbana, IL: University of Illinois at Urbana-Champaign.

Wildner-Bassett, M. (1994) Intercultural pragmatics and proficiency: 'Polite' noises for cultural appropriateness. *International Review of Applied Linguistics* 32, 3–17.

Yoshida, K., Kamiya, M., Kondo, S. and Tokiwa, R. (2000) *Heart to Heart: Overcoming Barriers in Cross-Cultural Communication*. Tokyo: Macmillan Languagehouse.

Appendix 8.1: Use of strategies by JEB, JEA and AE

		Direct	Regret	Positive	Account	Gratitude	Future	Indefinite	Alternative	Empathy	Good
JEB N = 35	N %	16 46%	24 69%	7 20%	30 86%	1 3%	2 6%	0 0%	0 0%	0 0%	0 0%
JEA N = 35	N %	17 49%	17 49%	13 37%	32 91%	70 20%	6 17%	0 0%	0 0%	0 0%	0 0%
AE N = 46	N %	30 65%	10 22%	17 37%	39 85%	17 37%	8 17%	1 2%	2 4%	2 4%	4 9%

Chapter 9
Enhancing the Pragmatic Competence of Non-native English-speaking Teacher Candidates (NNESTCs) in an EFL Context

ZOHREH R. ESLAMI and ABBASS ESLAMI-RASEKH

Introduction

Although language proficiency is often listed as an area of interest for non-native English-speaking teachers (NNESTs) in many papers (Mahboob, 2004; Medgyes, 1994; Pasternak & Bailey, 2004; Samimy & Brutt-Griffler, 1999), there is lack of research on enhancing the language proficiency of NNESTs in general, and their pragmatic competence in particular.

Pragmatic competence is a central component in Bachman's (1990) model of language competence and incorporates the ability to use the language to express a wide range of functions as well as interpret their illocutionary force in discourse according to the sociocultural context in which they are used. In Bachman's model, pragmatic competence is not subordinated to knowledge of grammar and text organization but co-ordinated with formal linguistic and textual knowledge and interacts with 'organizational competence' in complex ways. In order to communicate appropriately in a target language, pragmatic competence in the secondo/foreign language (L2) must be reasonably well developed. However, L2 learners often show an imbalance in pragmatic and grammatical competence in interlanguage (Celce-Murcia *et al.*, 1995; Koike & Pearson, 2005), and pragmatic competence often lags behind grammatical competence (Olshtain & Blum-Kulka, 1985). Research findings (Alcón, 2005; Bardovi-Harlig & Dörnyei, 1998; Bardovi-Harlig & Griffin, 2005) strongly suggest that without a pragmatic focus, foreign language teaching raises students' metalinguistic awareness but it does not contribute much to develop their metapragmatic consciousness in L2 to be able to distinguish between what is and is not appropriate in given contexts. Blum-Kulka *et al.* (1989: 10) submit that 'even fairly advanced language learners' communicative acts regularly contain pragmatic errors, or deficits, in that they fail to convey or comprehend the intended illocutionary force or politeness value'. Therefore, there is a need for L2 instruction to focus on pragmatics of the language, and researchers in this area generally point out the positive impact of instruction aimed at raising learners' pragmatic awareness (Bardovi-Harlig & Griffin, 2005; Eslami-Rasekh *et al.*, 2004; Kasper, 1997; Koike & Pearson, 2005).

Research shows that non-native English-speaking teacher candidates (NNESTCs) feel insecure about their English language proficiency and their pragmatic competence may be weaker than their organizational competence (Eslami-Rasekh, 2005b; Pasternak & Bailey, 2004). In addition, English as a Second Language (ESL) teacher education programs do not seem to focus on pragmatic aspects of language and to train the teacher candidates in teaching the pragmatic dimensions of language (Biesenback-Lucas, 2003; Rose, 1997). Available teacher preparation sources (Bardovi-Harlig & Hartford, 1997 is an exception) typically include chapters on how to teach the four major skills which would result in some declarative knowledge of grammar but not pragmatics. Bardovi-Harlig and Hartford (1997), Eslami-Rasekh (2005b) and Rose (1997) are the only sources who have addressed the issue of pragmatics in ESL teacher education programs. As Rose (2005) submits, while most studies have focused on the production of the target pragmatic features or their use in interaction, instruction aimed at improving learners' pragmatic comprehension has received far less attention (Rose, 2005: 388). Furthermore, as Schauer (2006) submits, although a number of interventional studies have investigated the development of learners' productive pragmatic competence and some have studied the development of learners' pragmatic awareness, there is paucity of research in the development of pragmatic awareness and production of one learner sample. In response to such assertions and in order to fill the gap in the literature on interlanguage pragmatics, this study investigates the effect of instruction on the pragmatic awareness and production of NNESTCs in English as a Foreign Language (EFL) contexts.

Background

EFL contexts are sometimes labeled as impoverished L2 contexts because developmental pragmatic research conducted in these settings reports that in contrast to second language learning environments, the range of speech acts and realization strategies is quite narrow, and the typical interaction patterns restrict pragmatic input and opportunities for practicing discourse organization strategies (Alcón, 2005; Kasper, 2001; Lörscher & Schulze, 1988; Rose, 1999). Large classes, limited contact hours and little opportunity for intercultural communication are some of the features of the EFL context that hinder pragmatic learning (Eslami-Rasekh *et al.*, 2004; Rose, 1999). Bardovi-Harlig and Hartford (1996) point out, for example, that the pragmatic input teachers provide for students was status-bound, and as a consequence they could not serve as direct models for the learner. Similar findings are reported by Nikula's (2002) study, which reveals a tendency towards directness in teachers' performance explained in terms of the unequal power relationship of classroom discourse. It is also shown that pedagogical materials are inadequate as a reliable source of pragmatic input for classroom language learners (Alcón & Safont, 2001; Bardovi-Harlig, 1996; Vellenga, 2004) and unlikely to result in pragmatic development.

As a result, arguments have been put forward for the necessity of instruction in pragmatics (Bardovi-Harlig, 2001). The rationale for the need of instruction in pragmatics is provided by Schmidt's (1993) argument that simple exposure to the target language is not enough for developing pragmatic competence because pragmatic functions and relevant contextual factors are often not salient to learners and so not likely to be noticed even after prolonged exposure. In the same vein, Kasper (1997) holds that in purely meaning-oriented L2 use, learners may not detect relevant input features, and that to achieve learners' attention, input should be made salient through 'input enhancement'. It is believed that input enhancement will raise the learners' consciousness about the target feature. Input enhancement is defined by Fukuya and Clark (2001) as an implicit instructional technique that provides no metapragmatic information. However, Takahashi (2001) proposes a much broader view of input enhancement. She distinguishes three different degrees and types of input enhancement: explicit teaching, featuring metapragmatic explanation about form-function relationships of the target structures; form-comparison, in which students compare their own speech acts realizations with those of native speakers; and form-search, in which students identify the target strategies in provided scenarios.

As Rose (2005) states, most instructional pragmatic studies include learners coming from English, Japanese, Cantonese, German, Hebrew and Spanish as their first language (L1). Future research needs to expand the range of L1 and target languages to enable investigators and language educators to better assess whether and to what extent findings from studies of a particular L1 or target language my be transferable to other language pairings. Furthermore, as noted by Bardovi-Harlig and Griffin (2005), most interlanguage pragmatics research has utilized production tasks (Bardovi-Harlig, 2001), with more limited focus on judgment and perception of speech events (Cook, 2001) and speech acts (e.g. Bergman & Kasper, 1993; Koike, 1996; Olshtain & Blum-Kulka, 1985). Similarly, Rose (2005: 388) states that while most studies have focused on the production of the target features or their use in interaction, instruction aimed at improving learners' pragmatic comprehension has received far less attention.

This study was conducted to respond to the lack of research on the effect of instruction on learners from less studied L1 backgrounds (Persian), and to expand interventional studies that investigate the enhancement of both awareness and production aspects of pragmatic competence in an EFL context (Bardovi-Harlig & Griffin, 2005; Rose, 2005; Schauer, 2006). The study focuses on a less studied group of learners (NNESTCs), with high instrumental motivation to develop their language competence in general and their pragmatic competence in particular. The effect of metapragmatic instruction (Kasper, 1997) on the speech act awareness and production of Iranian NNESTCs in an EFL context is investigated.

The Study

Design and research questions

This research adopted a quasiexperimental, pretest/posttest design (pre-test-treatment-post-test). The researcher in this study was interested in comparing students' pragmatic competence before and after the intervention. The independent variable was the treatment with two different levels, and the dependent variable was students' pragmatic awareness and productions. Our study was designed to examine the effectiveness of planned pedagogical action directed towards the acquisition of the speech acts of requesting and apologizing. Taking into account the findings of interventional studies that show that instruction enhances the pragmatic competence of learners (House, 1996; Rose & Kwai-Fun, 2001; Takahashi, 2001), we formulated the following research questions:

(1) Does metapragmatic instruction in speech act patterns and strategies have a positive effect on Iranian NNESTCs' pragmatic awareness?
(2) Does metapragmatic instruction in speech act patterns and strategies have a positive effect on Iranian NNESTCs' pragmatic production ability?
(3) Is there any interaction between metapragmatic instruction in speech act patterns and strategies and Iranian NNESTCs' pragmatic awareness and production ability?

Following DeCoo (1996), in our instructional approach we did not make a dichotomous division between 'explicit' and 'implicit' instruction. Rather our approach to instruction centered around purposeful class activities (informed eclecticism) in the form of teacher-ronted discussion, peer work, pedagogic tasks, small-group discussion, roleplays, semi-structured interviews, introspective feedback and metapragmatic assessment tasks.

This instruction might be viewed as one form of what Larsen-Freeman and Long (1991: 323–324) term as 'comprehensible input-rich classroom instruction'.

Participants

Two groups of NNESTCs participated in this study. The first group (Group A) consisted of 25 MA students studying Teaching English as a Second Language (TESL) at Najafabad Azad University in Iran. They went through the ESL methodology course with a pragmatic focus. There were 15 females and 10 male students in this group. Their age range was between 23 and 30 years of age. The second group (Group B) included 27 MA students studying TESL at the same university who went through the same ESL Methodology course without a pragmatic focus. There were 17 female and 10 male students in this group. Their age range was between 23 and 28 years of age. The participants had studied English in classroom settings for about nine years and had a bachelor's degree in a related filed (English Translation, TESL or English literature). The semester when data was collected was the first semester in the MA program for all the students. None of them had spent any time in English-speaking countries. In addition, two American female graduate students were trained and asked to judge and rate the pragmatic appropriateness of the participants' language productions on a Likert scale ranging from 1 (least appropriate) to 5 (most appropriate).

Instruments

In addition to a language proficiency test, the Comprehensive English Language Test (CELT), error recognition task ERT) and discourse completion task (DCT) were the two main instruments used to collect the data for this study. The ERT was used to measure participants' awareness of appropriate language use and DCT was used to collect a sample of participants' production of speech acts.

Error recognition task (ERT)

Following Bardovi-Harlig and Dörnyei's (1998) study and based on Farhady's (1980) functional language testing procedure, the error recognition task was constructed. Based on the pilot-tested items of the production test (DCT), the pragmatically inappropriate and/or grammatically incorrect responses provided by Iranian students were selected as distracters for the error recognition task. The pragmatically correct options were taken from native speakers' responses to DCTs reported in the interlanguage pragmatic literature and also from Bardovi-Harlig and Dörnyei's (1998) study. The pragmatic problems included bare imperatives used for making a request without an alerter, lack of explanation and denial of offense when an apology was needed, the simple use of apology formula without any intensifiers when they were needed, and overuse of polite forms or explanations where simple request or apology was needed. The ERT was developed to measure the NNESTCs' pragmatic awareness. The ERT was piloted to make sure it worked as it was intended (both native (15) and non-native speakers of English (20) were used for this phase).

The reliability of the test was established through the KR-21 formula (KR-21 = 0.88). The validity of the instrument was established ($r = 0.81$) through concurrent validation with CELT administered to the non-native English-speaking participants in the pilot study.

The speech acts of requesting and apologizing were selected as teaching targets in this study. The rationale for the selection of these two speech acts was that these speech acts are considered as the most frequent speech acts used in daily communication and also they are the most empirically explored speech acts in the cross-cultural or interlanguage pragmatics literature (Kasper & Rose, 2002). The rich information on the realization patterns of these speech acts provided in the literature was used for the metapragmatic instruction and assessment of these speech acts in our study.

The ERT consisted of written scenarios on speech acts of requesting and apologizing. The test items included three categories: (a) eight items with sentences that were pragmatically appropriate, but ungrammatical, (b) eight items with sentences that were grammatical, but pragmatically inappropriate, and (c) eight items with sentences that were both grammatical and pragmatically appropriate. There were 24 items on the questionnaire. The participants were asked to judge if the utterance was pragmatically appropriate and grammatically correct, and if they said no, to specify if the problem was grammatical or related to pragmatics. In this case, they were asked to provide an explanation. Following is an example of a pragmatically inappropriate item taken from Bardovi-Harlig and Dörnyei's (1998) study.

The teacher asks Peter to help with the plans for the class trip.
T: OK, so we'll go by the bus. Who lives near the bus station? Peter, could you check the bus times for us on the way home tonight?
P: No, I can't tonight. Sorry.
Was the last part of the above conversation appropriate/grammatical? Yes _____ No_____ .
If you marked 'No' above, what do you think was the problem:
a) pragmatically inappropriate or b) grammatically incorrect
If you marked (a) above, can you provide some explanation for it?

Participants got the score of '1' if they correctly identified the items and '0' if not.

Discourse Completion Task (DCT)

Given that higher pragmatic awareness does not necessarily translate into appropriate pragmatic production (Bardovi-Harlig & Dörnyei, 1998), the study used a DCT to get NNESTCs' responses to the scenarios provided. Kasper and Dahl (1991: 9) defined DCT as 'written questionnaires including a number of brief situational descriptions, followed by a short dialogue with an empty slot'. The questionnaire for DCT in this study followed such a format. The participants were asked to complete the last sentence with responses which they thought fit the given context.

The DCT, similar to the ERT, contained requests and apologies. There were 16 items on the DCT (eight on apologies and eight on requests). Participants were given a scenario and asked how they would reply, as in the following example:

You meet your classmate, Maria, after school. You like to ask her out for a cup of coffee. What would you say to her:
You:

The DCT situations centered on a student's family, social and academic life. The situations were of various forms for each speech act accounting for the major situational variables of degree of imposition (offense for apologies), social distance and power of the interlocutors. All situations were thus carefully designed to facilitate participants' identifications with the role they had to play, taking into account the contextual variables of distance and dominance in shaping the choice of the required speech act strategy. Two bilingual faculty members and the two researchers reviewed the situations for cultural appropriateness and naturalness to students living in Iran. The final version was administered to a group of students (30) similar to the participants of the study to ensure that the DCT elicited the intended speech acts and also to find suitable distractors for the ERT. Their grammatically incorrect or pragmatically inappropriate responses were used for the ERT in this study.

Two native American English university students rated participants' pre and post DCT performances. Hudson *et al.*'s (1995) rating scale was used to train the raters. This rating scale contains six components: the ability to use correct speech acts, expressions, amount of information, levels of formality, directness and politeness. In this study, the last three components were combined as one (level of politeness) due to the overlapping elements of speech existing among the three components. The researchers explained the conceptual meanings of 'the ability to use correct speech act', 'expressions', 'the amount of information' and 'levels of politeness' to the raters.

The two native raters rated participants' performance based on a five-point rating scale ranging from 1 (not appropriate) to 5 (highly appropriate). The raters were also familiarized with the most frequently used strategies by native speakers for realizing requests and apologies and the role of contextual variables. The value for inter-rater reliability was reached to an acceptable level of agreement ($r > 0.90$).

Teaching procedure and materials

A set of programmed instructional materials explaining the realization and interpretation patterns, rules, strategies and tokens of the two speech acts under study were prepared and presented to the experimental group. Following Bardovi-Harlig's (1996) tentative 'speech acts framework', the materials compiled started with presenting descriptions of the notions of speech acts, levels of directness, types and factors of variability, and face-keeping strategies Olshtain and Cohen's (1990) speech act set was used to present the major sociopragmatic and pragmalinguistic patterns and strategies of realizing and interpreting the two speech acts at the 'explicit' and 'implicit' levels considering both 'internal' and 'external' modifications. Following DeCoo (1996), in our instructional approach we did not make a dichotomous division between 'explicit' and 'implicit' instruction. Rather our approach to instruction centered around purposeful class activities (informed eclecticism) in the form of teacher-fronted discussion, peer work, pedagogic tasks, small-group discussion, roleplays, semi-structured interviews, introspective feedback and metapragmatic assessment tasks. The treatment lasted for 14 weeks, and 30 minutes of each class time (3-hour class) was allocated to pragmatic related activities.

More specifically, in the experimental group, a number of research papers on different speech acts, cross-cultural pragmatics, interlanguage and instructional pragmatics (e.g. Bardovi-Harlig, 2001; Blum-Kulka et al., 1989; Rose & Kwai-Fun, 2001; Welzman, 1989) were used to familiarize the students with the research in this area. In addition, participants were asked to serve as researchers and do their own ethnographic research. Most of the classroom activities used aimed at both raising students' pragmatic awareness and providing them with opportunities for communicative practice (Kasper, 1997). The aim was to expose learners to the pragmatic aspects of language (L1 and L2) and provide them with the analytical tools they need to arrive at their own generalizations concerning contextually appropriate language use. In addition, these activities were designed to make learners consciously aware of differences between the native and target language speech acts. The rationale for this approach is that such differences are often ignored by learners and go unnoticed unless they are directly addressed

(Schmidt, 1993). The emphasis was placed on both the linguistic manifestations of the speech acts (pragmalinguistics) and the sociopragmatic aspects (i.e. the situation, the participants, the status of those involved, etc.). Students observed particular pragmatic features in various sources of oral or written 'data', ranging from feature films to fictional and nonfictional written and audiovisual sources.

A student-discovery procedure based on students' obtaining information through observations, questionnaires and/or interviews was used (Tarone & Yule, 1989). To collect data in English in an EFL setting is not as easy as in ESL settings. Therefore, students were asked to use movies, books, TV programs and Internet sources to get access to examples of speech acts. These uses of media provide natural language samples because they were not originally designed for teaching purposes but for genuine communication (Alcón, 2005; Rose, 1997; Washburn, 2001).

For an apology speech act, for example, students observed the strategies and linguistic means by which apologizing is accomplished – what formulae are used, and what additional means of expressing apologies are employed, such as explaining, offer of repair, promise of forbearance and so forth (pragmalinguistics). Also, students examined in which contexts the various ways of expressing apologies are used. After observing a certain number of cases, students analyzed their data and summarized their findings and presented it to their groups or to the class. Other in-class activities included roleplays of situations that elicit the speech act under discussion and on-the-spot analyses of these performances through the explicit metapragmatic explanations and discussions.

Some other activities used to increase the pragmatic awareness and production of the students included translation activities and examples of pragmatic miscommunications. Students were asked to collect a sample of the related speech acts in their L1 and translate it into English. This activity highlighted how cultural norms are reflected in the language, why pragmatic translations of instances of language use can be challenging and the peculiarities of literal translations (Eslami-Rasekh, 2005a).

Another appealing activity used was to present and share examples from cross-cultural (mis)communications (Rose, 1999). Students collected various examples and offered tentative explanations for the pragmatic peculiarities in the exchanges.

Results

This section contains information about the analysis of the data using both descriptive statistics, repeated-measures MANOVA analysis and follow-up Scheffe-test results of post hoc group mean comparisons. The significance level was set at $p < 0.05$.

Based on the results of the CELT, the participants were considered as advanced learners of English in language proficiency. However, to account for possible differences in the pragmatic competence of the two groups a pretest posttest design was used. The pragmatic awareness and production tests were used both as pre- and post-tests. The descriptive statistics in Table 9.1 depict the distribution of the scores of the two *groups* [control (Con.) versus experimental (Exp.)] on various *tests* at multiple points in *time* ['awareness' pretest (awarepre) and posttest (awarepost) versus 'production' pretest (prodpre) and posttest (prodpost)]. It is worth noting that the highest possible score of the awareness test was 24 and that of the production test was 80 (16×5). However in the data analysis we accounted for this difference by adapting a scale for the former proportionate exactly to the latter.

As mentioned earlier, the repeated-measures MANOVA was implemented to compare the multiple mean performances of the groups involved in this study in order to detect any statistically meaningful differences among them and determine the possible effects of independent variable [instruction group on multiple dependent variables, i.e. speech act awareness and production abilities (repeated measure, pretest and posttest)] or interactions among them. In this analysis, the experimental variables are arranged in a $2 \times 2 \times 2$ [*group* (control versus experimental) × *test* ('Awareness test' versus 'production test') × *time* (pretest versus posttest)] factorial design.

Table 9.1 Summary of descriptive statistics of 'awareness' and 'production' pretest and posttest scores

No.	Test	Group	N	Mean	sd	sd	Min	Max
1	Awarepre	Con.	27	30.70	6.89	1.25	18.00	45.00
2	Awarepre	Exp.	25	30.00	6.40	1.16	15.00	42.00
3	Awarepost	Con.	27	31.50	6.90	1.26	21.00	48.00
4	Awarepost	Exp.	25	52.00	8.67	1.58	36.00	69.00
5	Prodpre	Con.	27	36.51	7.31	1.33	23.00	53.00
6	Prodpre	Exp.	25	32.96	9.64	1.75	13.00	51.00
7	Prodpost	Con.	27	37.76	7.78	1.41	24.00	55.00
8	Prodpost	Exp.	25	51.48	9.01	1.65	35.00	68.00

Comparison of groups

The comparison of the control and experimental groups indicates that there was a meaningful difference between the scores of the subjects. The results are shown in Table 9.2, which shows that there were statistically significant differences among groups (control versus experimental) on their scores ($F = 68.99$, $p = 0.000$). These meaningful differences, though very important for the following analyses, are not enough to answer our research question on the effectiveness of instruction for the enhancement of pragmatic competence. One tempting conclusion of this significance of group differences might be that the experimental group outperformed the control group, evoking the idea that the explicit metapragmatic instruction did work. But this difference would not really address the most important question of the amount of change from one time to another, which is most particularly established by the significance of Time effect and its interaction with Group – i.e. Group × Time interaction.

Comparison of time (within-subject) effect

This analysis is based on the inclusion of the variable Time, which represents the amount of change from pretest time to posttest time for each Test considering Group effects at the same time. Table 9.3 shows the results of the follow-up repeated-measures MANOVA comparison of Time. As can be seen in Table 9.3, there were statistically meaningful differences between pretest and posttest scores. In other words, there was a significant Time effect ($F = 716.37$, $p = 0.000$), indicating that the mean change from one time (pretest) to another (posttest) is noticeably

Table 9.2 Group comparison

Source of variation	SS	DF	MS	F	Sig.
Within cells	15765.76	50	135.91		
Constant	629047.40	1	629047.40	4628.35	0.000
Group	9376.59	1	9376.59	68.99	0.000

Table 9.3 Comparison of pretest versus posttest (time)

Source of variation	SS	DF	MS	F	Sig.
Within cells	1986.29	50	17.12		
Time	12266.46	1	12266.46	716.37	0.000
Group × time	10170.60	1	10170.60	595.97	0.000

significant. Most importantly, significant effect was found for Group × Time interaction ($F = 593.97$, $p = 0.000$), displaying that experimental group showed much more significant change or improvement from pretest time to posttest time. That is, the treatment or the metapragmatic instruction was highly effective.

Comparison of test (within-subject) effect

Another factor investigated in this study was pragmatic awareness versus production (Test), designed as the dependent variables of the study. The results of the analysis are shown in Table 9.4. The results indicate that significant effect was found for the Test ($F = 8.95$, $p = 0.003$) factor. Additionally, there was a statistically meaningful Group × Test interaction ($F = 11.10$, $p = 0.001$), specifying that there were differences between the experimental and control groups on the two tests.

More clearly, the significance of Group × Test interaction, as noted above, indicates that the significance of Test effect exists not between the performance of one specific (control or experimental) group on one test and the same group's performance on the other test but between the control and experimental group separately. In addition, the significance of Group × Test × Time interaction, which will be shown in the next section, will add further clarity to the issue that the significant Test effect lies between the Groups separately from pretest Time to posttest Time.

Comparison of test by time within-subject effect

The results from this analysis presented in Table 9.5 indicate that significant effect was found for the Test × Time interaction ($F = 5.79$, $p = 0.018$). In addition, there was a statistically meaningful Group × Test × Time interaction ($F = 4.38$, $p = 0.039$). Consequently, the results show that there is significant interaction between metapragmatic instruction and NNESTCs' awareness and their production ability of speech acts. However, where this interaction lies needs further analysis. The results of follow-up Scheffe test analysis will make it clear if the instruction worked for one ability better than the other ability between the groups or not.

Table 9.4 Comparison of tests (awareness versus production)

Source of variation	SS	DF	MS	F	Sig.
Within cells	8061.16	50	69.49		
Test	622.21	1	622.21	8.95	0.003
Group × test	771.40	1	771.40	11.10	0.001

Table 9.5 Comparison of Test (awareness versus production) × Time within-subject effect

Source of variation	SS	DF	MS	F	Sig.
Within cells	2984.49	50	25.73		
Test × test	149.08	1	149.58	5.79	0.018
Group × test × time	112.62	1	112.62	4.38	0.039

The results of the Scheffe test

Our design is composed of eight combinations of the involved factors and thus includes eight group mean performances to be compared by using the Scheffe test for post hoc multiple comparisons of means. These groups are exhibited in Table 9.6.

The results of the Scheffe Test are displayed in Table 9.7. Notice that an asterisk (*) denotes 'pairs' of groups that are significantly different at the *0.05 level of significance*. The results from this post hoc comparison of group means shown in Table 9.7 indicate that the experimental group's performances on the posttests of both 'awareness' and 'production' tests were significantly higher than that group's pretests as well as the control group's pretest and posttest performances on the same tests separately. More precisely, in the absence of the explicit metapragmatic instruction, the performances of both groups on the speech act *'awareness'* and *'production'* tests were more or less the same. However, things dramatically changed for the experimental group on the posttests after the intervention. That is, the metapragmatic instruction in speech act patterns, rules and strategies did work for the experimental group. It is worth noting that no significant difference was found between the performances of the groups on 'production test' and their performance on the 'awareness test' at the pretest time. More importantly, no significant difference was found between the improvements of the experimental group's performances on one of the two tests of pragmatic awareness and pragmatic production. This indicates that the students' awareness as well as production abilities of speech acts improved (significantly) as a result of the treatment.

Discussion and General Conclusion

Although a number of interventional studies have investigated the development of learners' productive pragmatic competence and some others have studied the development of learners' pragmatic awareness, there is paucity of research in the development of pragmatic awareness and production of one learner sample (Schauer, 2006). Also, as Rose

Table 9.6 Group classification used by the Scheffe test

	Aware-pre	Aware-post	Prod-pre	Prod-post
Control	1 ($x = 30.7$)	3 ($x = 31.5$)	5 ($x = 36.51$)	7 ($x = 37.76$)
Exper.	2 ($x = 30$)	4 ($x = 52$)	6 ($x = 32.96$)	8 ($x = 51.48$)

Table 9.7 The results of the Scheffe test

No.	Comparison	Observed difference	Critical difference	Sig.
1	3 vs. 4	0.7	10.22	
2	8 vs. 7	20.5	10.22	*
3	8 vs. 4	22	10.22	*
4	7 vs. 3	0.8	10.22	
5	11 vs. 12	3.55	10.22	
6	16 vs. 15	13.75	10.22	*
7	16 vs. 12	18.52	10.22	*
8	15 vs. 11	1.25	10.22	
9	3+4 vs. 11+12	−8.77	14.45	
10	7+8 vs. 15+16	−5.74	14.45	
11	11+15 vs. 3+7	12.07	14.45	
12	12+16 vs. 3+7	22.24	14.45	*
13	12+16 vs. 11+15	10.17	14.45	
14	12+16 vs. 4+8	2.44	14.45	
15	4+8 vs. 11+15	7.73	14.45	
16	4+8 vs. 3+7	19.8	14.45	*
17	16 vs. 3	20.78	10.22	*
18	12 vs. 7	1.46	10.22	
19	15 vs. 4	7.76	10.22	
20	8 vs. 11	15.49	10.22	*

*Denotes significant differences at 0.05 level

(2005: 388) submits, while most studies have focused on the production of the target features or their use in interaction, instruction aimed at improving learners' pragmatic comprehension has received far less attention (Rose, 2005: 388). In response to such assertions the present study was conducted.

The aim of the study was to provide more insights into the effects of instruction on the pragmatic awareness and production development of advanced learners of English (NNESTCs in an MA program) in a foreign language environment. The development of learners' ability to correctly identify grammatical inaccuracies and pragmatic violations and to produce pragmatically appropriate speech acts was examined. The results of this study support the learnability of L2 pragmatics in EFL contexts. That is, with the pedagogical focus on pragmatic competence, pragmatic awareness and production can be acquired in the classroom, or more specifically in the FL classroom Our finding is consistent with claims that pragmatic awareness can indeed be acquired with pedagogical focus on pragmatic competence (Bardovi-Harlig & Dörnyei, 1998; Niezgoda & Röver, 2001).

It is worth mentioning that this SLA-oriented interventionist study, like other similar studies, as Kasper (1989) argues, is based on 'three interrelated hypotheses': the *noticing* hypothesis (Schmidt, 1993), *output* hypothesis (Swain, 1996) and *interaction* hypothesis (Long, 1996). The first two hypotheses relate to 'different stages in the language learning process'. According to the noticing hypothesis, in order for the *input* to be turned into *intake* and thus made available for further processing, it needs to be registered under awareness. The second hypothesis suggests some important *acquisitional* roles for productive language use: during utterance production, learners may notice gaps in their interlanguage knowledge; output is one way of creating and testing a hypothesis about L2; productive language use beyond entirely formulaic speech requires analyzed knowledge that is not called upon in comprehension; and automatization of language representations requires repeated productive use, as any skilled behavior does. The third hypothesis, namely the interaction hypothesis, integrates the first two hypotheses, proposing that 'negotiation for meaning, and especially negotiation for work that triggers interactional adjustment by the native or more competent interlocutor, facilitates acquisition because it connects input, internal learner capacities, particularly selective attention, and output in productive ways' (Long, 1996: 451). Moreover, some SLA theorists believe that L2 learners may not detect relevant input features in purely meaning-based L2 use. Accordingly, they argue that in order for noticing to happen, input might have to be made salient through input enhancement, which will raise the learners' consciousness about the target features.

The study contributes to the theory of interlanguage pragmatic development. As noted earlier, pragmatic ability is part and parcel of a non-native speakers' communicative competence and must be incorporated in a model of communicative ability. This study revealed that interlanguage pragmatic development does not seem impervious to metapragmatic instruction. The findings here are considered as compelling evidence that certain aspects of L2 pragmatics – both pragmalinguistic and sociopragmatic – do not develop sufficiently without instruction. It should be noted that the participants in this research were a highly select group of learners with high instrumental motivation who have made English the focus of their careers. However, as the results of the pretest show, they still had not developed enough pragmatic competence to be able to identify the pragmatic infelicities in speech acts. Accordingly, it is justified that some form of 'input-rich instruction' is necessary for the development of pragmatic competence. As Kasper and Rose (2002: 52) state, teachers, no matter native or non-native, should sufficiently be socialized to L2 pragmatic practices, so that they can comfortably draw on those practices as part of their communicative and cultural repertoire, and their metapragmatic awareness enables them to support student learning of L2 pragmatics effectively. As has been noted for second and foreign language education generally (e.g. Rampton, 1990), language teachers have to be experts in the target language rather than native speakers of it. Likewise, L2 language socialization, an integral aspect of L2 teaching, relies on teachers' cultural, pragmatic and interactional expertise in L2 and is not conditional on native speaker status.

This study is important in terms of curriculum and pedagogy for the education of language teachers. The findings revealed that students did not acquire many pragmatic aspects of speech act comprehension and production in the absence of pertinent instruction, implying that some form of instruction is necessary. According to Kasper (1997), L2 classrooms afford L2 learners the opportunity to reflect on their communicative encounters and to experiment with different pragmatic options. For foreign language learners, however, the classroom may be the only available setting where they can try out what using the foreign language feels like, and how more or less comfortable they are with various aspects of L2 pragmatics.

In addition, it is no doubt that the prerequisite for pragmatic instruction is the availability of especially prepared and appropriately tuned materials. To this end, material developers/writers can, following Bardovi-Harlig (1996), adopt a 'speech acts framework' in planning, developing or writing instructional materials both for its 'accessibility' and for the 'availability of descriptions of language use' in that framework. Moreover, teacher education methodology textbooks should have pragmatic component of language as one important area to be included in the content of the language teacher education program.

As for teaching methods or class activities and tasks, teachers can adopt activities through one of the inductive, deductive, implicit or explicit approaches to instruction (see Kasper, 1997) or through an informed eclectic approach. In addition, the prerequisite for the success of the instruction is that language teachers should be educated to become knowledgeable of pragmatics in general, and speech acts in particular.

Our analysis did not account for possible differences on the effect of instruction on the different speech acts considered as the learning targets in this study. Further studies are needed to investigate which speech acts or pragmatics aspects of language are easier to develop and which ones are more difficult. Also further research is needed to compare the differential effects of different teaching approaches. Our study focused only on one type of pragmatic intervention. Additionally since the effect of different instructional treatments may vary depending on learners' individual variables, such as age, motivation, language proficiency level and learning style, further research is needed to examine the effect of different instructional approaches based on these differences. It would also be desirable to examine if a delayed posttest would yield results similar to our findings.

The pedagogical activities used in this study enhanced these students' pragmatic ability. It is our hope that it informed these prospective English language teachers to identify the pragmatic abilities in the L2 that second language learners need. Kasper (1997: 113) emphasizes the necessity of inclusion of pragmatics in a teacher education program by asserting, 'Raising teachers' awareness of cross-culturally diverse patterns of linguistic action, including those performed under the institutional constraints of language classroom, must play an essential role in the education in and development of language teaching professionals'. It is our hope that the pragmatically oriented classroom activities and the readings in intercultural and interlanguage pragmatics have also promoted the teachers' awareness of the importance of teaching pragmatics in their ESL/EFL classroom.

References

Alcón, E. (2005) Does instruction work for performing pragmatics in the EFL context? *System* 33 (3), 417–435.

Alcón, E. and Safont, P. (2001) Occurrence of exhortative speech acts in ELT materials and natural speech data: A focus on request, suggestion and advice realization strategies. *Studies in English Language and Linguistics* 3, 5–22.

Bachman, L. (1990) *Fundamental Considerations in Language Testing*. Oxford: Oxford University Press.

Bardovi-Harlig, K. (1996) Pragmatics and language teaching: Bringing pragmatics and pedagogy together. In L.F. Bouton (ed.) *Pragmatics and Language Learning* (Vol. 7, pp. 21–39). Urbana, IL: University of Illinois at Urbana-Champaign.

Bardovi-Harlig, K. (2001) Evaluating the empirical evidence: Grounds for instruction in pragmatics? In K.R. Rose and G. Kasper (eds) *Pragmatics in Language Teaching* (pp. 13–32). Cambridge: Cambridge University Press.

Bardovi-Harlig, K. and Dörnyei, Z. (1998) Do language learners recognize pragmatic violations? Pragmatic versus grammatical awareness in instructed L2 learning. *TESOL Quarterly* 32 (2), 233–262.

Bardovi-Harlig, K. and Griffin, R. (2005) L2 pragmatic awareness: Evidence from the ESL classroom. *System* 33 (3), 401–415.

Bardovi-Harlig, K. and Hartford, B.S. (eds) (1997) Beyond methods: Components of second language teacher education. The McGraw-Hill Second Language Professional Series: Directions in second language learning. Newyork: McGraw Hill.

Bardovi-Harlig, K. and Hartford, B.S. (1996) Input in an institutional setting. *Studies in Second Language Acquisition* 18, 171–188.

Bergman, M.L. and Kasper, G. (1993) Perception and performance in native and non-native apology. In G. Kasper and S. Blum-Kulka (eds) *Interlanguage Pragmatics* (pp. 82–107). New York: Oxford University Press.

Biesenback-Lucas, S. (2003) Preparing students for the pragmatics of e-mail interaction in academia: A new/forgotten dimension in teacher education. *Teacher Education Interest Section Newsletter* 18 (2), 3–4.

Blum-Kulka, S., House, J. and Kasper, G. (1989) Investigating cross-cultural pragmatics: An introductory overview. In S. Blum-Kulka, J. House and G. Kasper (eds) *Cross-cultural Pragmatics: Requests and Apologies* (pp. 1–34). Norwood, NJ: Ablex.

Celce-Murcia, M., Dörnyei, Z. and Thurrell, S. (1995) Communicative competence: A pedagogically motivated model with content specifications. *Issues in Applied Linguistics* 6, 5–35.

Cook, H.M. (2001) Why can't learners of Japanese as a foreign language distinguish polite from impolite speech styles? In K. Rose and G. Kasper (eds) *Pragmatics in Language Teaching* (pp. 80–102). Cambridge: Cambridge University Press.

DeCoo, W. (1996) The induction–deduction opposition: Ambiguities and complexities of the didactic reality. *International Review of Applied Linguistics* 34, 95–118.

Eslami-Rasekh, Z. (2005a) Enhancing the pragmatic competence of NNEST candidates. *TESOL NNEST Newsletter* 7 (1), 4–7.

Eslami-Rasekh, Z. (2005b) Raising the pragmatic awareness of language learners. *ELT Journal* 59 (2), 199–208.

Eslami-Rasekh, Z., Eslami-Rasekh, A. and Fatahi, A. (2004) Using metapragmatic instruction to improve advanced EFL learners pragmatic awareness. *TESL EJ* 8 (2) A2, 1–12.

Farhady, H. (1980) Justification, development, and validation of functional language tests. Unpublished PhD thesis, University of California, Los Angeles.

Fukuya, Y.J. and Clark, M.K. (2001) A comparison of input enhancement and explicit instruction of mitigators. In L. Bouton (ed.) *Pragmatics and Language Learning* (Vol. 10, pp. 111–130). Urbana, IL: University of Illinois at Urbana-Champaign.

House, J. (1996) Developing pragmatic fluency in English as a foreign language. *Studies in Second Language Acquisition* 18, 225–253.

Hudson, T., Detmer, E. and Brown, J.D. (1995) *Developing Prototypic Measures of Cross-Cultural Pragmatics*. Honolulu: University of Hawai'i at Manoa, Second Language Teaching & Curriculum Center.
Kasper, G. (1989) Interactive procedures in interlanguage discourse. In W. Oleksy (ed.) *Contrastive Pragmatics* (pp. 189–229). Amsterdam: Benjamins.
Kasper, G. (1997) The role of pragmatics in language teaching education. In K. Bardovi-Harlig and B. Hartford (eds) *Beyond Methods: Components of Second Language Teacher Education* (pp. 113–136). New York: McGraw-Hill.
Kasper, G. (2001) Classroom research on interlanguage pragmatics. In K.R. Rose and G. Kasper (eds) *Pragmatics in Language Teaching* (pp. 33–60). Cambridge: Cambridge University Press.
Kasper, G. and Dahl, M. (1991) *Research Methods in Interlanguage Pragmatics*. Honolulu: Second Language Teaching & Curriculum Center, University of Hawaii at Manoa.
Kasper, G. and Rose, K.R. (2002) *Pragmatic Development in a Second Language*. (Also *Language Learning*: Supplement 1, 52). Mahwah, NJ: Blackwell.
Koike, D.A. (1996) Transfer of pragmatic competence and suggestions in Spanish foreign language learning. In S.M. Gass and J. Neu (eds) *Speech Acts across Cultures* (pp. 257–281). Berlin: Mouton de Gruyter.
Koike, D.A. and Pearson, L. (2005) The effect of instruction and feedback in the development of pragmatic competence. *System* 33 (3), 481–501.
Larsen-Freeman, D. and Long, M.H. (1991) *An Introduction to Second Language Acquisition*. London: Longman.
Long, M.H. (1996) The role of the linguistic environment in second language acquisition. In W.C. Rithie and T.K. Bhatia (eds) *Handbook of Second Language Acquisition* (pp. 413–468). San Diego: Academic Press.
Lörscher, W. and Schulze, R. (1988) On polite speaking and foreign language classroom discourse. *International Review of Applied Linguistics in Language Teaching* 26, 183–199.
Mahboob, A. (2004) Native or non-native: What do students enrolled in an intensive English program think? In L.D. Kamhi-Stein (ed.) *Learning and Teaching from Experience: Perspectives on Non-native English-speaking Professionals* (pp. 121–149). Ann Arbor, MI: The University of Michigan Press.
Medgyes, P. (1994) *The Non-Native Teacher*. London: MacMillan.
Niezgoda, K. and Röver, C. (2001) Pragmatic and grammatical awareness: A function of the learning environment? In K.R. Rose and G. Kasper (eds) *Pragmatics in Language Teaching* (pp. 63–79). Cambridge: Cambridge University Press.
Nikula, T. (2002) Teacher talk reflecting pragmatic awareness: A look at EFL and content-based classroom settings. *Pragmatics* 12 (4), 447–467.
Olshtain, E. and Blum-Kulka, S. (1985) Degree of approximation: Non-native reactions to native speech act behavior. In S.M. Gass and C. Madsen (eds) *Input in Second Language Acquisition* (pp. 303–325). New York: Newbury House.
Olshtain, E. and Cohen, A. (1990). The learning of complex speech act behavior. *TESL Canada Journal* 7, 45–65.
Pasternak, M. and Bailey, K.M. (2004) Preparing non-native and native English-speaking teachers: Issues of professionalism and proficiency. In L.D. Kamhi-Stein (ed.) *Learning and Teaching from Experience: Perspectives on non-native English-speaking Professionals* (pp. 155–176). Ann Arbor, MI: The University of Michigan Press.
Rampton, B. (1990) Displacing the 'native speaker': Expertise, affiliation, and inheritance. *ELT Journal* 44, 97–101.

Rose, K.R. (1997) Pragmatics in the classroom: Theoretical concerns and practical possibilities. In L.F. Bouton (ed.) *Pragmatics and Language Learning* (Vol. 8, pp. 267–295). Urbana, IL: University of Illinois at Urbana-Champaign.

Rose, K.R. (1999) Teachers and students learning about requests in Hong Kong. In E. Hinkel (ed.) *Culture in Second Language Teaching and Learning* (pp. 167–180). Cambridge: Cambridge University Press.

Rose, K.R. (2005) On the effects of instruction in second language pragmatics. *System* 33 (3), 385–399.

Rose, R.K. and Kwai-Fun, C.N. (2001) Inductive and deductive teaching of compliments and compliment responses. In K.R. Rose and G. Kasper (eds) *Pragmatics in Language Teaching* (pp. 145–170). Cambridge: Cambridge University Press.

Samimy, K. and Brutt-Griffler, J. (1999) To be a native or non-native speaker: Perceptions of non-native speaking students in a graduate TESOL program. In G. Braine (ed.) *Non-native Educators in English Language Teaching* (pp. 127–144). Mahwah, NJ: Erlbaum.

Schauer, G.A. (2006) The development of ESL learners pragmatic competence: A longitudinal investigation of awareness and production. In K. Bardovi-Harlig, J.C. Félix-Brasdefer and A. Omar (eds) *Pragmatics and Language Learning* (Vol. 11, pp. 135–163). Honolulu: University of Hawai'i at Manoa, National Foreign Language Resource Center.

Schmidt, R. (1993) Consciousness, learning and interlanguage pragmatics. In G. Kasper and S. Blum-Kulka (eds) *Interlanguage Pragmatics* (pp. 21–42). New York: Oxford University Press.

Swain, M. (1996) Three functions of output in second language learning. In G. Cook and B. Seidlhofer (eds) *Principle and Practice in Applied Linguistics* (pp. 245–256). Oxford: Oxford University Press.

Takahashi, S. (2001) The role of input enhancement in developing pragmatic competence. In K.R. Rose and G. Kasper (eds) *Pragmatics in Language Teaching* (pp. 171–199). Cambridge: Cambridge University Press.

Tarone, E. and Yule, G. (1989) *Focus on the Language Learner*. Oxford: Oxford University Press.

Vellenga, H. (2004) Learning pragmatics from ESL & EFL textbooks: How likely? *TESL-EJ* 8 (2), 1–17. On WWW at http://cwp60.berkeley.edu:16080/TESL-EJ/ej30/a3.html.

Washburn, G.N. (2001) Using situation comedies for pragmatic language teaching and learning. *TESOL Journal* 10 (4), 21–26.

Welzman, E. (1989) Requestive hints. In S. Blum-Kulka, J. House and G. Kasper (eds) *Cross-Cultural Pragmatics: Requests and Apologies* (pp. 71–95). Norwood, NJ: Ablex.

Part 3
Investigating How Pragmatics Can Be Tested in Foreign Language Contexts

Chapter 10
Investigating Interlanguage Pragmatic Ability: What Are We Testing?

SAYOKO YAMASHITA

Introduction

'The primary purpose of a language test is to provide a *measure* that we can interpret as an indicator of an individual's language ability' (Bachman & Palmer, 1996: 23). This is also true for testing learners' pragmatic ability or interlanguage pragmatics, which Kasper and Blum-Kulka (1993: 3) defined as 'a non-native speaker's use and acquisition of linguistic action patterns in a second language'. As there have not been many test development studies to date in the area of interlanguage pragmatics (Garcia, 2004; Hudson *et al.*, 1992, 1995; Liu, 2006; Roever, 2005; Yamashita, 1996) compared to the number of speech act studies carried out strictly for research purposes, it is not an easy task to obtain a comprehensive picture of what is an appropriate measure of interlanguage pragmatics. There is, however, a growing interest in this area due to the important role of pragmatic competence in the development of communicative competence and thus its importance in language teaching itself.

In this chapter, I would like to discuss various possible components for testing interlanguage pragmatics and the need for both production-type and comprehension-type interlanguage pragmatics testing. I will first briefly review the literature in interlanguage pragmatics and testing. Second, I will discuss issues related to learners' pragmatic ability. Third, I will talk about components of testing interlanguage pragmatic ability. Finally, I will describe instruments or methods of testing interlanguage pragmatic ability. After a brief summary of the discussion, future perspectives in testing interlanguage pragmatic ability will be presented.

Theoretical Overview

Pragmatic competence

Pragmatics is defined as 'the study of people's comprehension and production of linguistic action in context' (Kasper & Blum-Kulka, 1993: 3). A more specific definition can be given as 'pragmatics is the study of language from the point of view of users, especially of the choices they make, the constraints they encounter in using language in social interaction and the effects their use of language has on other participants in the act of communication' (Crystal, 1985: 240). Indeed, pragmatics deals with language users, constraints that they face and interaction effects with others in social interaction. 'Pragmatic knowledge enables us to create or interpret discourse by relating utterances or sentences and texts to their meaning, to the intentions of language users, and to relevant characteristics of the language use setting' (Bachman & Palmer, 1996: 69).

With the expansion of the communicative competence framework (Canale, 1983; Canale & Swain, 1980), language learners' pragmatic ability or interlanguage pragmatics is placed in a model of communicative language ability, which Bachman (1990: 84) described as 'consisting of both knowledge, or competence, and the capacity for implementing, or executing that competence in appropriate, contextualized communicative language use'. He proposed to include three components in a model of communicative language ability, namely language competence, strategic competence and psychophysiological mechanisms. Bachman's language competence model is divided into two components, organizational competence, which is subdivided into grammatical and textual competence, and pragmatic competence, which is subdivided into illocutionary competence and sociolinguistic competence (Bachman, 1990: 87).

The components under pragmatic competence in Bachman's model (1990) guided the theoretical direction for the measurement of interlanguage pragmatics. He described illocutionary competence in reference to the theory of speech acts and language functions, functions further categorized as ideational, manipulative or interactional, heuristic and imaginative functions (see Bachman, 1990 for more detail). All of these functions seem to be important for the learners to acquire as part of their pragmatic competence in a second or foreign language context. This competence will be tested as interlanguage pragmatic competence.

The other part of pragmatic competence in his model is sociolinguistic competence. Bachman (1990) listed three sensitivities and an ability-sensitivity to differences in dialect or variety, sensitivity to differences in register, sensitivity to naturalness and ability to interpret cultural references and figures of speech.

Pragmatic competence includes the types of knowledge that are employed in the contextualized performance and interpretation of socially appropriate illocutionary acts in discourse, in addition to organizational competence (Bachman, 1990). Pragmatic ability for the language learner then is to be able to comprehend the pragmalinguistic action as a listener and also be able to produce it as a speaker in a target language (TL) and following its cultural norms, using one's own pragmatic knowledge of a

TL. As for measuring learners' pragmalinguistic ability in a test, both comprehension and production should be equally important. Pragmatic failure (Thomas, 1983) could occur when learners misunderstand what a speaker of a TL says, and/or when they produce inappropriate expressions that do not meet the TL pragmatics or cultural norms.

Testing

Testing is one type of measure according to Bachman (1990). While measurement is the process of quantifying the characteristics of persons according to explicit procedures and rules such as different types of measures, including rankings, ratings and tests, and its quantification involves the assigning of numbers, letter grades or labels, such as excellent or good, among others, an observation of an attribute must be replicable, for other observers, in other contexts and with other individuals in order to be considered as a measure (Bachman, 1990).

As one type of measurement, a test is designed to elicit a specific sample of an individual's behavior, and 'the value of tests lies in their capability for eliciting the specific kinds of behavior that the test user can interpret as evidence of the attributes or abilities which are of interest' (Bachman, 1990: 22). When developing and evaluating a test of interlanguage pragmatics, the consideration of the validity, or a question of 'does the test measure what it is intended to measure?' is important.

Among several ways of evaluating validity, construct validation is a process of investigating what a test measures and in construct validation one validates a test against a theory (Palmer & Groot, 1981). 'Construct validity is used to refer to the extent to which we can interpret a given test score as an indicator of the ability, or construct(s), we want to measure with respect to a specific domain of generalization' (Bachman & Palmer, 1996: 21). Bachman and Palmer further expressed that we need to determine the extent to which the test task corresponds to tasks in the Target Language Use (TLU) domain or 'authenticity', and to determine the extent to which the test task engages the test taker's areas of language ability, or 'interactiveness'. They then raise questions whether or not it is sufficient to justify using a test. For example, using a multiple-choice test that was originally made for testing grammatical knowledge for measuring writing ability is not sufficient. Defining the construct to include only one area of language knowledge is inappropriately narrow, as the construct involved in the TLU domain involves other areas of language knowledge, as well as metacognitive strategies, and may involve topical knowledge and affective responses as well (Bachman & Palmer, 1996: 23). This is also true for a test of interlanguage pragmatic competence. Naturally including only speech acts as the construct in a pragmatics test is not sufficient, as Roever (2005) mentioned. An approach such as including implicatures and/or routines besides speech acts, adapted by Roever (2005) and Garcia (2004), is needed in an interlanguage pragmatics test.

Content validity is another important area to be considered in test construction. Content validity is the process of investigating whether the selection of tasks one observes in a test is representative of the larger set of tasks of which the test is assumed to be a sample (Palmer & Groot, 1981: 2). In fact, it refers to the degree to which a test is a representative sample of the content of whatever the test was designed to measure (Brown, 1996). We need to select tasks that we believe are representative of the target samples.

The perception of the pragmatics of a TL or gaining an understanding of what a native speaker (NS) is saying is another important facet of pragmatics, as a serious discrepancy would occur in communication if a learner failed to understand the appropriate meaning or pragmatic function of a speaker's utterances. Currently, only a limited number of pragmatics testing studies that target learners' pragmatic comprehension are available (Garcia, 2004; Roever, 2005).

Interlanguage Pragmatics Issues

Misunderstandings between speakers

Misunderstandings are a central issue in cross-cultural or interlanguage pragmatics, which occur both between NSs, and a NS and a learner. Cross-cultural pragmatic misunderstanding occurs between people from different cultural backgrounds. A group of the National Language Research Institute (Shinpro 'Nihongo' Dai 2-han, 1999a, 1999b) conducted a cross-cultural contrastive study to find out how speakers of different languages and with different cultural backgrounds interpret pragmalinguistic behaviors either differently or universally. They used a video-prompt method composed of six short video clips taken from Japanese TV dramas. Each of the six scenes contained various speech act combinations including claim-apology, gratitude-return, apology-excuse-warning, request-apology-explanation and so forth, and also other non-speech act strategies. They showed the videos to three groups of people, Japanese in Japan, that is NSs, who have never lived overseas for more than three months; Japanese who were living in five countries at the time of the study, namely, Brazil, France, South Korea, the USA and Vietnam; and people from those five countries listed above who were living in Japan at the time of the data collection. The total number of subjects was 990. Among many research questions, one question asked to what extent the ways of thinking of Japanese people and of foreigners living in Japan differed towards pragmalinguistic behaviors in the video clips. They were asked how they would react toward each situation if it happened in

Japan or happened in the five other countries. They were asked how they would react toward each situation shown if it happened in Japan or in one of the five other countries. This was done to explore whether or not any differences observed among the subjects could be attributed to their respective cultural backgrounds, or the physical location where they viewed the videos. One of the findings revealed that speech acts themselves varied depending on the culture, and the speaker's usage depended on where the speaker resided. The most striking finding was that values toward some speech acts were not relevant to another culture. Moreover, foreign people somewhat overgeneralized the target culture. For example, there is a tendency in Vietnam or in Korea that the apology speech act is not very relevant when a person in the video clip bumps into another person. Japanese living in those countries tended to be less apologetic or avoid an apology when they were asked what they would say in such a situation because they thought that people do not apologize in such a situation in those countries. In contrast, Vietnamese and Koreans living in Japan tended to be overapologetic compared to the native Japanese speakers' norm, because they believed that Japanese apologize quite frequently. Nishihara (1999) warned that pragmatic standards for a country or a culture may not be universal, thus when we conduct an international or intercultural study or survey, we need to be cautious not to overgeneralize our own beliefs. As for developing an interlanguage pragmatics test, it is valued and emphasized that we should base our test on empirical studies. However, most of the cross-cultural pragmatic studies were based on Western norms. Studies of pragmalinguistics based on non-Western cultural backgrounds might shed light on a better understanding of cross-cultural pragmatics, which would be, as Kasper (1992) stated, a base for interlanguage pragmatics.

Misunderstandings between a NS and a learner can naturally occur very often due to the learner's weak understanding of the target culture pragmatics, or due to differences in their cultural backgrounds. Thomas (1983) reports an incident that occurred when a Japanese graduate student for whom she was the thesis adviser made an inappropriate request in English when she submitted her thesis draft. Thomas became furious when her student said, 'Please read my draft and give me some comments'. She thought that the student was too direct and very impolite to tell her what she must do as a thesis adviser. In Japanese society, though, it is very common for a junior member to ask a senior member by 'acknowledging' or directly stating what the senior person does for the junior. This is regarded as more polite and even expected in Japanese academia. NSs are usually very patient if low-level learners make such mistakes, but they can misunderstand learners' pragmatic errors if their level is advanced because the learners can use the language grammatically and syntactically well. In Thomas' case, the learner had obviously been affected by L1 pragmatic transfer. Naturally, we cannot solely depend on these anecdotal episodes to design a test, but for a test developer it might be helpful if there was a database or corpus of pragmatic misunderstanding or pragmatic transfer samples of learners from different cultural backgrounds. Corpus linguistics might contribute to this area a great deal in the very near future (Aijmer, 1996; Aijmer & Altenberg, 1991; Tottie, 1991).

Participating in a conversation as a listener

Listeners' responses are called backchannels. Many researchers have studied the functions of backchannels used in English. While Orestrom (1983) took it as a supportive function (i.e. the non-primary speaker sends a signal to the primary speaker to show his or her understanding or agreement), Erickson (1979) and Schegloff (1982) described them as the interactional functions and contextual cues that contribute to conversation. The non-primary speaker serves to pass an opportunity to produce a full turn or regulative function (Schegloff, 1982). The Japanese term *aizuchi* is sometimes used for backchannel to indicate its unique aspects in the Japanese language. Maynard (1986, 1990) and White (1989) found that Japanese *aizuchi* is different from English backchannels regarding the frequency of listener responses, which shows their attentive listening and encourages the primary speaker to keep talking. It sometimes co-occurs with the primary speaker's speech producing simultaneous talk. Moreover, Japanese sometimes use *aizuchi* or nodding when they do not understand or do not agree with what the primary speaker is saying (Cutrone, 2005). These Japanese *aizuchi* might cause some native English speakers to be discouraged from keeping the floor or cause other serious misunderstandings (Cutrone, 2005).

Preface utterances such as 'As you know', 'I remind you' and 'Of course' are intended to be taken as reminders, and also affect the listener's participation. They indicate that the speaker believes the addressee already knows the proposition expressed (Green, 1996). These preface expressions are sometimes difficult for the learner to catch. When I was teaching Japanese as a foreign language in Texas, I frequently met a Hispanic–American lady at the Board of Education. When she spoke to me, she often finished her utterance with 'Do you know what I'm saying?' I thought at first that I needed to paraphrase what she told me and responded to her. Whenever she told me so, I was reviewing what she was saying to me in my head. Soon I learned that she used the expression as a simple sentence ending marker or a discourse marker. Knowing and being able to react properly to such expressions also depends on learners' pragmatic competence or ability. Even though we may not need to push learners too much to produce such sentences, such ability could be tested using multiple-choice-type questions.

Understanding metalanguage and metapragmatics is another important ability of a listener. Metalanguage is language which comments on, describes or examines what happens at the level of language itself, such as the example 'This is strictly off the record, but...' (Mey, 1993: 269). In contrast, the metapragmatic level is where we discuss theoretical issues in pragmatics having to do with pragmatics, and an example is when a comment by someone such as 'You did a great job' is followed by 'and I'm not being polite' (Mey, 1993: 270). Here a speaker expressed something, and added the pragmatic function verbally in order to emphasize or to avoid misunderstanding. Mey (1993) further wrote that metapragmatics should be concerned with the circumstances and conditions that allow us to use our language, or prevent us from using it adequately, as in the above example. The pragmatic ability of language users not only deals with whether or not they can produce pragmatic expressions appropriately or adequately, but also concerns how a receiver or listener interprets their utterances. If speakers are concerned about a recipient's possible misunderstanding, they may try to avoid it. This kind of ability of seeing and commenting on the possible consequence of one's own utterance is also an important part of a learner's pragmatic ability and should be part of testing that ability.

Understanding the unsaid and assessing the unsaid

Speaker hinting (using a hinting word or expression or something unsaid) is expecting that the listener knows what the speaker wants (Gibbs, 1983). When cultures differ, the extent to how explicitly people express themselves differs. Consequently, how well people understand what is said also differs. Hayata (1999) reported a case of an encounter of a Japanese person and a French person. She described a situation when the French person turned off a light in a university hallway in Paris where the Japanese person was sitting on a bench. The Japanese person was upset, thinking that the French person did not care about other people nearby when he turned off the light. Another Japanese person living in France for over 30 years laughed when she heard her complaint and said, French people will shout in such a case, '"Don't turn off the light! I am here!" Why didn't you shout him?' The episode might suggest how explicitly people communicate verbally is different depending on their cultural norm. Misunderstanding occurs when Japanese do not say enough. Sasaki (1994) cited another episode of an American businessman's misunderstanding of a Japanese businessman's hinting. When the American businessman visited a Japanese company to get an advertisement, the Japanese businessman said, 'The color coordination is fashionable; this kind of journal has surely not existed before. We will be considering it.' The American businessman was excited about the reaction of the Japanese saying *consider* it. On the other hand, the Japanese person who accompanied him instantly said, 'Mr. X, it's not a deal! If so, he would have asked us the deadline and other details; "will be considering" means "will *not* do any further".' As for interlanguage pragmatic ability, understanding things that are unsaid or hinting are as important as understanding implicature or routines. How we could test such ability is a challenge for test developers.

Avoiding a speech act to accommodate a target culture norm

Yamashita (1996) reported a number of examples in which participants in her study purposely avoided producing expected speech acts suggested in her discourse completion tests (DCTs). In one case some participants in the role of job interviewee did not refuse to attend a company tour offered by an interviewer, even though the DCT scenario said that the 'interviewee' cannot attend a tour due to another appointment and hinted that the offer should be refused. Another example from her DCTs is a situation in which someone asks the boss for a piece of memo paper at a meeting. The purposes of these particular DCTs were to elicit refusal and request speech acts respectively, carefully controlling the degree of imposition, power and distance. She did not assume avoidance of these speech acts in responses. However, some learners (American English-speaking participants learning Japanese as a foreign or second language) reported that they purposely avoided performing the acts by saying that they believed that Japanese would not refuse or request in such situations if the speaker were a junior member speaking with a boss. Native Japanese speakers' responses also support their comments. The above DCTs could be used as a test battery for learners of English to test their English interlanguage pragmatics ability, but may not be reliable as a testing battery for interlanguage pragmatics of Japanese.

Nonverbal behaviors

Whether or not we actually say something, nonverbal actions such as gestures including hand waves, head nods, facial expressions or eye movements can mean as much as verbal utterances alone or even more. Kelly *et al.* (1999) found that people were more likely to interpret an utterance as an indirect request when speech was accompanied by a relevant pointing gesture than when speech or gesture was presented alone. Jungheim (2006) investigated how learners of Japanese as a second language and Japanese NSs interpret a Japanese refusal gesture, the so-called *hand fan*, and found that the learners are significantly poorer than NSs at interpreting the refusal gesture. Many gestures are culturally specific. I have experiences of not being able to understand nonverbal messages in English. When I was studying at a graduate school in the USA, I had trouble interpreting what an American professor was implying while she was saying something and positioned her second and third fingers of both hands next to her ears and moved up and down. It took me a while to understand that she was imitating parentheses and trying to tell the students that what she was saying was a key word. Students could miss an important message if they did not understand this. Nonverbal behaviors play an important role in daily life and academic contexts. The Gesture Test (Gestest) for assessing the comprehension of English gestures and the Nonverbal Ability Scales (NOVA) (see Jungheim, 1995) for assessing nonverbal behavior in conversations were developed within the communicative competence framework. The former used multiple-choice questions with a video prompt to test the comprehension of a series of culturally specific gestures and the latter used a series of rating scales to evaluate learners' use of gestures, gaze and head nodding in an interview task. Broader units of analysis beyond the verbal message may also be needed for understanding learners' pragmatic ability.

Estimating the level of a learner's language proficiency

Learners' levels of language proficiency are usually assessed by scores on a proficiency test, a placement test or comprehensive examination administered by an institution. These traditionally measure a general language ability which includes knowledge of grammar, morphology, semantics, syntax and phonology, or skill categories such as listening, speaking, reading and writing. Pragmalinguistics is not yet regularly included in these tests. This is partly because the theories of communicative competence and communicative language teaching have not been fully developed and rigorous empirical studies need to be carried out.

The mismatch of learners' linguistic ability and pragmatic ability is another issue. Especially regarding interlanguage pragmalinguistics, learners' abilities differ depending on their learning backgrounds as either foreign language learners or second language learners. Empirical studies show some of the differences. Yamashita (1996) reported examples of two beginning Japanese learners' performances on roleplays to elicit a 'refusal' speech act. While a Japanese as a foreign language (JFL) learner tried to explain the situation or reason for the refusal linguistically to an interlocutor, but naturally had great difficulty doing that due to her limited grammatical and vocabulary knowledge, and as a result performed poorly, a Japanese as a second language (JSL) learner with two years of experience living in Japan performed his roleplay quite differently. He took the same placement test as the above JFL learner and was placed in the beginners' level based on his placement test scores for grammar, vocabulary, reading and listening. Instead of trying to explain the situation in his roleplay, he started his conversation with a hedge word and a pause, the typical Japanese hedge system of 'Chotto... (Well...),' and then he repeated the interlocutor's words in an interrogative form, just adding an interrogative marker 'ka' as in 'Raishuu desu ka? (Next week?)' (Yamashita, 1996: 70). The two learners' performances were quite different on the pragmalinguistic level, and naturally the JSL learner had an advantage, having been exposed to the target culture pragmatics. We can easily imagine that L2 learners' comprehension of L2 pragmatics must be more developed while they are living in their L2 country. If the placement test had have included a section on pragmatic ability, his placement might have been different. As Blum-Kulka and Olshtain (1986: 174) have reported, '...in terms of pragmatic competence, length of stay is a much more interesting measure than level of linguistic proficiency'. When we design a proficiency test, we need to ask ourselves, should we include a pragmalinguistic section, and if the answer is 'yes', how?

Components of a Test of Interlanguage Pragmatic Ability

Roever (2005) chose three components for his web-based language (pragmatics) test, namely speech acts, implicatures and routines. He intended to elicit test-takers' knowledge of commonly used strategies and beliefs about which practices are acceptable in the target speech community, rather than their individual preferences. The validation was exemplified by the comprehensive use of Messick's (1989) validation framework for language testing. As this is the first systematic pragmatic test containing multiple components that are based on empirical studies, I would like to review those components.

Speech acts

Numerous cross-cultural pragmatic studies have been conducted for empirical research purposes to study speech acts such as requests, apologies, refusals, complaints and suggestions, among many others (Beebe *et al.*, 1990; Blum-Kulka, 1982; Cohen *et al.*, 1986; Gass & Neu, 1996; House & Kasper, 1987; Ikoma, 1993; Kasper, 1989; Olshtain & Weinbach, 1987; Takahashi & Beebe, 1987, 1993; Trosborg, 1995). Most studies have focused on a particular speech act to examine how people realize each speech act and tried to find variations in strategies used by the participants. Among those studies, the Cross-Cultural Speech Act Realization Project (CCSARP) (Blum-Kulka *et al.*, 1989) was the pioneering study and very influential as a large international project. They studied the realization of requests and apologies cross-culturally and presented lists of the strategies. Many coding categories were suggested for naming realization of requests and apologies. Because of the results of this extensive empirical study, speech acts are unique items for testing pragmatic ability.

Using three distinctive speech acts, those of requests, apologies and refusals, as test items, Yamashita (1996) investigated different measures, including DCTs, multiple-choice tests, self-assessment and roleplay tests, and found that they were reasonably reliable and valid, except for the multiple-choice test. Yamashita (1996), however, pointed out that the area that these tests can cover is very limited (i.e. only involves three speech acts), whereas Austin (1962) estimated there are somewhere between 1000 and 10,000 illocutionary forces or speech acts in English (see also Flowerdew, 1990). It does not seem to be appropriate to only use a few speech act items to test learners' pragmatic ability and claim that the learner is at a certain level for pragmatic ability. We need to include other speech acts such as giving orders, making promises, giving thanks and so forth to test interlanguage pragmatics. Moreover, I would like to stress that speech acts are not the only component for testing interlanguage pragmatics, as we will see next.

Conversational implicatures

Conversational implicature was discussed by Grice (1975) with the notion of the Cooperative Principle. Participants in a conversation are expected to make their contributions to the conversation informative (quantity), truthful (quality), relevant (relation) and clear (manner). Bouton (1988) conducted an empirical study on conversational implicature to see how implicature is understood by English as a second language (ESL) and English as a foreign language (EFL) learners and NSs of English. He found that there were differences in interpreting implicatures between relatively proficient learners and NSs of English. He further studied the same participants in a longitudinal design (first arrived, 18 months later and 54 months later) using different types of implicatures such as Criticism, Sequence, Pope Q, Relevance Maxim and Scalar Maxim (see Bouton, 1994). He found that learners (non-native speakers of English) should become proficient if they live in an English-speaking community long enough, but the process is quite long, and also unguided learning in this area seems slow. Kubota (1995) replicated Bouton's study in an EFL context.

In Garcia (2004), two types of implicatures were used in her test of pragmatic comprehension, specific implicatures, single utterances that required the listener to infer what the speaker meant, and general implicatures, which involved using expectations of the context to figure the speaker's intention from the interaction overall. In her test, the test taker listens to fairly long dialogues (e.g. 30 turns in a conversation) and a few multiple-choice questions are given regarding speech acts and implicatures in each set. One example question from Garcia's study (2004: appendix A), looks like this:

> 5. Consider the whole dialogue. What does the woman think?
> [PC, Implicature General]
> (a) She thinks the man is lying.
> (b) She thinks the man is argumentative.
> (c) She thinks the man is honest.*
> (d) She thinks the man is wrong.

Roever (2005) included items testing idiosyncratic implicature (general conversational implicature) and formulaic implicature (Pope Q type and indirect criticism) in his implicature section. A typical example of his web-based written questions looks like this (Roever, 2005: 122).

101. Jack is talking to his housemate Sarah about another housemate, Frank.

> Jack: 'Do you know where Frank is, Sarah?'
> Sarah: 'Well, I heard music from his room earlier.'
> 1. Frank forgot to turn the music off.
> 2. Frank's loud music bothers Sarah.
> 3. Frank is probably in his room.
> 4. Sarah doesn't know where Frank is.

Pragmatic routines

Routine 'is a property of utterances or an expression that is appropriate to a situation of a certain kind or a strategy which is appropriate relative to certain communicative ends' (Coulmas, 1981). Many routines are universal phenomena such as greetings. However, according to different cultures, there are variations which are for learners difficult to understand and sometimes cause misunderstanding (Coulmas, 1981). Being able to master and use routines of a TL are beneficial for learners as they provide speech with a natural and proficient flavor, and often such routine expressions such as 'What does it mean?' or 'Please speak slowly' help solve learners' recurrent communication problems. Moreover, for both NSs and learners, routinized speech serves an important function when speakers need time to arrange their thoughts and to prepare the next conversational moves. In other words, routines are a means of guiding a person's normal participation in social interaction (Coulmas, 1981).

Roever (2005) differentiates between situational routines and functional routines after Coulmas (1981). Situational routines are limited in their appropriate appearance to a specified situational condition such as an institutional routine. 'What brings you here?' is a typical situational routine that a medical doctor says to a patient when he starts a medical interview. Functional routines, on the other hand, have much variation depending on the context and can apply to a variety of conditions. 'I was wondering if...,' or 'Do you mind if...?' Roever (2005) found that EFL learners performed significantly worse on situational than on functional routines, and ESL learners performed flawlessly on the situational routines on the same testing instrument.

Methods of Testing Pragmatic Ability

Various methods or measures of testing pragmatic ability have been proposed, which have been included in research studies in order to test production and comprehension. I would like to discuss each measure below in the following order: DCTs, multiple-choice tests, picture prompts, video prompts and roleplays.

Discourse completion tests (DCTs)

The most popular method in cross-cultural and interlanguage pragmatics is known as DCTs. DCTs can be used as both a production test to elicit speech acts and a comprehension test to measure learners' comprehension of speech acts. The DCT provides learners with an opportunity for a display of knowledge that is precluded for many non-native speakers by the cognitive demands of face-to-face interaction (Bergman & Kasper, 1993: 101). Some negative characteristics of this method have been reported, such as (1) the waffling effect or verbosity (Edmondson & House, 1991); (2) the differences of the intended speech acts and elicited speech acts (Wolfson *et al.*, 1989; Yamashita, 2005); (3) differences of the length of oral responses and written DCT responses (Rintell & Mitchell, 1989; Yamashita, 1998a, 2001); and (4) DCTs' misguiding written descriptions (Yamashita, 1998b). Despite the above weaknesses, DCTs have been regarded as very effective tools for cross-cultural and interlanguage pragmatics studies due to the fact that they can be used to gather a large amount of data easily and the data obtained from this method have been considered as compatible with natural speech occurrences. DCTs are administered using both production methods and multiple-choice methods. There may be some difficulties when production DCTs are used as a testing tool as rater involvement might cause a reliability problem.

Multiple-choice tests

Multiple-choice tests including multiple-choice DCTs have also been used as a comprehension measure of interlanguage pragmatics and are discussed elsewhere (Roever, 2005; Rose, 1994; Rose & Ono, 1995; Yamashita, 1996). The problems with multiple-choice DCTs reported in Yamashita (1996) seem to be due to their translation from English DCTs. She hinted that some strategies that appeared in the multiple-choice DCTs were not applicable in the Japanese context, or there was no applicable one in the choices. Regarding his multiple-choice DCTs, Rose (1992) suggested that the Japanese utterance with a certain discourse marker (i.e. hinting ending) indicates a hearer's filling in the gap, but no single choice could indicate that.

The multiple-choice test format has also been used to test implicature (Bouton, 1988, 1994; Garcia, 2004; Roever, 2001), formulaic or routine expressions (Hagiwara, 2007; Read & Nation, 2004; Roever, 2001), and politeness (Tanaka & Kawade, 1982). Multiple-choice tests are used quite often in traditional grammar tests, as their strongest feature is the ability to test easily in a short period of time and to facilitate analysis. Tanaka and Kawade (1982) used multiple-choice questions containing a picture of each situation, a written description of each situation and six polite responses or choices for each situation. Their multiple-choice design worked for their own research purposes, as it was designed for studying politeness levels of requests, it does not reflect differences in pragmatic-based strategies. The need for multiple-choice test formats, however, seems to be growing with the increasing number of web-based tests drawing a great deal of interest.

Roleplays

Roleplays are possible to simulate conversational turns and to have the interlocutor apply conversational pressures that are not present in a DCT (Cohen & Olshtain, 1994). As video equipment has become widely used in second language acquisition research, more and more cross-cultural and interlanguage pragmatics studies have been conducted using video-taped roleplays (Yamashita, 1996). The advantage of using the roleplay method in testing pragmatics is that the full discourse context and sequential organization in terms of negotiation of meaning, the strategy choice and politeness investment can be examined (Kasper & Dahl, 1991). Naturally nonverbal parts of authentic conversation are also reflected in roleplay. The problem of using a roleplay in an actual testing situation is that it is time consuming and requires interlocutor training. It might be feasible for testing learners' pragmatics ability if we set up a rubric for interlanguage pragmatics roleplay testing just like the American Council on the Teaching of Foreign Languages (ACTFL) test guidelines (ACTFL, 1986, 1989).

Picture prompts

Picture prompts, including illustrations and cartoons, have been used to elicit interlanguage pragmatic features instead of using written descriptions. Picture prompt interlanguage pragmatics tests are particularly useful when young learners' second language acquisition is investigated. Rose (2000) investigated cross-sectional speech act acquisition by primary school pupils in Hong Kong using young learner-friendly cartoons. Most interlanguage pragmatics empirical studies have used intermediate to advanced learners as subjects and avoid novice and beginners due to their difficulty reading written prompt descriptions. Yamashita (2001) developed Picture Response Tests (PRTs) to solve the above problem and also to avoid the effects of written prompts. In her pilot study, she found that learners tend to be affected by written prompts. One particular written prompt described the situation neutrally, but if learners used the description as it appeared there in an utterance, it would show their irresponsibility. Surprisingly, all NS participants changed the description (i.e. using a different type of verb form) to show that the utterance was more apologetic. Picture prompts can also be used effectively in web-based tests.

Video prompts

Video prompts have been used for different purposes, such as (1) to grasp a learner's beliefs toward a target culture pragmatic norm in general; (2) to comprehend a learner's interpretation of target culture pragmatics; and (3) to elicit a learner's pragmatic production. It contains various aspects of interlanguage interaction, not only verbal including voice tones and prosodic (e.g. 'uhmmm'), but also conversational partners' facial expressions, gestures and silent pauses, as well as visual cues and background to the situation. Such rich information far surpasses written elicitation measures. Naturally there are also weaknesses in using video prompt. A specialist will be required to produce such videos, and the budget will be more than that of paper and pencil tests due to the need for equipment to show it to test takers. Evaluation standards should also be developed. Using video prompts on web-based pragmatics tests can be expected to become more feasible in the future, but further research in this area is needed.

Summary

As a summary of the above discussion regarding components and methods of interlanguage pragmatics testing, I would like to present Figure 10.1. It summarizes the methods and components that have been tested (marked with *) and *hypothetical* test components (marked with ●) that have not yet been tested, but that may be included in pragmatics

Measurement / Method of testing	Production		Comprehension
Components	Written	Performance	Multiple-choice MCQ=multiple choice questions
Speech Act	DCT(w/p)*1	Roleplay(w)*2	MCQ (w/p)*3
Implicature	●	●	MCQ(w)*4
Routine	●	●	MCQ(w)*5
Formulaic	●	●	MCQ(w)*6
Politeness	●	●	MCQ (w/p)*7
Nonverbal behavior	●	Roleplay(w)*8	MCQ (v)*9
-Back-channeling	●	●	●
-Dialect and language variation	●	●	●
-Discourse markers	●	●	●
-Indirectness	●	●	●
-Metapragmatics	●	●	●
-Phatic expressions	●	●	●
-Pre-sequence (e.g., "You know")	●	●	●
-Prosodic (e.g., "uhmmm")	●	●	●
-Register (Written or Spoken)	●	●	●
-Turn-taking	●	●	●

Note: Abbreviations in ( ) shows Prompt:

w=written prompt, p=picture, illustration, or cartoon prompt; v=video prompt

[-] before component represents hypothetical component

*1 Hudson et al. (1995), Liu (2006), Roever (2005), Rose (1994), Yamashita (1996, 2001)

*2 Hudson et al. (1995), Yamashita (1996)

*3 Garcia (2004), Hudson et al. (1995), Liu (2006), Roever (2005), Rose (2000), Yamashita (1996)

*4 Bouton (1988), Garcia (2004), Roever (2005)

*5 Roever (2005)

*6 Hagiwara (2007)

*7 Tanaka and Kawade (1982)

*8 Jungheim (1995)

*9 Jungheim (1995)

Figure 10.1 Test developments of interlanguage pragmatics

testing in the future. Written and performance tests are categorized under production measurement because they deal with test-takers' written or performed samples or outcomes. Multiple choice questions (MCQs) are categorized under Comprehension measurement, because test takers show only their pragmatic knowledge by selecting an appropriate answer choice. Potential components for interlanguage pragmatics tests are listed under 'Nonverbal behavior' in the component column on the far left. We can see that interlanguage pragmatics tests that have been conducted to date are very limited.

Interlanguage pragmatics has dynamic facets. Adding such components to testing measures in the future will allow us to obtain a more comprehensive picture of learners' interlanguage pragmatic abilities.

Future Perspectives in Testing Pragmatic Ability: Rethinking Assumptions

I would like to conclude this chapter with a few questions for future research.

(1) What are the constructs of interlanguage pragmatics?

Speech acts seem to be an established component for interlanguage pragmatics for testing, and implicature and routines have also come to be used as additional components. As pragmatics is used in practical situations in daily life, a language for specific purposes approach can also focus on such areas as pragmatics in daily life, college life, the workforce and medical encounters. Understanding pragmatics makes conversation effective and natural, not only for NSs, but in particular for learners. Phatic expressions, prosodics, turn-taking, backchanneling and many others are all useful pragmatic features to master, but the methods of testing such features have not been fully developed yet. I presented the above features in Figure 10.1 as a hypothetical list of components for interlanguage pragmatics together with the tests that have actually been conducted. Empirical studies are needed in order to claim that each component is a representative construct in interlanguage pragmatics and thus can be used in testing. As for content validity, whether or not a representative sampling from the TL use domain can generalize to the entire domain is an issue. All subcomponents need to be shown to correlate highly or to be controlled by the same underlying factor (Roever, 2001).

(2) Should we test production or comprehension in order to measure interlanguage pragmatic ability?

As the DCT method was introduced to elicit interlanguage speech act production at the research level, this particular method has been widely utilized. It had a great impact on research in cross-cultural pragmatics. However, it has a certain weakness, especially when it is used as an interlanguage pragmatic *testing* measure. Learners need to be able to fully understand the written description in order to produce (write) expected pragmatic utterances. Learners' reading ability might not match their pragmatic ability. Moreover, learners might be fully aware of what is going on, but might not yet be able to produce a pragmatic reaction due to the lack of linguistic ability. Roleplay performance tests have the same problems as the DCT as a testing measure. Both DCTs and roleplay tests need to be evaluated by experienced raters if they are used as testing measures. Regarding comprehension, Garcia (2004: 1–2) listed several points that learners need to be able to do to comprehend meaning pragmatically: (1) understand a speaker's intentions; (2) interpret a speaker's feelings and attitudes; (3) differentiate speech act meaning, such as the difference between a directive and a commissive; (4) evaluate the intensity of a speaker's meaning, such as the difference between a suggestion and a warning; (5) recognize sarcasm, joking and other facetious behavior; and (6) be able to respond appropriately. These are all very important points for learners' comprehension of pragmatics. Interlanguage pragmatic measures should test the above comprehension abilities besides production ability.

(3) Is a paper and pencil test the best way to test interlanguage pragmatics?

Because pragmatics does not operate according to strict rules such as grammar, which usually involves right or wrong answers, showing one's pragmatic ability only by a paper and pencil test is sometimes difficult. The DCT method has been widely used in interlanguage pragmatics research and testing, but assessing the learner's production elicited by the test and scoring it would be a difficult task. A hundred test takers may produce a hundred different answers in an interlanguage pragmatics test. Multiple choice tests might have a similar kind of problem. Imagine if the learner chose, 'Fine, thank you, and you?' to a written question such as, 'What would you think you would say, if someone approaches you and says, "How are you?" – Select the most appropriate response from the following choices.' What you would answer might be different depending on the situation, whom it is you are speaking with or the interlocutor, or even your mood at a particular point. Even though I support the inclusion of such a feature as phatic expressions (i.e. greetings as seen above) in a pragmatics test, much consideration of how we should test or present it is needed. Is it appropriate to test it by written questions and ask the test taker to answer it by paper and pencil? It is different from a grammar test in which the learner selects the verb form 'went' as the past tense of the verb 'go', which is the only correct answer.

The use of visual prompts discussed earlier (e.g. pictures and videos) will be a strong and effective tool for future interlanguage pragmatics testing. Creating, editing and implementing visual prompts in pragmatics tests is getting easier due to the advancement of technology. It will give a sense of 'authenticity' or real life-like domain to test takers. Moreover, 'interactiveness' is a strong feature of visual prompts by which test takers can relate the topical content of it to their own topical knowledge. More and more web-based tests are being developed using video prompts due to their authenticity and interactiveness.

In conclusion, I would like to emphasize that there should be more components besides speech acts to test interlanguage pragmatics. Testing only a limited area does not represent or describe a whole picture of the learner's pragmatic ability. Naturally, it is easier to say this rather than actually conduct it. We should expand our research agenda to understand the construct of pragmatics in more depth. Additionally, both production ability and comprehension ability are important regarding pragmatic ability. Sometimes learners can understand what is said (including implicature), but cannot produce. Both skills should be tested. Lastly, visual prompts will be used more and more as a strong tool for testing, especially for pragmatics testing because they can effectively illustrate authentic situations and topics. Therefore, more research studies regarding developing interlanguage pragmatics testing are needed.

Acknowledgement

I would like to express my sincere gratitude to Nick Jungheim for his valuable advice and comments.

References

Aijmer, K. (1996) *Conversational Routines in English*. London: Longman.
Aijmer, K. and Altenberg, B. (1991) *English Corpus Linguistics*. London: Longman.
American Council on Teaching of Foreign Languages (ACTFL) (1986) *ACTFL Proficiency Guidelines*. New York: ACTFL.
American Council on Teaching of Foreign Languages (ACTFL) (1989) *ACTFL Testers Training Manual*. New York: ACTFL.
Austin, J.L. (1962) *How To Do Things with Words*. Oxford: Oxford University Press.
Bachman, L.F. (1990) *Fundamental Considerations in Language Testing*. Oxford: Oxford University Press.
Bachman, L.F. and Palmer, A.S. (1996) *Language Testing in Practice*. Oxford: Oxford University Press.
Beebe, L.M., Takahashi, T. and Uliss-Weltz, R. (1990) Pragmatic transfer in ESL refusals. In R.C. Scarcella, E. Anderson and S.D. Krashen (eds) *Developing Communicative Competence in a Second Language* (pp. 55–73). Rowley, MA: Newbury House.
Bergman, M.L. and Kasper, G. (1993) Perception and performance in native and nonnative apology. In G. Kasper and S. Blum-Kulka (eds) *Interlanguage Pragmatics* (pp. 82–107). Oxford: Oxford University Press.

Blum-Kulka, S. (1982) Learning to say what you mean in a second language: A study of speech act performance of learners of Hebrew as a second language. *Applied Linguistics* 3 (1), 29–59.

Blum-Kulka, S. and Olshtain, E. (1986) Too many words: Length of utterance and pragmatic failure. *Journal of Pragmatics* 8, 47–61.

Blum-Kulka, S., House, J. and Kasper, G. (1989) (eds) *Cross-Cultural Pragmatics: Requests and Apologies*. Norwood, NJ: Ablex.

Bouton, L. (1988) A cross-cultural study of ability to interpret implicatures in English. *World Englishes* 17, 183–196.

Bouton, L. (1994) Conversational implicature in a second language: Learned slowly when not deliberately taught. *Journal of Pragmatics* 22, 157–167.

Brown, J.D. (1996) *Testing in Language Programs*. Upper Saddle River, NJ: Prentice Hall Regents.

Canale, M. (1983) From communicative competence to communicative language pedagogy. In J. Richards and R. Schmidt (eds) *Language and Communication* (pp. 2–27). London: Longman.

Canale, M. and Swain, M. (1980) Theoretical bases of communicative approaches to second language teaching and testing. *Applied Linguistics* 1, 1–47.

Cohen, A., Olshtain, E. and Rosenstein, D. (1986) Advanced EFL apologies: What remains to be learned? *International Journal of Sociology and Language* 62, 51–74.

Cohen, A.D. and Olshtain, E. (1994) Researching the production of second language speech acts. In E. Tarone, S. Gass and A.D. Cohen (eds) *Research Methodology in Second Language Acquisition* (pp. 143–156). Hillsdale, NJ: Lawrence Erlbaum Associations.

Coulmas, F. (ed.) (1981) *Conversational Routine*. The Hague: Mouton.

Crystal, D. (1985) *A Dictionary of Linguistics and Phonetics* (2nd edn). Oxford: Blackwell.

Cutrone, P. (2005) A case study examining backchannels in conversations between Japanese–British dyads. *Multilingua* 24, 237–274.

Edmondson, W.J. and House, J. (1991) Do learners talk too much? The waffle phenomenon in interlanguage pragmatics. In R. Philippson, E. Kellerman, L. Selinker, M. Sharwood Smith and M. Swain (eds) *Foreign Language Pedagogy Research: A Commemorative Volume for Claus Faerch* (pp. 273–287). Clevedon and Philadelphia: Multilingual Matters.

Erickson, F. (1979) Talking own: Some cultural sources of miscommunication in interracial interviews. In A. Wolfgang (ed.) *Nonverbal Behavior: Applications and Cultural Implications* (pp. 99–126). New York: Academic Press.

Flowerdew, J. (1990) Problems of speech act theory from an applied perspective. *Language Learning* 40 (1), 79–105.

Garcia, P. (2004) Pragmatic comprehension of high and low level language. *TESL-EJ* 8 (2). On WWW at http://www-writing.berkeley.edu/TESL-EJ/ej30/a1.html.[d1]

Gass, S. and Neu, J. (eds) (1996) *Speech Acts across Cultures: Challenge to Communication in a Second Language*. Berlin: Mouton de Gruyter.

Gibbs, R.W. (1983) Do people always process the literal meanings of indirect requests? *Journal of Experimental Psychology: Learning, Memory, and Cognition* 9 (3), 524–533.

Green, G.M. (1996) *Pragmatics and Natural Language Understanding*. Mahwah, NJ: Lawrence Erlbaum.

Grice, H.P. (1975) Logic and conversation. In P. Cole and J. Morgan (eds) *Syntax and Semantics* (Vol. 3, pp. 41–58). New York: Academic Press.

Hagiwara, A. (2007) Utterance comprehension in Japanese: A quantitative study using MCQ. Paper presented at the meeting of the 17th International Conference on Pragmatics and Language Learning, University of Hawai'i at Manoa.

Hayata, M. (1999) Zainichi Furansujin-zaifutsu nihonjin chousa no shuhen kara [Study of French living in Japan and Japanese living in France]. In Shinpro 'Nihongo' Dai 2-han (ed.) *Video Shigeki ni-yoru Gengo Koudou Ishiki Chousa Houkokusho: Shiryo hen* [*Study of Consciousness toward Linguistic Behaviors of Japanese by Video Stimulation: Book of Data*] (pp. 379–382). Tokyo: National Language Research Institute. Ministry of Education of Japan, Scientific Research Grant No. 09NP0701.

House, J. and Kasper, G. (1987). Interlanguage pragmatics: Requesting in a foreign language. In W. Lorscher and R. Schulze (eds) *Perspectives on Language and Performance* (pp. 250–288). Tubingen, Germany: Narr.

Hudson, T., Detmer, E. and Brown, J.D. (1992) *A Framework for Testing Cross-Cultural Pragmatics.* Honolulu, HI: University of Hawai'i Press.

Hudson, T., Detmer, E. and Brown, J.D. (1995) *Developing Prototypic Measures of Cross-cultural Pragmatics* (Technical Report # 7). Honolulu: University of Hawai'i at Manoa, National Foreign Language Resource Center.

Ikoma, T. (1993) Sorry for giving me a ride: The use of apologetic expressions to show gratitude in Japanese. Unpublished PhD thesis, University of Hawai'i.

Jungheim, N.O. (1995) Assessing the unsaid: The development of tests of nonverbal ability. In J.D. Brown and S. Yamashita (eds) *Language Testing in Japan* (pp. 149–165). Tokyo: Japan Association for Language Teachers.

Jungheim, N. O. (2006) Learner and native speaker perspectives on a culturally-specific Japanese refusal gesture. *International Review of Applied Linguistics in Language Teaching* 44 (2), 125–143.

Kasper, G. (1989) Variation in interlanguage speech act realization. In S. Gass, C. Madden, D. Preston and L. Selinker (eds) *Variation in Second Language Acquisition: Discourse and Pragmatics* (pp. 37–58). Clevedon, UK: Multilingual Matters.

Kasper, G. (1992) Pragmatic transfer. *Second Language Research* 8, 203–231.

Kasper, G. and Blum-Kulka, S. (eds) (1993) *Interlanguage Pragmatics.* Oxford: Oxford University Press.

Kasper, G. and Dahl, M. (1991) Research methods in interlanguage pragmatics. *Studies in Second Language Acquisition* 13, 215–247.

Kelly, S.D. Barr, D.J., Church, R.B. and Lynch, K. (1999) Offering a hand to pragmatic understanding: The role of speech and gesture in comprehension and memory. *Journal of Memory and Language* 40, 577–592.

Kubota, M. (1995) Teachability of conversational implicature to Japanese EFL learners. *IRLT Bulletin* 9, 35–67. Tokyo: The Institute for Research in Language Teaching.[d2]

Liu, J. (2006) *Measuring Interlanguage Pragmatic Knowledge of EFL Learners.* Frankfurt am Main: Peter Lang.

Maynard, S. (1986) On back-channel behavior in Japanese and English casual conversation. *Linguistics* 24 (6), 73–105.

Maynard, S. (1990) Conversation management in contrast: Listener responses in Japanese and American English. *Journal of Pragmatics* 14 (1), 397–412.

Messick, S. (1989) Validity. In R.L. Linn (ed.) *Educational Measurement* (pp. 13–103). New York: Macmillan.

Mey, J. (1993) *Pragmatics.* Oxford: Blackwell.

Nishihara, S. (1999) Kenkyu no gaiyo. In Shinpro 'Nihongo' Dai 2-han (ed.) *Video Shigeki ni-yoru Gengo Koudou Ishiki Chousa Houkokusho: Bunseki hen* [*Study of Consciousness toward Linguistic Behaviors of Japanese by Video Stimulation: Book of Analysis*] (pp. 1–14). Tokyo: National Language Research Institute. Ministry of Education of Japan, Scientific Research Grant No. 09NP0701.

Olshtain, E. and Weinbach, L. (1987) Complaints: A study of speech act behavior among native and nonnative speakers of Hebrew. In M. Papi and J. Vershueren (eds) *The Pragmatic Perspective* (pp. 195–208). Amsterdam: Benjamin.

Orestrom, B. (1983) *Turn-taking in English Conversation*. Lund, Sweden: Lund University Press.

Palmer, A.S. and Groot, P.J.M. (1981) An introduction. In A.S. Palmer, P.J.M. Groot, and G.A. Trosper (eds) *The Construct Validation of Tests of Communicative Competence* (pp. 1–11). Washington, DC: Teachers of English to Speakers of Other Languages.

Read, J. and Nation, P. (2004) Measurement of formulaic sequences. In N. Schmitt (ed.) *Formulaic Sequences* (pp. 23–35). Amsterdam: John Benjamins.

Rintell, E.M. and Mitchell, C.J. (1989) Studying requests and apologies: An inquiry into method. In S. Blum-Kulka, J. House and G. Kasper (eds) *Cross-Cultural Pragmatics: Request and Apologies* (pp. 248–272). Norwood, NJ: Ablex.

Roever, C. (2001) A web-based test of interlanguage pragmalinguistic knowledge: Speech acts, routines, and implicatures. Unpublished PhD thesis, University of Hawai'i.

Roever, C. (2005) *Testing ESL Pragmatics*. Frankfurt am Main: Peter Lang.

Rose, K. (1992) Method and scope in cross cultural speech act research: A contrastive study of requests in Japanese and English. Unpublished PhD thesis, University of Illinois at Urbana-Champaign.

Rose, K. (1994) On the validity of discourse completion tests in non-Western contexts. *Applied Linguistics* 15 (1), 1–14.

Rose, K. (2000) An exploratory cross-sectional study of interlanguage pragmatic development. *Studies in Second Language Acquisition* 22, 27–67.

Rose, K. and Ono, R. (1995) Eliciting speech act data in Japanese: The effect of questionnaire type. *Language Learning* 45 (2), 191–223.

Sasaki, M. (1994) In S. Nishihara (ed.) Kakkokugo Washa to Nihonjin tono Gokai no Jirei-Eigo Washa no Baai [Examples of misunderstanding between speakers of other languages and Japanese: Case of English speakers). In *Zainichi Gaikokujin to Nihonjin tono Gengo-koudouteki Sesshoku ni-okeru Sougo 'Gokai' no Mekanizumu* [*Mechanism of Misunderstanding between Foreigners in Japan and Japanese at Linguistic Interaction*] (pp. 34–48). Tokyo: National Language Research Institute. Ministry of Education of Japan, Scientific Research Grant No. 04451093.

Schegloff, E. (1982) Discourse as an interactional achievement: Some uses of 'UH-HUH' and other things that come between sentences. In D. Tannen (ed.) *Georgetown University Roundtable on Language and Linguistics, Analyzing Discourse: Text and Talk* (pp. 71–93). Washington: Georgetown University Press.

Shinpro 'Nihongo' Dai 2-han (1999a) *Video Shigeki ni-yoru Gengo Koudou Ishiki Chousa Houkokusho: Bunseki hen* [*Study of Consciousness toward Linguistic Behaviors of Japanese by Video Stimulation: Book of Analysis*]. Tokyo: National Language Research Institute. Ministry of Education of Japan, Scientific Research Grant No. 09NP0701.

Shinpro 'Nihongo' Dai 2-han (1999b) *Video Shigeki ni-yoru Gengo Koudou Ishiki Chousa Houkokusho: Shiryo Hen* [*Study of Consciousness toward Linguistic*

Behaviors of Japanese by Video Stimulation: Book of Data]. Tokyo: National Language Research Institute. Ministry of Education of Japan, Scientific Research Grant No. 09NP0701.[d3]
Takahashi, T. and Beebe, L.M. (1987) The development of pragmatic competence by Japanese learners of English. *JALT Journal* 8, 131–155.
Takahashi, T. and Beebe, L.M. (1993) Cross-linguistic influence in the speech act of correction. In G. Kasper and S. Blum-Kulka (eds) *Interlanguage Pragmatics* (pp. 138–158). Oxford: Oxford University Press.
Tanaka, S. and Kawade, S. (1982) Politeness strategies and second language acquisition. *Studies in Second Language Acquisition* 5, 18–33.
Thomas, J.A. (1983) Cross-cultural pragmatic failure. *Applied Linguistics* 4, 91–112.
Tottie, G. (1991) Conversational style in British and American English: The case of backchannels. In K. Aijimer and B. Altenberg (eds) *English Corpus Linguistics* (pp. 254–271). London: Longman.
Trosborg, A. (1995) *Interlanguage Pragmatics*. Berlin: Mouton de Gruyter.
White, S. (1989) Backchannels across cultures: A study of Americans and Japanese. *Language in Society* 18 (1), 59–76.
Wolfson, N., Marmor, T. and Jones, S. (1989) Problems in the comparison of speech acts across cultures. In S. Blum-Kulka, J. House and G. Kasper (eds) *Cross-Cultural Pragmatics: Requests and Apologies* (pp. 174–196). Norwood, NJ: Ablex.
Yamashita, S. (1996) *Six Measures of JSL Pragmatics* (Technical Report # 14). Honolulu: University of Hawai'i at Manoa, National Foreign Language Resource Center.
Yamashita, S. (1998a) What do DCTs and roleplays assess? Paper presented at the meeting of the American Association for Applied Linguistics, Seattle, WA.
Yamashita, S. (1998b) The book fell or I dropped the book – A cross-cultural comparison. Paper presented at the meeting of the 18th Annual Second Language Research Forum (SLRF), University of Hawaii at Manoa.
Yamashita, S. (2001) Using pictures for research in pragmatics: Eliciting pragmatic strategies by picture response tests. In T. Hudson and J.D. Brown (eds) *A Focus on Language Test Development* (pp. 35–56) (Technical Report # 21). Honolulu: University of Hawai'i at Manoa, National Foreign Language Resource Center.
Yamashita, S. (2005) 'I'm sorry, but could you be a bit more careful?': Pragmatic strategies of Japanese elderly people. In D. Tatsuki (ed.) *Pragmatics in Language Learning, Theory and Practice* (pp. 119–136). Tokyo: The Japan Association for Language Teaching (JALT).

Chapter 11
Raters, Functions, Item Types and the Dependability of L2 Pragmatics Tests

JAMES DEAN BROWN

Introduction

Researchers in L2 pragmatics have tested pragmatics ability using a number of different types of instruments, including at least the following types: (1) written discourse completion tasks (WDCT), (2) multiple-choice discourse completion tasks (MDCT), (3) oral discourse completion tasks (ODCT), (4) roleplays, (5) self-assessments and (6) roleplay self-assessments (RPSA). This chapter begins by reviewing the literature on pragmatics testing, and then turns to discussions of the design issues involved in pragmatics testing and the statistical analyses that can be used to improve pragmatics tests – including both classical theory and generalizability theory (G theory) approaches.

A study is also presented to illustrate how such statistical analyses can be applied. The study is based on pragmatics test results generated by 53 university students learning Korean, who took four of the six types of pragmatics tests listed in the first paragraph above. The four tests were designed to systematically measure three different functions and eight different item types, as rated (for three out of the four tests) by four native speakers of Korean.

A generalizability study (G study) was then conducted to investigate the relative magnitude of variance components for examinees, raters (when appropriate), functions, item types and their interactions for the four different types of pragmatics tests studied here. A decision study (D study) was then conducted to examine dependability estimates for various options available for designing each of the four different types of tests in terms of the numbers of raters, functions and item types so as to maximize the dependability of these four types of tests in light of whatever practical considerations testers, administrators or researchers may encounter in using L2 pragmatics tests in actual measurement and decision making.

Testing Pragmatics Ability

Research on pragmatics and intercultural pragmatics stretches back for decades (see the literature reviews in the other chapters of this book), so no attempt will be made to cover that literature here. However, literature focused solely on the testing of pragmatics has a much more recent genesis.

Hudson *et al.* (1992, 1995) can be seen as the first effort by language testers to systematically develop and examine the effectiveness of tests of pragmatics ability. They developed six types of tests: what they called written discourse completion tasks, multiple-choice discourse completion tasks, oral discourse completion tasks, self-assessments, roleplay discourse tasks and roleplay self-assessments. They administered these tests to English as a second language students and examined the resulting descriptive, reliability and validity statistics for the scores generated by all these measures; they found all but the MDCT worked reasonably well from a psychometric standpoint (for more on the empirical results of this study, see Hudson, 2001a, 2001b; Hudson *et al.*, 1995).

Yamashita (1996a, 1996b) extended this research to Japanese as a second language (JSL) settings. She translated the six types of English language tests developed by Hudson *et al.* (1992, 1995) into Japanese and then investigated the effectiveness of these six tests for measuring the pragmatics ability of JSL students at four different universities in Tokyo and Yokohama. Again, she found that five of the six worked quite well for these purposes, but that the multiple-choice version was not as effective as the others.

Yoshitake also extended this line of research by using such tests in an EFL setting in Japan. Her research (reported in Yoshitake, 1997; Yoshitake & Enochs, 1996) used four of the prototype English language tests (i.e. the discourse completion tasks, MDCTs, ODCTs and roleplays) in exactly the same form that was developed by Hudson *et al.* (1992, 1995) and investigated their effectiveness for testing EFL students at the International Christian University in Tokyo.

Brown (2000, 2001, 2004) and Hudson (2001a, 2001b) look back on this research, provide some comparisons and further analyses, and reflect on what it all means. One conclusion that surfaced out of this early research was that the multiple-choice variant of the discourse completion task did not work particularly well in paper-and-pencil format. However, it is important to note that Roever (2001, 2005) had much more success with his variant of multiple-choice format in a web-based pragmatics test, as did Tada (2005) in his computer-based video pragmatics test.

The data for the study presented in this chapter were first collected and analyzed in Ahn (2005). He translated four of the six types of English language tests developed by Hudson *et al.* (1992, 1995) into Korean, and then investigated their effectiveness for testing 53 Korean as a foreign language students at the University of California at Berkeley and the Defense Language Institute in Monterey, California. As Ahn was kind enough to let me use his data to do further analyses for this chapter, these 53 participants and four of the measures will be described below in more detail as background for the analyses reported in this chapter.

Design issues in pragmatics testing

In many respects, language testing is about the careful design of tests so they will prove reliable and valid, as well as the revision or redesign of tests based on statistical analyses intended to make them more reliable and valid. The items created for the various measures reported in all but two[1] of the studies discussed in the previous five paragraphs were all focused on the same four variables: speech acts, relative power, social distance and degree of imposition.

Three *speech acts* (requests, refusals and apologies) were the focus of all these studies (after the original work by Hudson *et al.*, 1992, 1995). These three speech acts were chosen because of their prominence in the literature. In addition, these test designers chose to test three other variables: relative *power*, social *distance* and degree of *imposition* for each of the three speech acts, because '...within the research on cross-cultural pragmatics, they are identified as the three independent and culturally sensitive variables that subsume all other variables and play a principled role in speech act behavior (Brown & Levinson, 1987; also see Fraser, 1990)' (Hudson *et al.*, 1995: 4). These three variables were defined as follows:

(1) *Power* is the relative difference between the listener and speaker due to rank, professional status, etc.
(2) *Distance* is the social distance between the listener and speaker due to familiarity or shared solidarity due to group membership.
(3) *Imposition* is the degree of imposition imposed by the speech act within the cultural context based on expenditure or obligation.

In order to test all combinations of power, distance and imposition, eight items were created for each of the three speech acts (with all possible combinations of plus or minus power, distance and imposition) for a total of 24 items for the WDCTs and ODCTs in this study (as shown in Table 11.1). For logistical reasons, the roleplays and RPSAs needed to be shorter, so they were designed to have only eight tasks, each of which included occasions for requests, refusals and apologies.

Table 11.1 Functions, item types and item numbers

Three functions	Eight item types*							
	+I+P+D	+I+P−D	+I-P+D	+I−P−D	−I+P+D	−I+P−D	−I−P+D	−I−P−D
Requests	Item 23	Item 14	Item 03	Item 22	Item 08	Item 16	Item 12	Item 05
Refusals	Item 10	Item 09	Item 15	Item 17	Item 21	Item 20	Item 24	Item 04
Apologies	Item 06	Item 13	Item 02	Item 07	Item 18	Item 01	Item 11	Item 19

* ± I, P and D = ± Imposition, Power and Distance, respectively

Using statistical analyses to design better pragmatics tests

The classical theory approach

One major concern in classical test theory is reliability. The *reliability* of a set of test scores is their consistency of measurement whether across time, forms, raters, items, etc. Reliability is estimated with a statistic that ranges from 0.00 to 1.00, indicating zero to 100% reliability (more on this later in the chapter).

One question that language testers often pose for themselves about test score reliability is the effect different test designs might have on the reliability of future versions of a test. We know that, all other factors held constant, tests with more items tend to be predictably more reliable than tests with fewer items. For instance, a tester might design a test with items that are working quite well and yet, because there are only 20 items, the test scores turn out to be reliable at a disappointing 0.70. The test designer, knowing that more of the same sorts of items might help make the test more reliable, might reasonably ask how many more items would be needed. The Spearman-Brown (S-B) prophecy formula was designed to help testers make just such design decisions. That formula can be represented as follows:

$$r_{revised} = \frac{n \times r_{original}}{(n-1)r_{original} + 1}$$

where: $r_{revised}$ is the reliability of the revised version of the test, $r_{original}$ is the reliability of the original version of the test and n is the number of times the test length is to be changed.

Let's say the tester wants to know what reliability could be reasonably expected if the test length were doubled from 20 items to 40 items (i.e. $n = 2$ in the above equation). Substituting in the $r_{original}$ of 0.70 and the n of 2 into the equation, and calculating the result, it turns out that a reliability of 0.82 could reasonably be expected from a new revised test:

$$r_{revised} = \frac{n \times r_{original}}{(n-1)r_{original} + 1} = \frac{2 \times 0.70}{(2-1)0.70 + 1} = \frac{2 \times 0.70}{(1)0.70 + 1} = \frac{1.40}{0.70 + 1}$$

$$= \frac{1.40}{1.70} = 0.82.$$

Similarly, if the test were made 2.5 times as long with 50 items, reliability of 0.85 would be predicted as follows:

$$r_{\text{revised}} = \frac{n \times r_{\text{original}}}{(n-1)r_{\text{original}} + 1} = \frac{2.5 \times 0.70}{(2.5-1)0.70 + 1} = \frac{1.75}{(1.5)0.70 + 1}$$

$$= \frac{1.75}{1.05 + 1.00} = \frac{1.75}{2.05} = 0.85.$$

Based on these predictions and practical considerations, the test designer might decide to make a new version with 40 items because the increase in reliability from 0.75 to 0.82 seems worth the effort. However, a further increase to 50 items would only raise the reliability from 0.82 to 0.85, and so might not seem worth the effort necessary to develop those additional items or the additional imposition on the students' test-taking time. These are the sorts of decisions the S-B prophecy formula affords test designers. How much bang for the buck can be gained in reliability by adding X number of items? All of which is useful from a very practical standpoint. Unfortunately, this classical theory approach only allows predicting what would happen for one variable at a time, items in the examples given above. In other words, we can estimate the effects of increasing the numbers of items or raters, but not both at the same time.

The generalizability theory approach

In 1963, Cronbach, Rajaratnam and Gleser changed all that when they proposed a new way of looking at test consistency called *generalizabilty theory* (G theory). Their work provided a useful extension of classical theory reliability estimation that offers language testers a framework for estimating the effects on test consistency of multiple factors all at the same time. G theory involves using analysis of variance (ANOVA) procedures to separate out and estimate the relative magnitudes of variance components attributable to various measurement facets in a generalizability study (G study). The researcher can then further investigate in a *decision study* (D study) how changes in the test design would probably affect the generalizability coefficient (G coefficient), which is analogous to a reliability coefficient. [For more on the roles of G and D studies in G theory, see Brown (2005b).]

The first published discussion of G theory in language testing was in Bolus *et al*. (1982), but G theory was first applied to actual language testing data in Brown (1982, 1984), which was an investigation of the relative effects of numbers of items and numbers of reading passages on the dependability of scores from an engineering English reading test. Other studies that applied G theory to language tests included Bachman *et al*. (1995), Brown (1988, 1989, 1990a, 1990b, 1991, 1993, 1999), Brown and Bailey (1984), Brown and Ross (1996), Kunnan (1992), Lynch and

McNamara (1998), Stansfield and Kenyon (1992) and Van Weeren and Theunissen (1987).

The new millennium is off to a good start with continued work involving G theory including the Brown and Hudson (2002: 184–197) discussion of applications of G theory to criterion-referenced language testing and Bachman's (2004: 176–188) introduction of some of the key G theory concepts. Other work that actually applies G theory includes at least the following studies: Brown (2005b), Kozaki (2004), Lee (2006), Molloy and Shimura (2005), Schoonen (2005), Shin (2002), Solano-Flores and Li (2006), Yamamori (2003), Yamanaka (2005), Yoshida (2004, 2006) and Zhang (2003, 2006). One area where G theory has not been applied in language testing is the testing of pragmatics ability.

Purpose

The central purpose of the study reported in this chapter was to analyze the effects of different numbers of examinees, functions, raters and item types on the dependability of different types of pragmatics tests and, in the process, explore the options available for designing more dependable pragmatics tests. To those ends, the following research questions were posed:

(1) What does the literature tell us about the reliability of the various types of L2 pragmatics tests that have been used?
(2) What can we extrapolate from the literature about the effects of numbers of items and raters on the reliability of the various types of L2 pragmatics tests that have been used?
(3) In the G study, what is the relative importance to test variance of numbers of raters, functions and item types in L2 pragmatics tests?
(4) In the D study, what are the effects of numbers of raters, functions and item types on the dependability of L2 pragmatics tests?

Method

Participants

The 53 participants in this study were all studying at the University of California at Berkley or the Defense Language Institute in Monterey, California.[2] These participants ranged in age from 18 to 48 years old. The participants varied in proficiency, but in order to be eligible for the study, participants needed, at minimum, to be able to read using the Korean alphabet (no Chinese characters were used in the test).

Eight of the participants (13%) were excluded from the study either because they gave up half way through a test, or did not return to take additional tests as they had promised. That left 53 participants. Of those, four did not fill in all the items. A total of 60 items were left blank. For purposes of analysis these 60 blank items were replaced by a 3 on the scale of 1–5. This substitution affected 60 out of a total of 5088 data points amounting to 1.18% (60/5088 = 0.011790.0118, or about 1.18%).[3]

Materials and procedures

At least six types of tests (with variations) have been used in the study of pragmatics: (1) multiple-choice discourse completion task, (2) self-assessment, (3) written discourse completion task, (4) oral discourse completion task, (5) discourse roleplay task (DRPT) and (6) roleplay self-assessment. For more information on all of these different formats, see Brown (2001, 2004), Hudson (2001a, 2001b), Hudson *et al.* (1992, 1995), Yamashita (1996a, 1996b) and Yoshitake (1997). In this study, based on the data from Ahn (2005), only the last four of these test types[4] were used. Each will be described in turn.

Written discourse completion tasks

The WDCT used in this study had 24 items that consisted of a situation description requiring a request, refusal or apology in one of the eight possible combinations of power, distance and imposition (see Table 11.1). The WDCT asked examinees to read 24 descriptions of situations and write what they would say next in spaces provided after each item. Four raters scored the answers on a five-point Likert scale (ranging from 1 for *very unsatisfactory* to 5 for *completely appropriate*) in terms of appropriateness in each of six categories: speech act, expression, amount/information, formality, directness and politeness. The basic scores analyzed here were the individual item scores assigned by each rater, which were calculated by averaging the ratings for the six categories listed in the previous sentence.

Oral discourse completion tasks

The ODCT used in this study also had 24 items, each of which consisted of a situation description requiring a request, refusal or apology in one of the eight possible combinations of power, distance and imposition (see Table 11.1). The ODCT asked examinees to listen to the 24 situation descriptions on Tape A and orally record what they would say next on Tape B. Again, four raters scored their answers on a five-point Likert scale (ranging from 1 for *very unsatisfactory* to 5 for *completely appropriate*) in terms of appropriateness in each of six categories: speech act, expression, amount/information, formality, directness and politeness. The basic scores analyzed here were the individual item scores assigned by each rater, which were calculated by averaging the ratings for the six categories listed in the previous sentence.

Discourse roleplay tasks

Because performing 24 roleplays would be particularly exhausting in terms of both time and energy, the DRPT was designed in a shorter version with eight tasks, each of which contained a request, a refusal and an apology. All eight possible combinations of power, distance and imposition were present across the eight tasks (Hudson *et al.*, 1995: 60). The DRPT asked examinees to read the directions and description for each task for two to three minutes then perform the roleplay with a native speaker of Korean. The eight tasks were videotaped and took an average of about 30 minutes to administer. The video tapes were scored by four raters separately for requests, refusals and apologies on five-point Likert scales (ranging from 1 for *very unsatisfactory* to 5 for *completely appropriate*). The basic scores analyzed here were the individual item scores assigned by each rater for each function.

Roleplay self-assessments

Like the DRPT, the RPSA necessarily contained only eight items. After all, it was based on the eight items in the DRPT, each of which consisted of a request, a refusal and an apology with all eight possible combinations of power, distance and imposition in the eight situations (Hudson *et al.*, 1995: 60). The RPSA asked examinees to watch their DRPT videotapes and rate their own performance for each function on each task on a five-point Likert scale (ranging from 1 for *very unsatisfactory* to 5 for *completely appropriate*).

Results and Discussion

The results of this study will be presented and discussed in this section in an order and manner that directly addresses the research questions posed earlier in the chapter. As such, this section will be organized around the research questions themselves, which will serve as headings.

What does the literature tell us about the reliability of the various types of L2 pragmatics tests that have been used?

A key concept to understanding this chapter is that of test reliability. Recall that *test reliability* is the idea that a test, whatever its purpose, should measure consistently, that is, examinees who take a test repeatedly or in several forms should produce scores that are similar each time. Traditionally, test score reliability is estimated using a coefficient that ranges from 0.00 for zero reliability to 1.00 for 100% reliability, with all values in between indicating relative degrees of reliability. Thus, all sets of test scores turn out to be reliable somewhere between 0.00 and 1.00 reliability, and of course, high reliability is usually desirable. For example, a set of scores with a reliability estimate of 0.96

would be considered quite consistent as the scores can be said to be 96% reliable and only 4% unreliable (1.00−0.96 = 0.04).

Internal consistency reliability is the most commonly reported type of reliability used to demonstrate the degree to which a set of test items is working together consistently in testing a particular group of examinees (for more on how internal consistency reliability fits with other types of reliability for different types of tests, see Brown 2005a: 169–219). The internal consistency reliability of language test scores is typically demonstrated by applying classical theory formulas like K-R20, K-R21 or Cronbach's alpha. These estimates can be interpreted as proportions of reliable variation in scores as explained above.

Table 11.2 shows reliability statistics for six pragmatics tests used in four different studies. Reliability statistics for the tests developed in the Hudson *et al.* (1992, 1995) ESL pragmatics testing project were not reported until Hudson (2001a, 2001b) revisited that project. The JSL pragmatics testing project (Yamashita, 1996a) included a number of different reliability estimates (internal consistency reliabilities, inter-rater reliabilities, intraclass correlations and standard errors of measurement), but only K-R21 and alpha are reported here. In contrast, the EFL study (Yoshitake, 1997) presented no reliability estimates and no item-level and rater-level data. However, in Brown (2001), I was able to calculate K-R21 estimates using Yoshitake's information about total numbers of items, score means and standard deviations.

Note that generally in Table 11.2 the reliability estimates indicate that these tests as they were administered to these groups have moderate to high consistency. The exceptions are for the MDCT in all studies reporting reliability for that test, as well as the WDCT and ODCT in Yoshitake's EFL study. Also noteworthy is the fact that the reliabilities in the Yamashita (JSL) study and Ahn (KFL) study are quite a bit higher than those for the Hudson *et al.* (ESL) study and Yoshitake (EFL) study. This suggests that, at least in these studies, the tests generally worked better in their translated Japanese and Korean versions than they did in their original English (whether administered in ESL or EFL situations). Naturally, that may have more to do with the sorts of students tested in the different studies than with the tests themselves, but it is nonetheless an interesting pattern.

What can we extrapolate from the literature about the effects of numbers of items and raters on the reliability of the various types of L2 pragmatics tests that have been used?

Recall from the introduction above that using the S-B prophecy formula can help testers make decisions about better ways to design a test. Recall also that one representation of the formula is as follows:

Table 11.2 Reliability estimates for previous pragmatics testing projects

Study reliability	WDCT	MDCT	ODCT	DRPT	DSAT	RPSA
Hudson et al. (1992, 1995)						
Alpha (from Hudson, 2001a)	0.86	–	0.78	0.75	–	–
Alpha (from Hudson, 2001b)	–	–	–	0.82	0.87	0.90
Yamashita (1996a, 1996b)						
K-R21	0.87	0.45	0.93	0.93	0.91	0.92
Alpha	0.99	0.47	0.99	0.99	0.94	0.95
Yoshitake (1997)						
K-R21 (calculated in Brown, 2001)	0.50	0.61	0.62	0.76	0.89	0.88
Ahn (2005)						
Split-half (adjusted)	0.91	–	0.95	0.99	0.90	0.97
Alpha (in original study)	0.97	–	0.95	0.99	0.95	0.97
Alpha (as the data were used here)	0.89		0.90	0.97	–	0.95

$$r_{revised} = \frac{n \times r_{original}}{(n-1)r_{original} + 1}.$$

Consider the situation faced by Yamashita (1996a, 1996b), where she found high reliability for five of her pragmatics tests (see Table 11.2, with alpha reliabilities of 0.99, 0.99, 0.99, 0.94 and 0.95 for the WDCT, ODCT, DRPT, DSAT and RPSA, respectively). However, the multiple-choice version (the MDCT in Table 11.2) scores produced an unacceptably low alpha estimate of 0.47. One possible cause of that low reliability might have been the relatively small number of 24 items. A reasonable question to ask would be the degree to which doubling the number of items from 24 to 48 (while holding all other factors constant) would affect the reliability of the scores on the MDCT. The S-B prophecy formula was designed to answer just such questions. Substituting 0.47 for $r_{original}$ and an n of 2 (for doubling the test length) into the equation, and calculating the result, it turns out that a reliability of 0.64 could be reasonably expected from a new double-length version of the test:

$$r_{revised} = \frac{n \times r_{original}}{(n-1)r_{original} + 1} = \frac{2 \times 0.47}{(2-1)0.47 + 1} = \frac{2 \times 0.47}{(1)0.47 + 1} = \frac{0.94}{0.47 + 1}$$

$$= \frac{0.94}{1.47} = 0.64.$$

Similarly, if the test were made three times as long at 72 items a reliability estimate of 0.73 would be predicted:

$$r_{revised} = \frac{n \times r_{original}}{(n-1)r_{original} + 1} = \frac{3 \times 0.47}{(3-1)0.47 + 1} = \frac{1.41}{(2)0.47 + 1} = \frac{1.41}{0.94 + 1.00}$$

$$= \frac{1.41}{1.94} = 0.73.$$

Thus it appears that tripling the length of the test with all other factors held constant will probably result in reliability of 0.73 or so for the MDCT. This reliability of 0.73 is obviously not in the range of reliabilities found for the scores on the other five tests. Nonetheless, if 0.73 reliability is sufficiently high for a particular testing purpose, the S-B prophecy formula has indicated how that can be achieved.

The opposite sort of reasoning might be equally useful. The DRPT in Ahn (2005) produced reliability of 0.99 with eight roleplays rated by four raters. This sort of design requires a serious investment of student and native speaker partner time, as well as a considerable amount of rater time, but it clearly also produces reliable test scores. However, if the test could be designed to use fewer roleplays or fewer raters without sacrificing much reliability, it would be considerably more efficient and useful. The S-B prophecy formula can also be used to calculate the effect of making a test *shorter*. For example, Ahn's eight-task DRPT was reliable at 0.99, and with four tasks, or half as long (i.e. 0.5 times as long), it turns out to be reliable at 0.98 as follows:

$$r_{revised} = \frac{n \times r_{original}}{(n-1)r_{original} + 1} = \frac{0.5 \times 0.99}{(0.5-1)0.99 + 1} = \frac{0.495}{(-0.5)0.99 + 1}$$

$$= \frac{0.495}{-0.495 + 1.00} = \frac{0.495}{0.505} = 0.98.$$

Thus, a shorter four-task revised version of the test would probably be almost as reliable as the eight task original version, but it would be much more efficient and useful.

Clearly then, the S-B prophecy formula can help us estimate what would happen if we redesigned a test while increasing or reducing the numbers of any one of the following: items, roleplays, raters, scoring categories, subtests, tests, etc. Unfortunately, however, it can only do so one variable at a time. In other words, the S-B prophecy formula *cannot* handle two or more of these variables simultaneously, which brings us to G theory, an approach that *can* handle two or more such variables simultaneously.

In the G study, what is the relative importance to test variance of numbers of raters, functions and item types in L2 pragmatics tests?

In this section, I will discuss the results of the G-study phase of this investigation. The focus of a G study is the derivation of variance components,[5] in this case variance components for the 53 persons taking each test, four raters, three functions (requests, refusals & apologies), eight item types (all possible combinations of relative power, social distance & degree of imposition, which are nested within functions because there are different items in each function) and all possible interactions of persons, raters, functions and item types.

Table 11.3 shows the variance components for persons (P), raters (R), functions (F), item types (T) and their interactions on the WDCT, ODCT and DRPT. Notice that, on the RPSA, there are no variance components for raters, or any of the interactions involving raters. That is because each examinee is doing one self-assessment, and by definition that means there can be only one rater. These variance components are used in rather formidable equations to actually calculate the dependability coefficients reported and discussed in the D study results reported in the next section

Table 11.3 Variance components for persons (P), raters (R), functions (F), item types (T) and their interactions on all four tests

Facet	df	WDCT	ODCT	DRPT	RPSA
P	52	0.398700	0.315082	0.799295	0.465925
R	3	0.052689	0.016991	0.022680	
F	2	0.000000	0.000000	0.006927	0.000000
T:F	21	0.040387	0.056076	0.020452	0.047261
PR	156	0.113538	0.068243	0.074100	
PF	104	0.017175	0.014818	0.006215	0.011087
PT:F	1,092	0.204787	0.251152	0.089424	0.492722
RF	6	0.000878	0.000000	0.002936	
RT:F	63	0.015429	0.015793	0.022325	
PRF	312	0.010400	0.000000	0.006173	
PRT:F	3,276	0.328452	0.298701	0.307124	
Total	5,087	1.182434	1.0368563	1.357651	1.016993

(for more detailed explanations, see Bachman, 2004; Brown, 1999; Brown & Ahn, unpublished; Brown & Hudson, 2002; or Brown & Ross, 1996).

Generally speaking, the persons (P) variance component indicates in relative terms how much variance is due to the examinees in the study. This persons variance is the consistent variance, that is, the variance that is spreading the people out in the sort of normal distribution useful in pragmatics research studies. The raters, functions and item types (R, F and T, respectively) variance components represent other sources of variance and all their interactions are potential sources of error variance. In fact, the degree to which they contribute to error is reflected in their magnitude relative to the persons variance component. Thus, a large persons variance component relative to the other variance components is desirable. Notice that the persons (P) variance components are relatively large for the WDCT, ODCT and DRPT at 0.398700, 0.315082 and 0.799295, which is a good sign for norm-referenced testing purposes. Also note that the persons variance component is largest for the DRPT and that all the other variance components are relatively low on the DRPT compared to the persons variance component, and even when they are compared to their counterparts for the WDCT and ODCT. Thus the DRPT appears to be the most dependable of these three measures in terms of variance components.

Turning now to the RPSA, the persons component is the second largest variance component, at 0.465925, surpassed by the interaction of persons and item types (nested within functions), or PT:F. This indicates that people are scoring themselves high or low on different item types from each other rather than scoring themselves equally high or low across the board (i.e. consistently) on all item types. This may simply be indicating, in part, that examinees are considering each item separately and self-assessing their performance differently on each. Nonetheless, this sort of interaction is problematic from the perspective of test consistency and must therefore be considered a source of error variance that will have a negative impact on dependability.

Table 11.4 transforms the variance component results by reframing them in terms of the percentage of total variance accounted for by each variance component. For some people, this table will be easier to understand even though it leads to the same conclusions discussed in the previous two paragraphs. In addition, looking at the sources of error variance here, notice that raters are a more important source of variance on the WDCT than on the ODCT and DRPT. Notice also that item types

Table 11.4 Percentages of variance for persons (P), raters (R), functions (F), item types (T) and their interactions on all four tests

Facet	df	WDCT	ODCT	DRPT	RPSA
P	52	33.72	3.39	58.87	45.81
R	3	4.46	1.64	1.67	
F	2	0.00	0.00	0.51	0.00
T:F	21	3.42	5.41	1.51	4.65
PR	156	9.60	6.58	5.46	
PF	104	1.45	1.43	0.46	1.09
PT:F	1092	17.32	24.22	6.59	48.45
RF	6	0.07	0.00	0.22	
RT:F	63	1.30	1.52	1.64	
PRF	312	0.88	0.00	0.45	
PRT:F	3276	27.78	28.81	22.62	
Total	5087	10.00	10.00	10.00	10.00

Raters, Functions, Item Types and Dependability of L2 Pragmatics   239

(nested within functions) (T:F) are a more important source of error on the WDCT, ODCT and RPSA than on the DRPT. Finally, notice that the functions are contributing almost no error variance with 0% for three of the tests and only half a percent for the other, and that the PF, RF and PRF interactions (i.e. those that involve functions) are also relatively low. Generally, these results indicate that it does not make much difference which functions or how many of them we include on our test. However, as raters and item types are relatively more important sources of error, we should make sure that we have ample numbers of each. Let's consider these issues from a different perspective in the next section.

In the D study, what are the effects of numbers of raters, functions and item types on the dependability of L2 pragmatics tests?

The variance components derived in the G study in the previous section are important because they help researchers understand the relative contribution of each variance component to error variance, but also because they serve as the building blocks for calculating dependability estimates (analogous to reliability estimates in classical theory) for varying numbers of raters, functions and item types. Table 11.5 shows examples of how norm-referenced dependability would likely vary if alternative test designs were used for the WDCT, ODCT, DRPT and RPSA.

Reading Table 11.5 is easier than it might at first seem. Notice there are two sets of headings that are the same. In each set, the first column, R, indicates the number or raters (1–4); the second, F, shows the number of functions (1–3); the third, T, gives the number of item types (1–8); and the fourth column is the total number of observations (obtained by multiplying the numbers of R, F and T). The next four columns, labeled WDCT, ODCT, DRPT and RPSA, give the dependability estimates that will likely result from the combination R, F and T represented by each row.

Thus, looking at the upper-left part of the table, with one rater, one function and one item type (a total of one observation) the WDCT, ODCT, DRPT and RPSA are estimated to be dependable at 0.37, 0.33, 0.62 and 0.48, respectively. Turning to the other end of the table in the lower-right corner, the results are given for conditions under which three of the tests were actually administered (with four raters, three functions and eight item types – for a total of 96 observations); notice that under these conditions, the WDCT, ODCT and DRPT are estimated to be dependable at 0.89, 0.90 and 0.97, respectively. The RPSA is not shown there because only one rater, the examinee, can logically ever be used. Thus results are

Table 11.5 The dependability of the WDCT, ODCT, DRPT and RPSA for different combinations of numbers of raters, functions and item types (R, F & T)

R	F	T	Total	WDCT	ODCT	DRPT	RPSA	R	F	T	Total	WDCT	ODCT	DRPT
1	1	1	1	0.37	0.33	0.62	0.48	3	1	1	3	0.52	0.45	0.78
1	1	2	2	0.49	0.47	0.74	0.64	3	1	2	6	0.65	0.60	0.86
1	1	3	3	0.56	0.54	0.79	0.73	3	1	3	9	0.71	0.67	0.89
1	1	4	4	0.59	0.59	0.81	0.78	3	1	4	12	0.74	0.72	0.91
1	1	5	5	0.62	0.62	0.83	0.81	3	1	5	15	0.77	0.75	0.92
1	1	6	6	0.63	0.65	0.84	0.83	3	1	6	18	0.78	0.77	0.92
1	1	7	7	0.65	0.66	0.85	0.85	3	1	7	21	0.79	0.78	0.93
1	1	8	8	0.66	0.68	0.85	0.87	3	1	8	24	0.80	0.80	0.93
1	2	1	2	0.50	0.47	0.74	0.65	3	2	1	6	0.66	0.61	0.87
1	2	2	4	0.60	0.60	0.82	0.78	3	2	2	12	0.76	0.73	0.91
1	2	3	6	0.65	0.65	0.85	0.84	3	2	3	18	0.80	0.78	0.93
1	2	4	8	0.67	0.69	0.86	0.87	3	2	4	24	0.82	0.81	0.94
1	2	5	10	0.69	0.71	0.87	0.89	3	2	5	30	0.83	0.83	0.94
1	2	6	12	0.70	0.72	0.88	0.91	3	2	6	36	0.84	0.84	0.95
1	2	7	14	0.71	0.73	0.88	0.92	3	2	7	42	0.85	0.85	0.95
1	2	8	16	0.71	0.74	0.88	0.93	3	2	8	48	0.85	0.86	0.95

Table 11.5 (Continued)

R	F	T	Total	WDCT	ODCT	DRPT	RPSA	R	F	T	Total	WDCT	ODCT	DRPT
1	3	1	3	0.57	0.55	0.79	0.74	3	3	1	9	0.73	0.69	0.90
1	3	2	6	0.65	0.66	0.85	0.84	3	3	2	18	0.80	0.79	0.93
1	3	3	9	0.69	0.70	0.87	0.89	3	3	3	27	0.83	0.83	0.94
1	3	4	12	0.70	0.73	0.88	0.91	3	3	4	36	0.85	0.85	0.95
1	3	5	15	0.72	0.74	0.88	0.93	3	3	5	45	0.86	0.86	0.95
1	3	6	18	0.72	0.75	0.89	0.94	3	3	6	54	0.87	0.87	0.95
1	3	7	21	0.73	0.76	0.89	0.94	3	3	7	63	0.87	0.88	0.96
1	3	8	24	0.73	0.77	0.89	0.95	3	3	8	72	0.87	0.88	0.96
2	1	1	2	0.47	0.41	0.73		4	1	1	4	0.54	0.47	0.81
2	1	2	4	0.60	0.56	0.83		4	1	2	8	0.68	0.62	0.88
2	1	3	6	0.66	0.63	0.86		4	1	3	12	0.73	0.69	0.91
2	1	4	8	0.70	0.68	0.88		4	1	4	16	0.77	0.74	0.92
2	1	5	10	0.72	0.71	0.89		4	1	5	20	0.79	0.77	0.93
2	1	6	12	0.74	0.73	0.90		4	1	6	24	0.81	0.79	0.94
2	1	7	14	0.75	0.75	0.91		4	1	7	28	0.82	0.80	0.94
2	1	8	16	0.76	0.76	0.91		4	1	8	32	0.83	0.81	0.94

Table 11.5 (Continued)

R	F	T	Total	WDCT	ODCT	DRPT	RPSA	R	F	T	Total	WDCT	ODCT	DRPT
2	2	1	4	0.61	0.57	0.83		4	2	1	8	0.69	0.63	0.88
2	2	2	8	0.71	0.69	0.89		4	2	2	16	0.78	0.75	0.93
2	2	3	12	0.75	0.75	0.91		4	2	3	24	0.82	0.80	0.94
2	2	4	16	0.78	0.78	0.92		4	2	4	32	0.84	0.83	0.95
2	2	5	20	0.79	0.80	0.92		4	2	5	40	0.86	0.85	0.95
2	2	6	24	0.80	0.81	0.93		4	2	6	48	0.87	0.86	0.96
2	2	7	28	0.81	0.82	0.93		4	2	7	56	0.87	0.87	0.96
2	2	8	32	0.81	0.83	0.93		4	2	8	64	0.88	0.88	0.96
2	3	1	6	0.68	0.65	0.87		4	3	1	12	0.75	0.71	0.91
2	3	2	12	0.76	0.75	0.91		4	3	2	24	0.83	0.81	0.94
2	3	3	18	0.79	0.79	0.92		4	3	3	36	0.86	0.85	0.95
2	3	4	24	0.81	0.81	0.93		4	3	4	48	0.87	0.87	0.96
2	3	5	30	0.82	0.83	0.93		4	3	5	60	0.88	0.88	0.96
2	3	6	36	0.82	0.84	0.94		4	3	6	72	0.89	0.89	0.96
2	3	7	42	0.83	0.85	0.94		4	3	7	84	0.89	0.89	0.96
2	3	8	48	0.83	0.85	0.94		4	3	8	96	0.89	0.90	0.97

given in the upper middle of the table for the current RPSA with one rater, three functions and eight conditions showing that the estimated dependability would be 0.95. Is that clear? If so, the rest of the table should be transparent.

Notice that, in general, for the examinees in this study, the DRPT and RPSA are more dependable than the WDCT and ODCT; and that within these pairs, the two vary in terms of which has higher dependability, depending on the combinations of R, F and T. Given infinite time and resources, it would seem to be best to do the DRPT with four raters, three functions and eight item types because the dependability would be a very high 0.97. However, with two raters and the same numbers of F and T, the dependability would still be 0.94, so this combination might prove to be a more practical test design that still remains highly dependable. Or perhaps three raters, three functions and four item types would be more practical in a particular setting because of the savings that would be realized in testing time while still maintaining good dependability at 0.95. And so forth...

Clearly, the point is that the information in Table 11.5 about the relative effects of raters, functions and types on the dependability of the WDCT, ODCT, DRPT and RPSA can be used to select which sort of test design to use, or more importantly, to rationally modify the test designs that will ultimately be used with the goal of minimizing the impact of important practical issues in a particular situation (like numbers of raters, time needed to take the test, rater and examinee fatigue, etc.) while maintaining whatever level of dependability is expected, needed or acceptable for the purposes of testing in that situation.

Conclusion

Recall that G theory is useful because (unlike the classical theory approach, which uses the S-B prophecy formula) it allows testers to simultaneously examine the effects of multiple facets on the dependability of test scores. In this chapter, I examined the effects of numbers of raters (1–4), functions (requests, refusals and apologies) and item types (all eight possible combinations of power distance and imposition).

The G study indicated that the DRPT, with the largest variance component for persons and the smallest components for the other facets and their interactions, is prone to producing the most consistent variance, especially when compared to the other tests in this study. In terms of error variance, the functions variance components and the interactions involving functions were very small or non-existent, indicating that the number and type of functions included in a pragmatics test may not have much effect on the dependability of the test. However, based on research design or validity concerns, we might still have sound reasons for using multiple functions of particular types.

In contrast, raters and item types were relatively important sources of error, though not equally so on all tests, so we should probably make sure we use ample numbers of each. The D study results shown in Table 11.5 provided information that can help in making decisions about how to best modify four types of pragmatics test designs so as to minimize the impact of raters, functions and item types while maintaining whatever level of dependability is acceptable for the pragmatics testing purposes in a given situation. Thus G theory has opened up new possibilities for testers, administrators and researchers to enhance the dependability of their tests of L2 pragmatics abilities and improve how well those tests work in research and practice.

Suggestions for future research

Virtually every study I have ever done has raised more questions than it has answered. This study is no exception, so I will end here by making some suggestions for directions toward which research on testing pragmatics might usefully turn:

(1) Would similar results be obtained if this study were replicated in different settings and for different languages?
(2) What sorts of G-study and D-study results would be obtained if similar studies were done for other sorts of pragmatics tests (e.g. the multiple-choice and self-assessment DCTs found in Hudson *et al.*, 1992, 1995; the cartoon oral production tasks used in Rose, 2000; and so forth)?
(3) What sorts of dependability estimates would be obtained if the testing purposes were criterion-referenced (i.e. for classroom testing purposes)?
(4) What other facets should be analyzed beyond the raters, functions and item types analyzed here? What about rating categories (for a start on this issue, see Brown & Ahn, unpublished)?
(5) What could multivariate generalizability theory additionally reveal about the simultaneous use of multiple measures of pragmatics ability?
(6) Given that dependable measures of pragmatics abilities can apparently be designed with various combinations of numbers of raters, functions, item types, etc., what validity considerations should be brought to bear on the testing of pragmatics ability?

Notes

1. The two exceptions are Roever (2001, 2005) and Tada (2005).
2. The data for this study were originally gathered for Ahn (2005) and further analyzed in Ahn and Brown (unpublished ms.). They are used here with the

permission of the author for further additional analyses not presented in the previous studies.
3. For more details on these participants, see Ahn (2005).
4. Self-assessment was not used because it was viewed as redundant with the RPSA and because the researcher did not want to put the participants through any testing that was not absolutely necessary. The multiple-choice discourse completion task was not used because it had previously been found to be ineffective in paper-and-pencil format for Hudson *et al.* (1992, 1995) and Yamashita (1996a, 1996b). Note that recently Roever (2001, 2005) had much more success with multiple-choice format in his web-based pragmatics testing project, and so did Tada (2005) in his computer-based video testing of pragmatics.
5. The technical details of how generalizability theory works and how these variance components are derived from analysis of variance procedures followed by calculation of estimated mean squares and then calculation of the variance components are well beyond the scope of this chapter (for more information, see Bachman, 2004; Brown, 1999; Brown & Ahn, unpublished; Brown & Hudson, 2002: 175–182; or Brown & Ross, 1996, or the references cited in those sources).

References

Ahn, R.C. (2005) Five measures of interlanguage pragmatics in KFL (Korean as a foreign language) learners. Unpublished PhD thesis, University of Hawaii at Manoa.
Bachman, L.F. (2004) *Statistical Analyses for Language Assessment*. Cambridge: Cambridge University Press.
Bachman, L.F., Lynch, B.K. and Mason, M. (1995) Investigating variability in tasks and rater judgments in a performance test of foreign language speaking. *Language Testing* 12 (2), 239–257.
Bolus, R.E., Hinofotis, F.B. and Bailey, K.M. (1982) An introduction to generalizability theory in second language research. *Language Learning* 32, 245–258.
Brown, J.D. (1982) Testing EFL reading comprehension in engineering English. Unpublished PhD thesis, University of California at Los Angeles.
Brown, J.D. (1984) A norm-referenced engineering reading test. In A.K. Pugh and J.M. Ulijn (eds) *Reading for Professional Purposes: Studies and Practices in Native and Foreign Languages* (pp. 213–222). London: Heinemann Educational Books.
Brown, J.D. (1988) *1987 Manoa Writing Placement Examination* (Technical Report #1). Honolulu: University of Hawai'i at Manoa, Second Language Teaching and Curriculum Centre.
Brown, J.D. (1989) *1988 Manoa Writing Placement Examination* (Technical Report #2). Honolulu: University of Hawai'i at Manoa, Second Language Teaching and Curriculum Centre.
Brown, J.D. (1990a) Short-cut estimates of criterion-referenced test consistency. *Language Testing* 7 (1), 77–97.
Brown, J.D. (1990b) *1989 Manoa Writing Placement Examination* (Technical Report #5). Honolulu: University of Hawai'i at Manoa, Second Language Teaching and Curriculum Centre.
Brown, J.D. (1991) *1990 Manoa Writing Placement Examination* (Technical Report #11). Honolulu: University of Hawai'i at Manoa, Second Language Teaching and Curriculum Centre.

Brown, J.D. (1993) A comprehensive criterion-referenced language testing project. In D. Douglas and C. Chapelle (eds) *A New Decade of Language Testing Research* (pp. 163–184). Washington, DC: TESOL.
Brown, J.D. (1999) Relative importance of persons, items, subtests and languages to TOEFL test variance. *Language Testing* 16 (2), 216–237.
Brown, J.D. (2000) Observing pragmatics: Testing and data gathering techniques. *Pragmatics Matters* 1 (2), 5–6.
Brown, J.D. (2001) Six types of pragmatics tests in two different contexts. In K.R. Rose and G. Kasper (eds) *Pragmatics in Language Teaching* (pp. 301–325). Cambridge: Cambridge University Press.
Brown, J.D. (2004) Observing pragmatics: Testing and data gathering techniques. *The Language Teacher* 20 (11) (reprinted from Brown, 2000).
Brown, J.D. (2005a) *Testing in Language Programs: A Comprehensive Guide to English Language Assessment* (new edn). New York: McGraw-Hill.
Brown, J.D. (2005b) Statistics corner, questions and answers about language testing statistics: Generalizability and decision studies. *Shiken: JALT Testing & Evaluation SIG Newsletter* 9 (1), 12–16. On WWW at http://jalt.org/test/bro_21.htm.
Brown, J.D. and Ahn, R.C. (unpublished) Effects of raters, functions, items, and item characteristics on L2 pragmatics tests. Unpublished manuscript, University of Hawai'i at Manoa.
Brown, J.D. and Bailey, K.M. (1984) A categorical instrument for scoring second language writing skills. *Language Learning* 34, 21–42.
Brown, J.D. and Hudson, T. (2002) *Criterion-referenced Language Testing*. Cambridge: Cambridge University Press.
Brown, J.D. and Ross, J.A. (1996) Decision dependability of item types, sections, tests, and the overall TOEFL test battery. In M. Milanovic and N. Saville (eds) *Performance Testing, Cognition and Assessment* (pp. 231–265). Cambridge: Cambridge University Press.
Brown, P. and Levinson, S. (1987) *Politeness: Some Universals in Language Usage.* Cambridge: Cambridge University Press.
Fraser, B. (1990) Perspectives on politeness. *Journal of Pragmatics* 14, 219–236.
Hudson, T. (2001a) Indicators for cross-cultural pragmatic instruction: Some quantitative tools. In K. Rose and G. Kasper (eds) *Pragmatics in Language Teaching* (pp. 283–300). Cambridge: Cambridge University Press.
Hudson, T. (2001b) Self-assessment methods in cross-cultural pragmatics. In T. Hudson and J.D. Brown (eds) *A Focus on Language Test Development* (pp. 57–74). Honolulu, HI: University of Hawai'i Press.
Hudson, T., Detmer, E. and Brown, J.D. (1992) *A Framework for Testing Cross-Cultural Pragmatics.* Honolulu, HI: University of Hawai'i Press.
Hudson, T., Detmer, E. and Brown, J.D. (1995) *Developing Prototypic Measures of Cross-Cultural Pragmatics* (Technical Report # 7). Honolulu: University of Hawai'i at Manoa, Second Language Teaching and Curriculum Centre.
Kozaki, Y. (2004). Using GENOVA and FACETS to set multiple standards on performance assessment for certification in medical translation of Japanese into English. *Language Testing* 21 (1), 1–27.
Kunnan, A.J. (1992) An investigation of a criterion-referenced test using G-theory, and factor and cluster analysis. *Language Testing* 9 (1), 30–49.
Lee, Y.-W. (2006) Dependability of scores for a new ESL speaking assessment consisting of integrated and independent tasks. *Language Testing* 23 (2), 131–166.

Lynch, B.K. and McNamara, T.F. (1998) Using G-theory and many-facet Rasch measurement in the development of performance assessments of the ESL speaking skills of immigrants. *Language Testing* 15 (2), 158–180.

Molloy, H. and Shimura, M. (2005) An examination of situational sensitivity in medium-scale interlanguage pragmatics research. In T. Newfields, Y. Ishida, M. Chapman and M. Fujioka (eds) *Proceedings of the May 22–23, 2004 JALT Pan-SIG Conference* (pp. 16–32). Tokyo: JALT Pan SIG Committee. On WWW at www.jalt.org/pansig/2004/HTML/ShimMoll.htm.

Roever, C. (2001) A web-based test of interlanguage pragmalinguistic knowledge: Speech acts, routines, implicatures. Unpublished PhD thesis, University of Hawai'i at Manoa, Honolulu, HI.

Roever, C. (2005) *Testing ESL Pragmatics*. Frankfurt-am-Main, Germany: Peter Lang.

Rose, K.R. (2000) An exploratory cross-sectional study of interlanguage pragmatic development. *Studies in Second Language Acquisition* 22, 27–67.

Schoonen, R. (2005) Generalizability of writing scores: An application of structural equation modeling. *Language Testing* 22 (1), 1–3.

Shin, S. (2002) Effects of subskills and text types on Korean EFL reading scores. *Second Language Studies* 20 (2), 107–113. On WWW at http://www.hawaii.edu/sls/uhwpesl/on-line_cat.html.

Solano-Flores, G. and Li, M. (2006) The use of generalizability (G) theory in testing of linguistic minorities. *Educational Measurement: Issues and Practice* 25 (1), 13–22.

Stansfield, C.W. and Kenyon, D.M. (1992) Research of the comparability of the oral proficiency interview and the simulated oral proficiency interview. *System* 20, 347–364.

Tada, M. (2005) Assessment of EFL pragmatic production and perception using video prompts. Unpublished PhD thesis, Temple University, Philadelphia.

Van Weeren, J. and Theunissen, T.J.J.M. (1987) Testing pronunciation: An application of generalizability theory. *Language Learning* 37 (1), 109–122.

Yamamori, K. (2003) Evaluation of students' interest, willingness, and attitude toward English lessons: Multivariate generalizability theory. *The Japanese Journal of Educational Psychology* 51 (2), 195–204.

Yamanaka, H. (2005) Using generalizability theory in the evaluation of L2 writing. *JALT Journal* 27 (2), 169–185.

Yamashita, S.O. (1996a) Comparing six cross-cultural pragmatics measures. Unpublished PhD thesis, Temple University, Philadelphia.

Yamashita, S.O. (1996b) *Six measures of JSL Pragmatics* (Technical Report # 14). Honolulu: University of Hawai'i at Manoa, Second Language Teaching and Curriculum Centre.

Yoshida, H. (2004) An analytic instrument for assessing EFL pronunciation. Unpublished PhD thesis, Temple University, Philadelphia.

Yoshida, H. (2006) Using generalizability theory to evaluate reliability of a performance-based pronunciation measurement. Unpublished manuscript, Osaka Jogakuin College.

Yoshitake, S.S. (1997) Measuring interlanguage pragmatic competence of Japanese students of English as a foreign language: A multi-test framework evaluation. Unpublished PhD thesis, Columbia Pacific University, Novata, CA.

Yoshitake, S. and Enochs, K. (1996) Self assessment and role play for evaluating appropriateness in speech act realizations. *ICU Language Research Bulletin* 11, 57–76.

Zhang, S. (2006) Investigating the relative effects of persons, items, sections, and languages on TOEIC score dependability. *Language Testing* 23 (3), 351–369.

Zhang, Y. (2003) Effects of persons, items, and subtests on UH ELIPT reading test scores. *Second Language Studies* 21 (2), 107–128. On WWW at http://www.hawaii.edu/sls/uhwpesl/on-line_cat.html.

Chapter 12
Rater, Item and Candidate Effects in Discourse Completion Tests: A FACETS Approach

CARSTEN ROEVER

Introduction

Testing second language (L2) learners' knowledge of speech acts productively through discourse completion tests (DCTs) is complicated by the need for rating responses. Not only does this require a significant outlay of resources, but the rating process itself introduces additional variance into scores as the measurement of learners' ability and of the difficulty of items is mediated by the raters. It is therefore desirable in practice that ratings are consistent, but it is just as important to understand inconsistencies and improve rater training to preempt them.

A useful tool for understanding the relationship between test-taker ability, rater judgments and item difficulty is many-facet Rasch measurement (MFRM), implemented in the program FACETS. This paper applies MFRM to data from a productive speech act test.

Testing Knowledge of L2 Speech Acts

Work on speech acts has been a central feature of acquisition and assessment research in interlanguage pragmatics. Assessment studies are more recent, with the first large-scale test development and validation study by Hudson *et al.* (1995) actually being a method comparison study, which employed traditional written DCTs, oral DCTs, multiple-choice DCTs, roleplays and self-assessments with Japanese ESL learners in Hawai'i. Their study was replicated by Yoshitake (1997) and adapted for English-speaking learners of Japanese by Yamashita (1996). Brown (2001) shows that the reliability of all the instruments was acceptable except the multiple-choice DCT, which had been especially difficult to construct due to the challenges of writing distractors that were clearly unacceptable but still attractive. This is a somewhat unfortunate finding, as the multiple-choice DCT was the instrument with the greatest practicality. Written and oral DCTs were less practical because they required human raters but could at least be administered to groups of test takers. The roleplay was the least practical instrument because it required one-on-one administration, videotaping and rating by human raters. Liu (2006) developed a multiple-choice DCT for Chinese EFL learners, which showed good reliability, but McNamara and Roever (2006) raise some concerns over the construct validity of Liu's instrument.

Roever (2005, 2006) also used a DCT as part of his web-based pragmatics test battery, but his approach differed in several respects from previous studies. Firstly, Roever's test was intended to be unspecific with regard to test-takers' first language (L1), whereas nearly all other assessment studies in interlanguage pragmatics had been focused on a specific L1–L2 pair, with the only exception being Bouton's (1994, 1999) test of ESL implicature.

Secondly, Roever's DCT constituted the speech act section of a larger test battery, which included 12-item multiple-choice tests of routines and implicature. So the DCT in Roever's study contributed to an understanding of learners' pragmalinguistic knowledge but it was not the only instrument used, and its construct relevance could be investigated by correlating it with the other test components. Roever (2005) shows fairly high correlations in the 0.6 range between the speech act section and the other sections with a multitrait–multimethod matrix indicating no clear evidence of a DCT method effect.

Thirdly, Roever's DCT was constructed differently than the DCTs used by Hudson *et al.* and their successors. Whereas Hudson *et al.* trialed but subsequently rejected rejoinders as a design feature of their DCTs, arguing that they interfered with the real-world authenticity of responses, Roever included them. He argued that real-world authenticity is less important in assessment instruments, which try to tap learners' knowledge rather than survey their actual usage (for which DCTs are problematic in any case, as Golato (2003) found). He constructed his rejoinders so that the situation prompt and the rejoinder together would elicit at least two speech act strategies. The data from Roever's study will be analyzed here using MFRM.

Many-facet Rasch Measurement

MFRM is an extension of the Rasch approach to test analysis (for a readable introduction, see McNamara, 1996). Mathematically equivalent to one-parameter item response theory, Rasch measurement relates estimates of item difficulty and test-taker ability, following the thoroughly sensible logic that high-ability test takers should perform nearly flawlessly on easy items, very well on mid-difficulty items and quite well on difficult items. Low-ability test takers, however, should perform relatively well on easy items, but quite poorly on mid-difficulty items and very poorly on difficult items. So item difficulty and test-taker ability are two sides of the same coin, and one can be inferred from the other.

This is quite a different view from classical test theory, which considers test-taker scores and item facility separately from each other.

MFRM, implemented through the computer program FACETS (Linacre, 2006), goes beyond simply investigating items and test takers but includes other facets of the testing situation, most commonly raters. In any setting where ratings of performance are involved, at least three facets of the testing situation interact to influence ratings: the ability of the test taker, the difficulty of the task and the harshness or leniency of the rater. A high ability test taker would be expected to perform better on tasks of greater difficulty than a low ability test taker, but if the high ability test taker has a harsh rater and the low ability test taker has a lenient rater, their ratings may look quite similar although their actual abilities are quite different. Similarly, a harsh rater would make tasks appear much more difficult than a lenient rater because the ratings candidates obtain from the harsh rater are lower. The advantage of relating the various facets of the measurement situation is that deviations from theoretical expectations can be flagged, which allows the identification of misfitting items, test takers or raters. For example, a misfitting item might be one where high-ability test takers perform less well than expected but low-ability test takers perform better than expected, a misfitting test taker might perform poorly on easy items but well on difficult items, and a misfitting rater might rate low-ability candidates higher than high-ability candidates. A test taker may be misfitting because they are not trying their best, e.g. answering randomly, and a rater may be misfitting if their ratings are erratic and inconsistent. Items may be misfitting because they measure something other than the construct under investigation.

The Rasch model is probabilistic, so it assumes that there will be some deviations from theoretical expectations simply due to chance, but if violations of the model's assumption exceed certain thresholds, this indicates a misfit. The Rasch model also identifies cases where the deviation from theoretical expectations is less than predicted. This situation is known as 'overfit', and it is particularly relevant for raters: an overfitting rater may not be using the full measurement scale, e.g. mostly assigning mid-level ratings but shying away from the extremes of the scale.

Determining what degree of misfit or overfit is 'too much' is not a straightforward business. The infit statistic computed by FACETS shows how far individual measurements deviate from theoretical expectations. The infit mean square has an expectation value of 1, and values above 1 indicate 'misfit', whereas values below 1 indicate 'overfit'. Linacre (2006) considers infit mean squares between 0.5 and 1.5 acceptable.

MFRM computes rather harshness or leniency by analyzing the differences between raters in rating the same candidates' performances on the same tasks. Similarly, it determines candidate ability by comparing ratings that candidates received (taking into account severity differences between raters) for their performances on items of differential difficulty. And it determines task difficulty by looking at the ratings given to candidates at different levels of ability, again taking into account rater harshness or leniency.

One strong advantage of MFRM is its ability to identify possible cases of measurement bias, i.e. where there seems to be an unexpected interaction between facets. This might occur where a normally harsh rater rates certain candidates leniently, or a generally difficult task is tackled successfully by a low-ability candidate, or where a lenient rater rates performances on one task much more harshly than on other tasks. Such unexpected interactions between elements are called 'bias terms' in MFRM, and they can be used to retrain raters where necessary. For example, if a rater assesses candidates of a certain L1 background more harshly than comparable candidates of a different L1 background, this rater can be made aware of their bias and trained not to lower their ratings of these candidates.

MFRM has mostly been used in oral proficiency testing. Traditionally, the focus has been on understanding rater behavior (Bachman *et al.*, 1995; Brown, 1995; Lumley & McNamara, 1995; Wigglesworth, 1993) but it has also frequently been employed to examine bias and unwanted interactions between test facets (Eckes, 2006; Lumley & O'Sullivan, 2005; O'Loughlin, 2002). In other uses, Bonk and Ockey (2003) explored the extent to which individual facets contributed to scores in a group oral test, Kozaki (2004) used FACETS for standard setting in a translation exam, and Weir and Wu (2006) investigated test form comparability with the help of FACETS.

This Study

While MFRM and FACETS have been employed in second language research for over a decade, they have not yet been applied to the rating of data from pragmatics assessments. This study will analyze data from Roever (2005) using MFRM, and incorporating three facets: test takers, items and raters. Putting all three facets in relation to each other will 'purify' each of the measures, and show item difficulty without influence of raters, rater similarity or difference without effect of test-taker ability, and test-taker ability unaffected by rater harshness or item difficulty. This will allow conclusions as to the measurement properties of the test, the sufficiency of rater training and characteristics that contribute to item difficulty or facility.

Research Questions

(1) What were the item characteristics of the 12 DCT items?
   (a) Were any speech acts more difficult than others?
   (b) Were high-imposition items more difficult than low-imposition items?
(2) Were the raters similar in harshness/leniency?
(3) Did the test differentiate well between test takers of different ability level?
(4) Were there any interactions between raters, test takers and items that would advantage or disadvantage test takers?

Methodology

Participants

The test-taker sample consisted of 41 participants, drawn from Roever's (2005) population of 240 NNS. Test takers belonged to nine subpopulations, as shown in Table 12.1.

Not all subpopulations are represented in the sample in exact proportion to their size because, particularly in lower-level groups, some test takers completed few of the speech act items, for which the

Table 12.1 Test takers

Group	Test takers	Total number in sample	Total N
3rd year EFL	4, 5, 6	3	24
4th year EFL	18, 19, 20, 21, 22, 23	6	41
5th year EFL	24, 25, 26	3	34
6th year EFL	27, 28, 29, 30	4	22
8th year EFL	31, 32	2	17
9th year EFL	33, 34, 35, 36, 37	5	8
Lower ELI at UHM	1, 2, 3	3	15
Upper ELI at UHM	7, 8, 9, 10, 11, 12, 13, 14, 15, 16, 17	11	46
Advanced NNS in USA/Japan	38, 39, 40, 41	4	33
Total		41	240

EFL, English as a foreign language; ELI at UHM, English Language Institute at the University of Hawai'i at Manoa; NNS, non-native speakers time allotted was probably too short. To provide sufficient numbers of ratable items, the majority of test takers included needed to have answered a sizeable number of items. However, to provide a representative sample of the whole population, some test takers with few ratable answers were also included.

Although the FACETS software can handle much larger numbers, this sample had to be constrained to 41 test takers, as this meant that potentially 492 responses had to be rated by each of the raters. Even after eliminating missing responses, each of the raters rated 403 individual speech act responses. While the responses are short and rating can be done quite quickly, it would not have been feasible to ask volunteer raters to rate more than this large number of responses.

Raters

The raters were three doctoral students in an Applied Linguistics program in the USA. Two of them were female (Tami and Lisa) and one was male (Stu). All three had extensive experience as ESL teachers.

Materials

The speech act section was one of three sections of a web-based test assessing second language learners' knowledge of American English pragmalinguistics. The other two sections assessed comprehension of implicature and recognition of situationally appropriate routine formulae. All sections consisted of 12 items, but the speech act section differed from the other two sections in several ways. Most importantly, it was the only productive section, and test takers typed out a response to a prompt. At 18 minutes, the time allotted for the speech act section was 50% longer than for the other sections, but Roever (2005, 2006) showed that it was still not sufficient; 24–30 minutes would have been more appropriate, but this would have made it practically impossible to administer the test in under an hour, which was important in order to recruit this volunteer population of test takers.

The speech act section contained four items for each of the speech acts apology, request and refusal, two of which were high imposition/severity of offense and two were low imposition/severity of offense. Items and their context settings are illustrated in Table 12.2.

All items consisted of a situational prompt, a space for the test taker to enter their response, and a rejoinder, which was visible at all times. Test takers were explicitly instructed to take the rejoinder into consideration when constructing their response, and to make sure the resulting exchange made sense. The following is a low-imposition apology item:

Table 12.2 Items

Item	Speech act	Imposition	Content
1	Request	Low	Ask instructor to speak more slowly
2	Apology	Low	Ruined borrowed magazine
3	Refusal	Low	Lend friend textbook
4	Request	Low	Ask colleague to take shift
5	Apology	Low	Make friend wait 15 minutes
6	Refusal	High	Help housemate move furniture
7	Request	High	Interview busy housemate for project
8	Apology	High	Miss project group meeting
9	Refusal	High	Borrow $500
10	Request	High	Borrow friend's apartment for party
11	Apology	High	Break colleague's precious vase
12	Refusal	Low	Water plants for housemate

(1) Ella borrowed a recent copy of *TIME Magazine* from her friend Sean but she accidentally spilled a cup of coffee all over it. She is returning the magazine to Sean.
Ella: _____
Sean: 'No, don't worry about replacing it, I read it already.'

The items were constructed to elicit two strategies each. In the case of the example item above, this might include an illocutionary force indicating device (IFID), e.g. 'I'm sorry about ruining your magazine' or 'Sorry', and an offer of repair ('I'll buy you a new one', 'I'll replace it'). While the situation itself would probably elicit a formulaic IFID even from a less proficient test taker, only the additional use of an offer of repair would complete the exchange satisfactorily (unless one assumes a fairly high degree of sarcasm on Sean's part). As Rose (2000) has shown, more advanced learners are more likely to provide such supportive moves.

Procedures

The speech act section was administered as part of the complete test battery. The test was administered under supervised conditions in computer labs at the test takers' institutions. All responses were captured by a scoring script, and while the implicature and routines sections were scored automatically, the speech act responses were sent to the researcher for manual scoring.

To investigate the effect of multiple ratings, speech act section responses from 41 test takers were compiled into rating booklets for the raters. Every response was inserted in the DCT prompt to provide adequate context for the raters. In a one-hour pre-rating training session, raters were instructed to consider in their rating whether the response makes sense in terms of the situational prompts and the following rejoinder. In other words, is the resulting conversational exchange coherent? For this to be the case the response needed to be comprehensible and have the required illocutionary force. At the same time, the response did not need to be flawless, so raters were asked to tolerate linguistic errors as long as they did not interfere with comprehensibility. In particular, raters were asked not to judge the appropriateness of responses in terms of whether they were sufficiently polite. It was not the purpose of this instrument (unlike Hudson *et al.*'s test, 1995) to investigate sociopragmatic knowledge, but rather pragmalinguistic ability. At the same time, extreme sociopragmatic mis-performance can lead to overall pragmatic failure, so raters were instructed to fail a response that was either grossly offensive or ridiculously overpolite.

The raters scored responses on a scale from 0 to 3, with 0 indicating an unacceptable response, 1 given for a severely flawed response which still succeeded in conveying the speech intention, 2 assigned to a generally good response with slight flaws and 3 awarded to responses that did not need any further improvement. Raters assessed the responses independently and returned the completed rating booklets to the researcher. A post-rating debriefing completed the rating process.

All ratings were entered into an SPSS spreadsheet and subsequently transferred to the FACETS program. As is commonly done in these analyses, the FACETS data specifications centered the raters and the items around 0 but allowed test-taker ability to float.

Results

The FACETS ruler

The most comprehensive part of the FACETS output is the 'ruler', a visual representation of the relationship between rater severity, item difficulty and test-taker ability. The measurement unit of a ruler is logits, a measure of probability. Candidates at 0 logits are of average ability, and they have a 50% chance of getting an item correct that is of average difficulty if they have a rater of average harshness. The higher a candidate's logit measure, the greater their ability. The higher an item's logit measure, the greater is its difficulty, and similarly, the higher a rater's logit measure, the greater their harshness. Figure 12.1 shows the FACETS ruler for this study.

Taking each test facet in turn, we can first see that tasks are located in a fairly narrow range between −1 and +1 logits. This indicates that none of the tasks are very difficult or very easy, and they should be manageable for a test taker of average ability. Similarly, the raters are also all very close to 0, which indicates that they are neither particularly harsh nor particularly lenient. So in other words, test-taker scores would not be greatly raised or lowered by rater effects.

The spread for test takers is much wider than for items or raters, which is to be expected in a diverse sample representing various ability levels. The majority of test takers are located around 0, showing that they have roughly average ability, but a large number is also in the negative logit

logit	items	raters	test takers		
			FL-9yr2		
1					
	apol-hi (8)		SL-hi5		
	req-hi (10) req-hi (7)				
			FL-adv1 SL-hi4	SL-hi7	
			FL-adv2		
	apol-lo (2) apol-lo (5)	Lisa			
			FL-6yr2 FL-6yr4	FL-9yr4	
			FL-9yr1 SL-hi11		
0			FL-adv3 SL-hi3		
		Stu	FL-4yr6 SL-hi8		
	ref-lo (3)	Tami	FL-9yr3 SL-hi9		
	apol-hi (11) req-lo (4)		FL-8yr2 SL-hi6		
			FL-8yr1 SL-low2		
	ref-lo (12) ref-hi (6) req-lo (1)		FL-6yr1 SL-hi2		
	ref-hi (9)		SL-low1 SL-low3		
			FL-4yr5		
			FL-9yr5 SL-hi10		
−1			FL-4yr3 FL-5yr1	FL-5yr3	SL-hi1
			FL-5yr2		
			FL-3yr3		
			FL-3yr2		
			FL-3yr1 FL-4yr4		
			FL-adv4		
−2			FL-4yr2		
			FL-4yr1		
			FL-6yr3		

Figure 12.1 FACETS ruler

range so they would be less than 50% likely to answer a mid-difficulty item correctly.

Another piece of information that the ruler provides is the match of test takers to items. If a test taker is at the same horizontal level in the ruler as an item, the test-taker's ability is perfectly matched to the item's difficulty and that test taker would have a 50% chance of getting the item correct. This is the case, for example, for test-takers SL-lo1 and SL-lo3 and item 9, test-taker SL-hi5 and item 8, and several others. For test-taker SL-hi5, all items except item 8 are easy, i.e. s/he would have a greater than 50% likelihood of getting them correct. Conversely, for anyone below test-takers SL-lo1 and SL-lo3, all items are difficult, i.e. they would have a less than 50% likelihood of getting them correct.

While the ruler is a good visual representation of the relative standing of all test facets, it does not show results with great precision, so FACETS produces tables with detailed information about each facet and their interactions.

The test facets: Raters, items and test takers

The FACETS report for three raters gives information about their harshness in logits, their fit in terms of the Rasch model and their exact agreement. Table 12.3 shows the rater characteristics of the three raters in this study. From the Measure column, we can conclude that Lisa is the harshest of the raters. Her positive logit value means that her ratings would lower candidates' scores, compared to what they would obtain with an average rater (logit value of 0). Stu is the closest to an average rater and Tami is slightly on the lenient side. It is noticeable that all raters are within 0.5 logits of each other, so their difference in severity is minimal.

The following section, Infit, is used to assess the quality of ratings and detect misfit and overfit. All raters in this study are within the acceptable range of 0.5 to 1.5 suggested by Linacre (2006), so no sizeable misfit or overfit is present.

Table 12.3 Rater characteristics

Measure		Infit		Exact agreements		Raters
Logit	se	Mean sq	Z std	Observed%	Expected%	
0.30	0.06	0.73	−4.5	50.4	38.9	Lisa
−0.11	0.06	1.25	3.6	56.5	38.9	Stu
−0.20	0.06	1.01	0.1	57.5	38.4	Tami

On demand, FACETS also produces overall agreement statistics, which indicate that out of 1201 agreement opportunities, raters had 658 exact agreements (54.8%). So for more than half of all ratings, raters agreed exactly. This exceeds the expectations of the Rasch model, which had predicted 38.8% exact agreement. FACETS calculates no traditional inter-rater reliability statistics.

FACETS also produces a detailed table about item characteristics, again showing each item's difficulty in logits, as well as the item fit (see Table 12.4). Optionally, the correlation between item score and total score can be included to obtain a traditional measure of item discrimination. From Table 12.4, it is apparent that items do not spread very much in terms of difficulty: the difference between the easiest and the hardest item is only 1.4 logits. This also means that these items are most appropriate for test takers of average ability but less so for very highly proficient test takers, who would need harder items, or very low-proficiency test takers, who would need easier items. Using Linacre's (2006) classification of misfit and overfit, none of the items are misfitting or overfitting. It is noteworthy that the three out of four request and apology items are of more than average difficulty, and all four refusal items are of below average difficulty. FACETS computes a separation reliability index for items similar to reliability in classical test theory. The reliability for this set of items was 0.95, which indicates a very reliable test overall.

The third test facet is the test takers, and FACETS produces a similar table as for the other two facets, raters and items (see Table 12.5). It shows measures of ability in logits as well as the fit of the test taker to the model. The test takers are spread much more widely than the items or the raters, ranging over 3.8 logits. Noticeably, most of them have below average ability. Three test takers seem to be misfitting (FL-adv2, FL-8yr2, FL-3yr2) and one is overfitting (SL-hi5).

Interactions: Bias report

The final important piece of information from a FACETS analysis concerns unexpected interactions. The program reports any interaction between test facets (raters, test taker and items) that may raise concerns. These interactions can be between pairs of facets (raters and task, raters and test takers, tasks and test takers) or all facets at the same time (raters, items and test takers).

The report for interactions between raters and tasks showed that Lisa and Stu both reacted to item 201 but interestingly in opposite ways: Lisa became more lenient but Stu became harsher in his judgments. No other rater-item interactions were observed.

Table 12.4 Item characteristics

Item	Speech act	Impos.	Measure		Infit		Item-total correlation
			Logits	se	MnSq	z std	
8	Apology	High	0.86	0.13	0.83	−1.1	0.36
10	Request	High	0.84	0.14	1.10	0.6	0.35
7	Request	High	0.75	0.13	1.16	1.0	0.32
2	Apology	Low	0.29	0.12	0.94	−0.4	0.48
5	Apology	Low	0.25	0.12	0.88	−0.9	0.37
3	Refusal	Low	−0.20	0.11	1.23	1.8	0.29
11	Apology	High	−0.28	0.11	1.04	0.3	0.32
4	Request	Low	−0.35	0.11	0.61	−3.6	0.49
1	Request	Low	−0.51	0.11	1.31	2.3	0.12
12	Refusal	Low	−0.52	0.12	1.09	0.7	0.35
6	Refusal	High	−0.52	0.11	0.89	−0.9	0.46
9	Refusal	High	−0.62	0.12	0.95	−0.3	0.27

Table 12.5 Test-taker characteristics

Logit measure	se	Mean square	z std	Test taker
1.29	1.06	0.55	0.0	FL-9yr2
0.91	0.55	0.18	−1.8	SL-hi5
0.74	0.21	1.05	0.3	FL-adv1
0.71	0.22	1.08	0.4	SL-hi4
0.67	0.51	0.67	−0.4	SL-hi7
0.55	0.20	1.56	2.2	FL-adv2
0.23	0.19	0.82	−0.8	FL-9yr4
0.20	0.19	0.78	−1.0	FL-6yr2
0.20	0.19	0.96	−0.1	FL-6yr4
0.10	0.19	0.95	−0.1	SL-hi11
0.10	0.19	1.14	0.7	FL-9yr1
0.03	0.18	1.35	10.6	FL-adv3
−0.04	0.19	1.19	0.9	SL-hi3
−0.10	0.18	0.58	−2.4	SL-hi8
−0.14	0.18	0.80	−1.0	FL-4yr6
−0.17	0.18	0.75	−1.3	FL-9yr3
−0.24	0.19	0.88	−0.5	SL-hi9
−0.27	0.18	0.80	−1.0	SL-hi6
−0.29	0.19	1.67	2.8	FL-8yr2
−0.42	0.23	0.91	−0.2	SL-low2
−0.44	0.18	0.88	−0.5	FL-8yr1
−0.47	0.18	0.84	−0.8	SL-hi2
−0.55	0.46	0.93	0.0	FL-6yr1
−0.58	0.19	1.02	0.1	SL-low3
−0.63	0.19	0.83	−0.8	SL-low1
−0.84	0.21	0.99	0.0	FL-4yr5
−0.91	0.20	1.28	1.2	FL-9yr5
−0.92	0.20	1.16	0.7	SL-hi10

Table 12.5 (*Continued*)

Logit measure	se	Mean square	z std	Test taker
−0.98	0.20	1.06	0.3	FL-5yr3
−1.00	0.21	0.80	−0.8	SL-hi1
−1.00	0.21	0.83	−0.7	FL-5yr1
−1.02	0.22	1.19	0.8	FL-4yr3
−1.14	0.24	1.05	0.2	FL-5yr2
−1.34	0.24	1.10	0.4	FL-3yr3
−1.36	0.38	1.83	1.7	FL-3yr2
−1.49	0.33	1.17	0.5	FL-3yr1
−1.51	0.25	1.40	1.3	FL-4yr4
−1.75	0.29	0.76	−0.6	FL-adv4
−2.00	0.30	0.61	−1.0	FL-4yr2
−2.46	0.39	0.77	−0.3	FL-4yr1
−2.50	1.76	Minimum		FL-6yr3

In terms of rater–test taker interactions, only one such interaction occurred, namely Lisa rating test taker FL-9yr2 (the highest scoring test taker) lower than expected, but the interaction proved to be minor and not a concern.

For test taker–task interactions, 1206 pairings were possible, of which 24 (2% of the total) showed significant bias values. In 21 out those 24 cases, the bias found was in the direction of overestimation, i.e. the particular task made it easier for the particular test taker to obtain a high score than would be expected.

Finally, a bias analysis considering test takers, tasks and raters simultaneously found only 2 out 1206 possible interactions between all three facets with significant bias values. So overall, bias in this measurement was very minor and had a negligible influence on results.

Discussion

The most practically relevant finding from this study is the similarity among the raters and the consistency with which they rated test-taker responses. One concern about any productive test instrument that requires rating is that the whole rating process is too resource intensive and introduces too much undesirable variance through the raters' interaction with tasks and responses. This was not the case here. Raters were very similar in their judgments, there were only two significant bias interactions between raters and tasks, and no significant bias interactions occurred between raters and test takers. At the same time, raters differed from each other to a small extent, which is normal and expected by a probabilistic model such as many-facet measurement. What accounts for this high degree of rater agreement despite relatively short rater training? Two factors are likely. One is the simplicity of the rating task. Raters were only asked to assess whether test takers' responses fit the situation and the rejoinder. They were not tasked with assigning a value to a much more vague construct like 'fluency', 'proficiency' or 'politeness'. This reduced the likelihood that raters had different conceptualizations of the construct they were supposed to assess. Undoubtedly, there was still room for disagreement, but raters' intuitions were quite similar when asked to determine whether the conversational snippet of the test-taker's response and the imaginary interlocutor's rejoinder made sense.

The second factor that probably helped in ensuring consistency was the use of rejoinders. By embedding the test-takers' responses in a situation and a rejoinder the decision as to whether the response 'fit' became much easier for raters than it would have been in a rejoinderless DCT. Situational prompts allow a wide range of responses, but rejoinders severely constrain what kind of response fits. Raters therefore did not have to speculate on the real-world likelihood of a response given the particular situation, but they could limit themselves to assessing a much narrower range of response options. In other words, it was easier for raters to recognize what kind of response was right or wrong. However, this line of reasoning must remain somewhat speculative unless the ratability of DCTs with or without rejoinders is compared.

Theoretical and practical implications

These findings indicate that knowledge of pragmalinguistic strategies for speech acts can be tapped by means of DCTs with rejoinders, and that this type of DCT produces construct-relevant data. This contention is supported in the FACETS analysis by the good fit of the items and the test takers to the measurement model. It is comforting that the recently much maligned DCT has this use in pragmatics research but it is equally important to realize that the construct investigated here was only knowledge of pragmalinguistic strategies. So findings allow conclusions about the learners' repertoire of strategies but they do not allow conclusion as to learners' ability to use those strategies in actual conversation. It remains a significant shortcoming of the DCT as a research and testing instrument that it cannot simulate the flow of conversation and show the distribution of strategies over various turns, pre- and post-head act. However, knowledge is arguably a precondition for use, so it is certainly useful to ascertain what learners know. At the same time, knowledge is decidedly not the same as ability for use, just like DCT data is not the same as conversational data.

In practical terms, DCTs with rejoinders can be constructed fairly easily, given how many DCTs there are available from the literature (e.g. Blum-Kulka *et al.*, 1989; Johnston *et al.*, 1998). It goes without saying that DCTs need to be carefully piloted before using them for any assessment purpose, and sufficient time must be allotted for their completion. Rater training can probably be kept fairly short, but raters will have disagreements, mostly with regard to politeness and appropriateness issues, and they may need constant reminding that politeness and appropriateness are of secondary importance in studies investigating pragmalinguistic knowledge. However, the high level of agreement between the raters means that it is certainly not necessary to have three raters assess responses. It is probably sufficient to have two raters, and for low-stakes situations it might be acceptable to have two raters overlap for a certain number of test takers but divide the rest of the population and single-rate it.

Finally, FACETS is a powerful tool for adjusting test scores according to item difficulty and rater severity. This ensures fair allocation of points where some test takers get rated by harsher raters and get assigned more difficult items from an item pool than other test takers. The drawback of using the adjusted scores is that test takers with the same raw score may receive different final scores, which is likely not to seem fair at all to the test takers with the lower scores.

Conclusion

This study used MFRM to investigate test-taker, item and rater facets in a DCT testing knowledge of pragmalinguistic speech act realization strategies. The analysis showed strong agreement between raters, few misfitting items or test takers, and very little unexplained interaction between facets. These findings support the defensibility of scores and inferences based on this instrument, and they are also promising in terms of future use of DCTs with rejoinders as assessment instruments.

Future research should investigate optimized ways of rater training and lower numbers of raters, as well as look in more detail at the rating process itself: how do raters arrive at their scores when rating responses on this instrument? A similar question goes for test takers: how do they use the prompt to construct their response? How does their ability interact with item difficulty to influence this process? And finally, the holy grail of structured testing of speech act knowledge remains this: is it possible to construct a test that extends over various turns and more closely approximates true conversation? This study provides an indication that rejoinders may help in this quest.

References

Bachman, L.F., Lynch, B.K. and Mason, M. (1995) Investigating variability in tasks and rater judgments in a performance test of foreign language speaking. *Language Testing* 12 (2), 239–257.

Blum-Kulka, S., House, J. and Kasper, G. (eds) (1989) *Cross-Cultural Pragmatics: Requests and Apologies*. Norwood, NJ: Ablex.

Bonk, W.J. and Ockey, G.J. (2003) A many-facet Rasch analysis of the second language group oral discussion task. *Language Testing* 20 (1), 89–110.

Bouton, L.F. (1994) Conversational implicature in the second language: Learned slowly when not deliberately taught. *Journal of Pragmatics* 22, 157–167.

Bouton, L. (1999) The amenability of implicature to focused classroom instruction. Paper presented at TESOL 1999, March, New York.

Brown, A. (1995) The effect of rater variables in the development of an occupation-specific language performance test. *Language Testing* 12, 1–15.

Brown, J.D. (2001) Six types of pragmatics tests in two different contexts. In K.R. Rose and G. Kasper (eds) *Pragmatics in Language Teaching* (pp. 301–325). Cambridge: Cambridge University Press.

Eckes, T. (2006) Examining rater effects in TestDAF writing and speaking performance assessments: A many-facet Rasch analysis. *Language Assessment Quarterly* 2 (3), 197–221.

Golato, A. (2003) Studying compliment responses: A comparison of DCTs and naturally occurring talk. *Applied Linguistics* 24, 90–121.

Hudson, T., Detmer, E. and Brown, J.D. (1995) *Developing Prototypic Measures of Cross-cultural Pragmatics* (Technical Report # 7). Honolulu: University of Hawai'i at Manoa, Second Language Teaching and Curriculum Centre.

Johnston, B., Kasper, G. and Ross, S. (1998) Effect of rejoinders in production questionnaires. *Applied Linguistics* 19 (2), 157–182.

Kozaki, Y. (2004) Using GENOVA and FACETS to set multiple standards on performance assessment for certification in medical translation from Japanese into English. *Language Testing* 21 (1), 1–27.

Linacre, J.M. (2006) *Facets Rasch Measurement Computer Program*. Chicago: Winsteps.

Liu, J. (2006) *Measuring Interlanguage Pragmatic Knowledge of EFL Learners*. Frankfurt: Peter Lang.

Lumley, T. and McNamara, T.F. (1995) Rater characteristics and rater bias: Implications for training. *Language Testing* 12, 54–71.

Lumley, T. and O'Sullivan, B. (2005) The effect of test-taker gender, audience and topic on task performance in tape-mediated assessment of speaking. *Language Testing* 22 (4), 415–437.

McNamara, T.F. (1996) *Measuring Second Language Performance*. London and New York: Addison Wesley Longman.

McNamara, T.F. and Roever, C. (2006) *Language Testing: The Social Dimension*. Oxford: Basil Blackwell.

O'Loughlin, K. (2002) The impact of gender in oral proficiency testing. *Language Testing* 19 (2), 169–192.

Roever, C. (2005) *Testing ESL Pragmatics*. Frankfurt: Peter Lang.

Roever, C. (2006) Validation of a web-based test of ESL pragmalinguistics. *Language Testing* 23 (2), 229–256.

Rose, K. (2000) An exploratory cross-sectional study of interlanguage pragmatic development. *Studies in Second Language Acquisition* 22, 27–67.

Weir, C. and Wu, J.R.W. (2006) Establishing test form and individual task comparability: A case study of a semi-direct speaking test. *Language Testing* 23 (2), 167–197.

Wigglesworth, G. (1993) Exploring bias analysis as a tool for improving rater consistency in assessing oral interaction. *Language Testing* 10, 305–335.

Yamashita, S.O. (1996) *Six Measures of JSL Pragmatics* (Technical Report #14). Honolulu: University of Hawai'i at Manoa, Second Language Teaching and Curriculum Centre.

Yoshitake, S.S. (1997) Measuring interlanguage pragmatic competence of Japanese students of English as a foreign language: A multi-test framework evaluation. Unpublished PhD thesis, Columbia Pacific University, Novata, CA.

For Product Safety Concerns and Information please contact our EU Authorised Representative:

Easy Access System Europe

Mustamäe tee 50

10621 Tallinn

Estonia

gpsr.requests@easproject.com